THE
BOTHAM
REPORT

THE
BOTHAM
REPORT

IAN BOTHAM
WITH PETER HAYTER

CollinsWillow
An Imprint of HarperCollins*Publishers*

First published in 1997
by CollinsWillow
an imprint of HarperCollins*Publishers*
London

© Mannez Promotions Ltd 1997

1 3 5 7 9 8 6 4 2

A CIP catalogue record for this book is
available from the British Library

ISBN 0 00 218770 1

Photographs supplied by Allsport, Patrick Eagar
and David Munden

Printed in Great Britain by The Bath Press, Bath

CONTENTS

*To my long-suffering family: Kathy, Liam, Sarah,
Becky, and the equally long-suffering
supporters of English cricket*

ACKNOWLEDGEMENTS

Once bitten, twice bitten. My grateful thanks to all those who assisted in the preparation of this book; to Tom Whiting, to the indefatigable Linda Hurcombe, the unflappable Amanda George, Samantha and Theresa Richards and the redoubtable Rosa Broome. Special thanks are due to Patrick Whittingdale, Mark Nicholas, John Heaton, David Roberts, Wayne Morton, Malcolm Berry, David Graveney, Dennis Silk and Rab C (David) Norrie who gave freely of their time; and to all those county chairmen, chief executives/secretaries, coaches and captains who contributed to the book through the questionnaire. Finally, to Mary, Max and Sophie: thanks for your patience, understanding and cups of tea.

Peter Hayter
Hesterhaven, Shropshire

A GAME IN CRISIS

'English cricket is in crisis, of that there is no doubt'

ON Saturday 28 December 1996, the third day of England's second Test against Zimbabwe in Harare, English cricket celebrated a bitter-sweet tenth anniversary.

It was ten years to the day when, on the 1986-87 tour of Australia, under captain Mike Gatting, England last won the Ashes; ten years to the day when England's descent to the bottom rung of international cricket began.

I remember the moment we achieved what Englishmen regard as the ultimate cricketing goal as though it was yesterday. One-nil up in the series with two matches to play, we arrived at Melbourne for the Christmas Test, confident that we would achieve the result that would give us the series. Our confidence was not misplaced. We won in three days and we were that good. Gladstone Small and I both took five wickets to dismiss the Australians for fewer than 150, then Chris Broad hit a century to set up victory by an innings. How sweet a moment it was when Merv Hughes swung a delivery from Phil Edmonds, our left arm spinner, into Gladstone's hands on the square leg boundary to bring the match to an end and signal the start of our celebrations.

Ten years later, on that fateful day in Harare, England were being bowled out by a team representing a country that wasn't even playing Test cricket when we last won the Ashes, dismissed for 156 in less than a full day's play. It was one of the most pathetic batting performances I've seen from an England team, but the fact that the overwhelming public reaction to it was one of resignation rather than shock underlined just how far English cricket had fallen during a decade in the doldrums.

Then Zimbabwe's young fighters completed England's indignity by winning the two final one-day games of the three-match series to secure a 3-0 whitewash.

David Lloyd, the England coach, on his first senior overseas tour, had already suffered ridicule back home for his comments after the tied first Test in Bulawayo, when, after a fracas with an official of the Zimbabwean Cricket Union he claimed, 'We murdered them. We hammered them. They know it, and we know it.' The team had also earned a reputation, unfair or not, for surliness.

For the armchair critics back home, England's final one-day defeat by 131 runs was meat and drink. Conservative MP Terry Dicks tucked in with the greatest relish. He said, 'I think the tour should be abandoned now. They should not be allowed to go out to the sun in New Zealand. They should be brought home in disgrace.' Now really gorging himself, he carried on, 'I would sack the management and half the team. I have never been so ashamed to be English.' Another Tory MP, Bill Cash, said English cricket had reached a new low. 'We have got to shake the whole thing up and produce some new talent,' he said. It wasn't just the rent-a-quote politicians who climbed into England. The former England captain Brian Close, my mentor as a young player at Somerset and a man whose opinions on cricket are usually direct and to the point said simply, 'The players want their arses kicking.'

Despite occasional upturns in form and the undoubted enthusiasm of new coach Lloyd, the underlying theme running through England's performances during 1996 was that as a cricketing nation we were going nowhere fast. The statistics said it all: nine Test matches were played in the twelve-month period, one against South Africa, three against India, three against Pakistan and two against Zimbabwe. England managed one solitary victory, the first Test of the summer against India at Edgbaston. They lost three, the first against South Africa to surrender the a five-Test series, two to Pakistan in the 2-0 defeat in the second half of the summer, and drew the other five matches – two against India, one against Pakistan and, most unforgivably in the eyes of politicians, players and punters alike, two Test matches in Zimbabwe.

In one-day international cricket, they did reach the quarter-finals of the 1996 World Cup – but after losing to every Test playing nation, and only because they managed to defeat Holland and the United Arab Emirates. In total, of the twenty-one matches completed, England won just six, losing fifteen. In all international cricket they played thirty-one matches, won seven, and lost eighteen. Whichever way you care to look at it, that record simply wasn't good enough. Certainly the sponsors of England's Test team, Tetley Bitter thought so as well.

When in the autumn of 1996 Tetley announced that their sponsorship would finish at the end of the 1997 Ashes series, they insisted it was because of 'changes in the brewing industry and changes in marketing strategy'. Those changes may well have had something to do with it. But it was the lack of change in the fortunes of the England team which persuaded them to make their decision.

Tetley had been sponsoring England's Test cricketers for four years. In September 1994 they announced a renewal of the sponsorship, which was intended to last until the end of the summer of 1999, during which they had intended to try and capitalise on the global exposure created by the Cricket World Cup being played in England.

But when Tetley informed the Test and County Cricket Board they would be exercising their contractual right to opt out of the deal two years early, it was a wake-up call that could be heard the length and breadth of the country. For the key element in their decision was their dissatisfaction with the continued lack of success at the top level. They simply didn't want to be associated with a losing team anymore.

When Tetley took up the sponsorship in 1992, they struck gold. Immediately after putting the Tetley logo on their shirts, England won their first Test series for eighteen months. Their 2-0 success on the 1992 tour to New Zealand was their first Test series victory away from home since England retained the Ashes in 1986-87. Following that, Graham Gooch's side finished runners-up to Pakistan in the World Cup in Australia and New Zealand. Tetley were rubbing their hands together in satisfaction at the success of their marketing ploy.

From that high point, however, England's record went from bad to worse. They lost eight of their next twelve series, beating only India and New Zealand and when that sequence culminated in 2-0 defeat by Pakistan in the summer of 1996, not surprisingly Tetley decided the time had come to stop backing a losing horse. It wasn't just the way the team played that persuaded Tetley to turn off the tap; the sponsors were also unhappy with the way England looked and the way they behaved. Market research had told them that although brand awareness had increased during the sponsorship with more people learning about their product, they were not necessarily drinking it – not even when England's latest abject performance drove them screaming to the bar.

By the time England played the final two one-day internationals in Zimbabwe in 1996, they had been joined by Lord MacLaurin, the new chairman of the English Cricket Board, and Tim Lamb, the chief executive. Perhaps for the future benefit of English cricket, it was as well they were there to watch England's surrender.

Tim Lamb spoke for himself and his boss when, on England's return from the second leg of the tour to New Zealand, at the annual general meeting of The Council of Cricket Societies, he said, 'The England team's performances over recent years have been extremely disappointing, and I think the way in which the England team have conducted themselves recently is also disappointing.

'Ian MacLaurin and I were absolutely horrified by what we saw in Zimbabwe. We were very very disturbed by some of the things we came across.

'We thought David Lloyd's comments in Bulawayo were completely inappropriate. We were not happy with the way the England team presented themselves. We understand their demeanour was fairly negative and not particularly attractive.

'I think the way they presented themselves in terms of their dress left a lot to be desired. That was a factor in Tetley Bitter not renewing their sponsorship. Things improved in New Zealand, but there is a long way to go.' A long way to go? Tim Lamb can say that again.

England did improve in New Zealand. It was almost impossible for them not to do so. But no one was getting carried away by the 2-0 score in the Test series, nor the 2-2 draw in the one-day international matches against New Zealand, who were, without doubt, one of the poorest international sides I've ever seen.

Mike Atherton's team could and should have won the series 3-0. The fact is, however, that the resilience of Danny Morrison and Nathan Astle in the first Test in Auckland and New Zealand's improved bowling in the third Test in Christchurch meant that without the captain's batting in that final Test, England may well have finished the Test series having drawn 1-1. Against a team comfortably the worst-rated in world cricket, that would have been a disaster. As Atherton explained after the series was over, had England not won that three Test series in New Zealand, he would have resigned, and rightly so.

I say that not because I think Atherton is a poor captain or an unworthy leader. He's an exceptional player and his batting performances have dug

England out of holes of their own creation more often than he, or they, would care to recall. No one who witnessed his magnificent 185 not out to save the second Test against South Africa at the Wanderers Ground in Johannesburg will ever have reason to doubt Atherton's commitment, determination, professionalism and sheer batting skill, nor his courage. But there comes a time in the career of a captain when no matter what he does, what plan he puts into operation, what words he imparts to his team, *nothing* works.

Having said that, Atherton has been on a hiding to nothing ever since he took over the captaincy from Graham Gooch in 1993. So was Gooch before him, so was David Gower before him, so was Mike Gatting before him. The reason? – the lack of world class talent produced by a domestic system that belongs in ancient history.

And I believe that fact was borne out by events during the summer of 1997. After starting in such breathtaking style, winning the Texaco Trophy series and the first Ashes Test England were finally exposed and outclassed against the unofficial world champions. There efforts were laudable and brave and all the rest, but in the end they were just not good enough to win. By the time the Ashes were surrendered Atherton was looking and playing as though he had had a gutful.

The new enthusiasm injected into proceedings by MacLaurin and Lamb at the start of the summer of 1997 had had an immediate affect. Glory be, England thrashed Australia in the Texaco Trophy series and then won handsomely in the first Ashes Test at Edgbaston. 'Crisis, what crisis?' came the cry from the counties once more.

And it was in this atmosphere of optimism that the two men at the head of the English game set their minds to devising their blueprint to take English cricket back to the top of the world game. By the time England had lost the Ashes by going down heavily in the fifth Test at Trent Bridge, MacLaurin's plan, *Raising the Standard* had been revealed. There were some good proposals from grassroots cricket all the way up to the top, but then came MacLaurin's baseball-style conference at the apex of the pyramid. Oh dear. Indeed, many counties realised MacLaurin had not gone far enough; thus the late push for his three-conference system to be replaced by straight promotion and relegation.

There are those who will react to the question 'What's wrong with English cricket' by saying 'nothing'. They will claim that fortunes in Test cricket are cyclical, and things will come right if we just wait long enough and leave them well enough alone. That is dangerous nonsense. I am not the only one who believes that either. Just ask Lord MacLaurin.

MacLaurin, to whom the counties turned at the end of 1996 as Chairman of the TCCB, soon to become the England and Wales Cricket Board, is the man who turned Tesco from a family-run business making £12 million worth of profits in 1976 into Britain's premier food retailer with a profit of £750 million for the financial year to April 1997. In 1976, by now managing director of the company he'd joined as a trainee in 1959, he took on and won a boardroom battle that changed the course of British retailing history. His principal opponent was no Tom, Dick or Harry, but Sir Jack Cohen, the chairman of Tesco, the business he had co-founded in 1926. And the bone of contention just happened to be the brainchild of Cohen and the cornerstone of Tesco's success for many years, Green Shield Stamps.

MacLaurin had done his homework and discovered that the stamps had become an unwanted anachronism. As he said, 'Stamps had been an integral part of Tesco's success, but it was very apparent to me visiting the stores, that the customers didn't want them anymore. They were costing us, Tesco's, £20 million per year to produce, and the customers were handing them back.' Certain that he was right and that the company needed to shed its 'pile 'em high, sell 'em cheap' image and be repositioned upmarket, MacLaurin would not be shaken off. It took five bitter recounts for him to win the boardroom vote 5-4 and earn the right to pursue his plans to transform the company.

He said, 'Before I attempted to turn Tesco around and into a world class act, people told me I was crazy. They said it simply couldn't be done. I heard the same things about taking on English cricket. But there is an awful lot to be done.

'I don't want to criticise what has gone on in the past, but we cannot shy away from the fact that England's Test team have not been in the top echelon of international cricket for some time.

'There are those who persist in claiming that success in cricket is cyclical, that if you wait long enough it'll all come right of its own accord. I simply don't believe that is true.

'You wouldn't last very long in my business if you just said "everything is cyclical". Just imagine if you went to the shareholders and told them, 'I'm terribly sorry that we've lost all this money this year, but I'm sure if you hang on and keep investing your cash, perhaps in a few years time we might make a profit.' We have to be realistic. If nothing is done to turn things round, the most pessimistic scenario is that the game will wither on the vine.' MacLaurin has a clear view of the alternative to decisive action. It goes like this: 'If we continue to do badly at international level and end up getting beaten by the Isle of Dogs, people will simply not pay to come and watch, and neither will the television companies whose money along with Test match receipts subsidises the first-class game. Then the counties will be in dire financial straits and the kids will ask, 'what was cricket?'

MacLaurin is right. But it was only after he presented an alternative so baffling as to be impossible to comprehend that some counties changed their tune and dropped their opposition to promotion and relegation.

For those among the county chairmen who don't believe things are as black as they are being painted, just consider these facts. Since retaining the Ashes in 1986-87 and prior to the start of the summer series of 1997, England had not won a full five or six Test series against anyone. Between the start of the 1987 home series against Pakistan and the final Test of the 1996-97 tour in New Zealand, England played 98 Tests. They won twenty of them – two versus Australia (out of 23), two against India (out of nine), six against New Zealand (out of 15), one against Pakistan (out of 16), one against South Africa (out of eight), two against Sri Lanka (out of three), six against West Indies (out of 25) and none against Zimbabwe (out of two).

They had won eight series, four against New Zealand, two each against India and Sri Lanka. In the period concerned they failed to win a Test series against Pakistan, Australia, South Africa, West Indies and later Zimbabwe and both single Test match victories against the Aussies had come after the Ashes had already been decided in their favour. That record put them right at the bottom of the unofficial ratings of world cricket, an assessment underlined by the fact that when Benson & Hedges, the sponsors of the 50-over domestic one day competition, brought out their annual yearbook at the end of the 1996 season, and named their Benson & Hedges Cricket Year World XI for that year, not one place was filled by an Englishman. Their XI was Gary Kirsten, South Africa; Nathan Astle, New Zealand; Sachin Tendulkar, India; Mark Waugh, Australia; Aravinda de Silva, Sri Lanka; Steve Waugh, Australia; Ian Healy, Australia; Shane Warne, Australia; Mushtaq Ahmed, Pakistan; Curtly Ambrose, West Indies; and Allan Donald, South Africa. In that team there was no place for Wasim Akram , Waqar Younis, Mohammed Azharuddin, Anil Kumble, Brian Lara, Courtney Walsh or Aamir Sohail.

Nor was there a place for any of the England side that played against

Pakistan in the final Test of that summer series of 1996; Mike Atherton, Alec Stewart, Nasser Hussain, Graham Thorpe, John Crawley, Nick Knight, Chris Lewis, Ian Salisbury, Dominic Cork, Robert Croft and Alan Mullally. And nor, if the XI had been selected at the end of England's series in New Zealand would have the selectors been unduly taxed by the claims of Craig White, Chris Silverwood, Darren Gough, Andrew Caddick and Phil Tufnell. In other words, not one of the best eleven players that England could produce to contest a Test match in 1996 was considered good enough to represent a World XI. In fact, throughout the 1990s so far, only four England players have been picked for the Benson & Hedges teams.

Further evidence that, in terms of international standing England players are just not good enough came with the publication of the *1997 Wisden Cricketers' Almanack*. One of the most keenly-awaited features included in the cricketers' bible is the annual nomination of their 'Five Cricketers of the Year'. Their selection for 1996 was Sanath Jayasuriya, the man who turned 'pinch-hitting' into a new cricketing art form during Sri Lanka's astonishing World Cup victory; Saeed Anwar, the Pakistan Test opener; Phil Simmons, the West Indies Test all-rounder who inspired his adopted county Leicestershire to the Championship; Mushtaq Ahmed, the Pakistan and Somerset leg-spinner; and Sachin Tendulkar, the Indian master. Sadly, England players were conspicuous by their absence.

According to Matthew Engel, the editor of *Wisden*: 'The 1996 cricket season in England was in some respects the most depressing in memory.

'The consistent failure of the England team is the biggest single cause of the crisis, but it is not the crisis itself. The blunt fact is that cricket in the UK has become unattractive to the overwhelming majority of the population.'

The statistics do not lie. England's ten-year record shows that we cannot compete against the best Test playing nations in the world. When we win, we win against New Zealand and India. But we're quite capable of losing to anyone.

English cricket is in crisis, of that there is no doubt. Not only are England's performances on the field in international and Test cricket simply not good enough, but the county clubs are living in a fool's paradise if they believe that they can exist through county cricket alone. During 1996, of the eighteen county cricket clubs, eleven received more than half their income from the Test and County Cricket Board from Test match receipts and television revenue. In the case of Derbyshire and Glamorgan, the figure they received was seventy per cent.

The counties depend for their survival on the England team performing properly, performing well and winning. If they continue to languish near the foot of the table of international cricket rankings, then it's not only sponsors like Tetley who will switch off.

The new England and Wales Cricket Board was able to broker a deal with Vodafone, to fill the gap caused by Tetley's withdrawal, but no one inside the Board was in any doubt that it was only the presence of MacLaurin at the head of the game that encouraged Vodafone, of which he was a non-executive director, that English cricket was worth the gamble. Nor should they be under any illusions that unless things change substantially for the better, this may be the last big-money payday of its kind.

If the results of England's national team do not start to improve hugely and quickly, I can imagine the following conversation taking place between the man chosen to replace MacLaurin after he walked out in despair and Sky television executives when the contract worth £60 million is up for renewal.

ECB man to Sky negotiator: 'Would you mind awfully if we had that £60 million again, please?'
Sky negotiator to ECB man: 'Sixty million for that? You must be joking. Come back when you've got something to sell.'

And then the game will be bankrupt.

I intend to trace how England's fortunes have dipped over the past ten years since that excellent victory under Mike Gatting's captaincy was achieved in 1986-87. I will highlight the mistakes, the arrogance, and the misjudgements that have plagued English cricket over the past ten years. I will discuss how counties have done a great disservice to the English national game by putting their needs ahead of the requirements of the Test side at most, if not all times. I will discuss the short-sightedness of those in charge of the English game in the past ten years of hurt. And I will suggest measures which I believe can be put in place immediately so that the job of rebuilding English cricket can start in earnest.

TEN YEARS
OF HURT
1987-1997

INTRODUCTION

*'From the moment when England secured the Ashes back in 1987,
it took ten years to persuade the men in charge of our game that
change had to come. Ten years of complacency. Ten years of waste.
Ten years of hurt.'*

WINNING the 1986-87 series against Australia down under should have created a platform from which England could seek to dominate world cricket for a decade.

Instead it might just have been the worst thing I and my colleagues could have done for the game in this country because the successes we achieved under Mike Gatting's captaincy merely served to paper over the cracks.

The feeling created by our performances down under, that everything in the English garden was rosy, turned out to be an illusion. Complacency was allowed to set in and complacency is death.

Australia reacted to their defeat by setting out long-term, clearly-defined goals to revive their fortunes at international level. They had lost to the Poms just once too often for comfort, realised a plan needed to be devised and stuck to it. Their rise to the status of unofficial world champions demonstrates just how well they put their strategy into practice.

We, on the other, hand proceeded as usual merely to look from one Test match and one Test series to the next.

Indeed, it was not until Mike Atherton was appointed captain to succeed Graham Gooch in 1993 that any kind of long-term selection strategy came into play. Atherton was appointed with a mandate for change, carte blanche to pick young players for the 1993-94 tour to West Indies and let them develop individually and as a team, no matter what short-term setbacks they might suffer. How long did the plan last? Three

Test matches. In came Raymond Illingworth as Chairman of Selectors and, over the next two seasons, back came Graham Gooch, Mike Gatting and John Emburey as players. There's long-term strategy for you.

From the moment England secured the Ashes back in 1987, it took ten years to persuade the men in charge of our game that change had to come. Ten years of complacency. Ten years of waste. Ten years of hurt.

When I review the performances of the England team during the decade in question one thing is immediately obvious, namely the apparently huge difference in the level of the talent available to England as opposed to that emerging elsewhere.

To the naked eye, the difference in quality is startling. While a steady stream of competent batsmen and the occasional high-class act like Mike Atherton have emerged, England have failed to produce one consistent world-class Test bowler, pace, swing, seam or spin, for a decade. When you look around world cricket the difference between the top cricketing nations and England in this respect tells it own story.

Just ponder this list of world-class Test match winners operating during the period in question – Shane Warne, Merv Hughes, Terry Alderman, Wasim Akram, Waqar Younis, Mushtaq Ahmed, Curtly Ambrose, Courtney Walsh, Allan Donald and Anil Kumble – and compare them with the best England have had to offer.

But great players are made as well as born. It is clear that, for too long, England players have reached Test level in spite of our domestic system rather than because of it. Thank goodness Lord MacLaurin understands that success is not merely cyclical and that change is absolutely fundamental for the future well-being of cricket in this country. In *Raising the Standard*, his plan to take English cricket back to the world summit, all those measures he is seeking to implement below first-class level demonstrate his clear sightedness and vision and, given a late change of mood among the most reactionary clubs, at the time of writing the possibility existed that he might even be given a mandate for real change.

But my reflections on England's struggles in the period 1987-1997 also concern the mistakes, the short-sightedness, the selfishness and the plain incompetence of those individuals who, despite all the constraints placed on them by the shortcomings of the county game, could and should have made a difference.

ONE
FROM HEROES TO ZEROES

'It was all a total fiasco. From Ashes winners eighteen months earlier England ended the summer of 1988 as the laughing stock of world cricket.'

It had started so brightly. Mike Gatting's success in leading England to victory on the 1986-87 tour down under represented a tremendous personal achievement. Written off as 'can't bat, can't bowl, can't field' no-hopers during the warm-up matches, we stuffed those words down the throats of our critics once the serious business started and won the Test series 2-1. There is no doubt that Gatting's captaincy was a major factor in the transformation.

Emphatically a player's captain, Gatt understood right from the start that if you treat cricketers like adults, giving them enough leeway when appropriate and a few hard words when necessary, you are far more likely to gain their confidence and get the best out of them rather than by simply attempting to impose your will on them. Even when early results tended to suggest otherwise, he knew that there was no cause for alarm and certainly no need to panic, and he was comfortable with the knowledge that, in terms of preparation, most senior Test players know what is best for them and don't need telling. Our results, winning the Ashes and the World Series competition, spoke for themselves.

Yet within little over a year after we returned from that wonderful tour, Gatting had been sacked and the England team thrown into turmoil. A year and a bit later he made the decision to turn his back on the England team by signing up for the 1989-90 'rebel' tour to South Africa. The story of how Gatt fell from grace underlines the confusion and lack of leadership from the top that dogged our national summer game for the best part of a decade.

Ever since Ted Dexter led the first England party to tour Pakistan in 1961-62, there had been rumblings of discontent over the standards and motives of the home umpires. England won the first Test ever played between the two countries in Pakistan, but from that initial success until the present day, we have never won there again. Prior to England's 1987 tour, no player or official had ever spoken out publicly on the subject, but a succession of England touring parties had considered this more than mere coincidence.

The build-up to the eruption that occurred at Faisalabad in the second Test of that 1987 tour had started during Pakistan's visit to England to play five Tests during the previous summer.

The trouble began even before a ball was bowled, when the Pakistan team, through their manager Haseeb Ahsan, officially objected to the TCCB over the presence on the Test umpiring panel of Ken Palmer and David Constant. Constant had been in the bad books of the Pakistan captain Imran Khan ever since their previous visit to England in 1982, when Imran believed he made a poor decision in the deciding Test of a three-match series at Headingley that he was convinced cost his side the match.

I happened to be batting at the time the incident occurred. After having bowled Pakistan out for 275, we were heavily in the mire at 77 for four with Imran himself bowling beautifully in conjunction with their leg-spin wizard Abdul Qadir. I decided that the best form of defence was attack and took on Qadir and my approach paid off as I made 57 out of a stand of 69 with David Gower in just over an hour. My efforts to break free of the Pakistan stranglehold were frustrating for Imran and his players, and their mood was not helped when Qadir felt certain he had found the edge of Gower's bat for a catch behind when he had made only seven. Had Gower gone then, Pakistan might well have seen off the tail and gone on to force victory. But Constant turned down huge appeals, Gower survived to make 74 and drag us to 256. I then took five wickets in their second innings of 199 and, set 219 to win, we got there by the narrow margin of three wickets, thanks in no small measure to the forty-two extras contributed by the Pakistan attack.

From where I was standing I honestly was not certain whether Gower had hit the ball or not, and neither, I am sure, could Constant have been. If he made a mistake, it was a genuine error, the kind that all umpires make because they are human. Imran saw it differently, as evidence, in effect, that he and his side were cheated by biased umpiring. Afterwards Imran hit out at Constant, claiming the decision had cost his side the match, and he carried those thoughts with him for the next five years.

What really riled Imran in 1987 was that although the TCCB had agreed to a request by the Indians, in that same summer of 1982, to have Constant taken off the list for their three-Test series with England, when the Pakistan management made the same request now they flatly refused on the grounds of prejudice. To a certain extent I can understand Imran's feelings. Although it may have been feeble of the Board to bow to India's wishes in 1982, not to comply with the Pakistan request was at best inconsistent and illogical and at worst bound to inflame any perceived sense of injustice they may have harboured.

The news of what had happened was leaked during the second Test at Lord's, in which Constant was standing and he stood again in the final match at The Oval. Both times Haseeb Ahsan publicly criticised Constant over his umpiring and at one stage described him as 'a disgraceful person.'

But this was by no means the only spark of controversy in a series that left everyone with a nasty taste in the mouth. Off the field there was trouble at Edgbaston during the third one-day international when some idiots, fuelled by booze and racial prejudice, fought with Pakistani youths on the terraces. Then in the first Test at Old Trafford, a rain-ruined match going nowhere, Pakistan managed to bowl 11 overs in an hour after tea on the second day. When Micky Stewart, the manager, commented on this, Imran reacted by saying: 'We get slagged off and called cheats and I object to that.' Then came the incidents at Headingley that some might say seemed to support the description Imran objected to. Both involved the Pakistan wicket-keeper Salim Yousuf.

After bowling us out for 136 in our first innings, Pakistan made 353 in reply. Chris Broad, whose batting in Australia the previous winter was a huge feature in our success, played at Imran's second delivery and the ball brushed his left hand after he had removed it from the bat handle. The laws state that the hand has to be in contact with the bat for a catch to be given. Without the benefit of television replays the appeal from the bowler was probably made in good faith, but what made the dismissal so unsatisfactory from England's point of view was that replays of the catch itself clearly showed that the ball bounced fractionally before arriving in Yousuf's gloves. Still, no one was too put out at this stage. Sometimes keepers and slip fielders genuinely do not know whether or not the ball has arrived on the bounce and, when considering whether a guy has attempted to deliberately pull a fast one, most players will give the fielder or keeper the benefit of the doubt. There was no doubt at all, however, over Yousuf's actions some time later. I edged a short delivery and instantly and instinctively looked around to follow the flight of the ball. I could see quite clearly that Yousuf dropped the ball, scooped it up again after it had hit the ground, *then* claimed the catch. I'm not proud of what I said to him, but it was a knee-jerk reaction in the heat of the moment. I called him, to his face, a cheat, although there might also have been a couple of adjectives thrown in for good measure. The umpire Ken Palmer intervened and had his say and I fully expected Imran to admonish his player for such a blatant offence which, after all, reflected no credit on him as captain. Nothing was forthcoming from Imran, although he did claim later that he would have reprimanded Yousuf had I not sworn at him!

All in all we were more than happy when the series was brought to a close, though disappointed with the 1-0 defeat, and in hindsight it would have been better all around had there been a cooling-off period of a few seasons before we met up again.

That was not to be, as almost immediately after the 1987 World Cup, in which we finished runners-up to Australia. Gatting led his men to Pakistan for a three-Test series, to be followed after Christmas by the Bicentennial Test with Australia and then a further three Tests in New Zealand.

And here is where Gatting and England were badly let down by the Test and County Cricket Board and most particularly by its chairman Raman Subba Row and chief executive A C Smith. It didn't take a genius to work out that there were likely to be repercussions over what had happened that summer. To me, the fact that the Board did not see fit to try and prevent trouble before it started smacks of complacency.

Instead they dispatched the players with little more than a cheery wave and let them walk into a political minefield unprepared and unprotected, and when the explosions began they made a ridiculous hash of clearing up the mess. It was obvious that Pakistan were desperate to win, more so than usual because of their third successive defeat in a World Cup semi-final, this time to Australia and most importantly this time in Lahore, and by the time Gatting and company arrived rumours were rife that Haseeb Ahsan, by now a Board member and the chairman of the selectors, was intent on orchestrating revenge for having his request to remove Constant and Palmer ignored by the TCCB.

Tit for tat ensued when the Pakistan board ignored England's protests over the appointment of the controversial umpire Shakeel Khan to stand in the first Test in Lahore and it did not take long for their dissatisfaction to boil over. England were convinced that several decisions had gone against them in the first innings; then at the start of the second Chris Broad decided to take matters into his own hands. Given out caught at the wicket by Shakeel Khan, Broad simply refused to walk and told all and sundry why. 'I didn't hit it,' he said. 'You can like it or lump it, I'm not going. I didn't hit it and I'm not out.' In fact, more than a minute elapsed before Broad was eventually persuaded by his batting partner Graham Gooch that no matter how unfair he thought the decision, it wasn't going to be overturned.

That was bad enough, but after the game things really got out of hand. Quite clearly Broad's actions were unpardonable and worth at least a heavy fine. But Peter Lush, the tour manager, driven no doubt by a sense of loyalty to his players, totally misread the situation. Instead of fining Broad he issued what he called a stern reprimand, then appeared tacitly to support the player's actions by criticising the umpiring and calling for neutral officials. All of which gave Gatting the green light to stir things up even more after the match had ended in an Abdul Qadir-inspired defeat. 'We knew what to expect,' said Gatt, 'but never imagined it would be so blatant. They were desperate to win, but if I was them I wouldn't be very happy about the way they did it.'

When the players arrived at the Montgomery Biscuit Factory at Sahiwal to play a three-day match against the Punjab Chief Minister's XI the mood darkened. Several of the players had nights they will never forget, however hard they try – wrapped from head to toe in clothes in order to keep the bat-sized mosquitoes at bay, they sweated and sweltered and never got a moment's kip. And by the end of the experience the entire party were convinced that they were the victims of plain sabotage. Instead of laughing at their situation, they got more and more stroppy, to such a point that the slightest provocation was bound to lead to an explosion.

It came three deliveries from the end of play on the second day of the second Test in Faisalabad and involved Gatting and the umpire Shakoor Rana – a man whose reputation for upsetting visiting teams was established when Jeremy Coney, the New Zealand captain led his team from the field during the Karachi Test in 1984-85 in protest at his decisions – and the fall-out eventually led to Gatting's removal from the position of England captain.

Gatting was first accused by Shakoor of moving a fielder without letting the batsman know, an allegation flatly denied by Gatting himself. According to Gatting and several fielders close to the incident, Shakoor then called the England captain a cheat and swore at him repeatedly. Gatting, fuelled by all the real and perceived injustices that he felt he and his side had had to put up with, swore back. While this made for gripping television, the behaviour of both men was wholly out of order.

By the following morning, the seriousness of the row became obvious when Shakoor refused to take the field unless and until he received a full apology from Gatting. Gatting, I understand, would have been happy to do so as long as Shakoor also apologised and plans were underway for a joint statement to be issued, until, wound up, it is believed, by the Pakistan captain Javed Miandad, who had taken over following Imran's first official retirement, Shakoor changed his mind. Gatting would not apologise unilaterally so, with the two sides stuck in stalemate, a whole day's play was lost.

When it became clear that the umpire would not allow the game to continue the England management and those at Lord's had two options. The first was to bend over backwards and bow to whatever demands Shakoor imposed on them, even to the point of forcing Gatting to apologise against his will.

Coincidentally, the next day, the rest day in the match, was also the occasion of the TCCB winter meeting at Lord's. Finally, understanding that the efforts of Lush to talk with high ranking Pakistan Board officials had come to nought, they issued the following statement:

'It was unanimously agreed that the current Test match in Faisalabad should restart today after the rest day. The Board manager in Pakistan Peter Lush, was advised of this decision and asked to take whatever action was necessary to implement it. In reaching their decision the members of the Board recognised the extremely difficult circumstances of the tour and the inevitable frustration for the players arising from those circumstances, but they believe it to be in the long-term interests of the game as a whole for the match to be completed. The Board will be issuing a statement on the tour when it is finished, but in the meantime the chairman and chief executive will be going to Karachi for the final Test next week.'

Peter Lush read the following statement:

'*The Test and County Cricket Board has instructed me as manager of the England team to do everything possible to ensure that this Test match continues today and that we honour our obligations to complete this tour of Pakistan. We have tried to resolve amicably the differences between Mike Gatting and umpire Shakoor Rana following their heated exchange of words which took place on the second day. We all hoped this could have been achieved in private and with a handshake. Umpire Shakoor Rana has stated that he would continue to officiate in this match if he received a written apology from Mike Gatting. The umpire has made it clear he will not apologise for the remarks he made to the England captain. In the wider interests of the game Mike Gatting has been instructed by the Board to write an apology to Shakoor Rana and this he has now done.*'

[viz:
Dear Shakoor Rana,

   I apologise for the bad language used during the 2nd day of the Test match at Fisalabad [sic].

Mike Gatting
11 Dec 1987]

The players had agreed to refuse to carry on if Gatt was forced to apologise but in the end settled for a strong statement of their own, expressing full support for Gatt and their anger at the Board for forcing him to act against his will.

   The second option, which the Board did not take but to my mind should have done, was to tell the players to pack their bags and prepare to come home, while informing the Pakistan Board that unless they put a stop to all this nonsense by instructing Shakoor to issue his apology, they would call off the remainder of the tour.

   Once back in England the Board should quietly have reminded Gatting of his responsibilities and told him that any further breaches of discipline from him and his players would result in the ultimate sanction of suspension.

   The fact that they chose the former rather than the latter option displayed fatal weakness from the men at the top. Their subsequent award of £1,000 to each player as a 'hardship bonus' was just a joke. In Australia and New Zealand the players' behaviour failed to improve. Broad and Graham Dilley were both fined for on-field incidents; on-field dissent often led by Gatting and then later supported by team manager Micky Stewart gave the squad a reputation for surliness they surely deserved.

From that moment Gatting was dead in the water as captain. Had the selectors made a clean break then England would have been able to approach the 1988 summer series against the West Indies as a fresh start. Gatting himself would have been able to re-focus his thoughts on maintaining his position as the best batsman in the side and the players would have understood the price of poor discipline. Instead, although the Board issued a directive to the selectors to take into account a player's behaviour as well as his form, Peter May, the chairman of selectors, re-appointed Gatting without a second thought. Such muddled thinking invited disaster.

And then came Rothley Court. Gatting's critics had waited eagerly for the slightest opportunity to pile in and, while England were achieving a creditable draw against Viv Richards' side in the first Test at Nottingham his behaviour at the team's hotel gave it to them with knobs on.

The day after the Trent Bridge Test had ended two national tabloids ran stories of a 'sex orgy' at Rothley Court involving unnamed players. The next day Gatting was named as one of them and by the afternoon of 9 June he was sacked. Gatting admitted to the selectors that he had invited a woman to his room for a birthday drink but denied any impropriety. The selectors said they accepted Gatting's version of events , then sacked him anyway. The saga then rumbled on when the Board fined Gatt £5,000 for publishing a chapter on the events of the Pakistan tour in his auto-biography *Leading From the Front* because of the contractual obligation not to comment on recent tours.

In between times the captaincy issue took on the nature of a game of pass the parcel. John Emburey was appointed for the second and third Tests, although increasingly unsure of his place. Chris Cowdrey, on the strength of Kent's performances in the Championship was then given the job when in spite of the fact that while a lovely bloke he resembled a Test match cricketer in name only. Finally, after Cowdrey had been ruled out of the final Test through injury, the selectors turned to Graham Gooch. Twenty-three players were used during the summer series. England lost 4-0. It was all a total fiasco. From Ashes winners eighteen months earlier England ended the summer of 1988 as the laughing stock of world cricket.

There was more, much more, to come, starting with the cancellation of England's 1988 winter tour to India.

TWO

TED LORD AND HIS BRAVE NEW WORLD

'His [Dexter's] habit of opening his mouth and walking straight into it had ensured that a man once considered merely an eccentric was developing a reputation for being dangerously out of touch.'

UNDER the captaincy of Graham Gooch England had made a better fist of things in the final Test of the 1988 summer series with West Indies. They still lost, by eight wickets, but at least England played as though they were a team rather than the disorganised rabble that had been on show previously, and they finally brought to an end a run of eighteen Test matches without success when they beat Sri Lanka in a one-off Test at Lord's.

On purely cricketing grounds Peter May, the retiring chairman of selectors, must have been relieved to be able to appoint Gooch to lead the winter tour party to India. But that feeling turned to dismay once again almost immediately. From the moment Gooch was appointed speculation was rife that the Indian government, hard-liners on the issue of sporting links with South Africa's apartheid regime, would object to Gooch's presence. And when, two days after the squad was announced on 7 September, the Indian government announced that no player 'having or likely to have sporting links with South Africa' would be granted a visa, the cancellation of the tour was only a matter of time.

In their defence the Board pleaded that there had been no objection to Gooch as a member of England's World Cup party the previous year, but the powers that be must have known that the Indian government had stretched a point so as not to cause problems.

In fact, earlier in the summer Gooch had already decided not to tour India with England in 1988 but to take up the offer from Robin Jackman, the former England bowler and now the Western Province coach, to spend the winter over there in South Africa. But when he was sounded out by Doug Insole of the TCCB and asked if he was prepared to travel to India as captain of the side, Gooch said yes.

Once again the Board had allowed their lack of foresight to make them look just plain daft. Why had they not foreseen the question of the blacklist? And if they had, was it not plain arrogance that led them to believe they could sweet-talk the Indian government if things got difficult?

Finally, after two seasons of complete shambles, the Test and County Cricket Board decided to take swift and decisive action over the future course of the running of the England cricket team and its public image.

Towards the end of the year it was decided that, in future, the England team should be the responsibility of an England committee, and the next step was to decide who should lead it. To that end the chairmen entrusted this task to a two-man working party comprising A C Smith, the chief executive, and Raman Subba Row, the chairman. Subba Row, the man who had sanctioned the £1,000 hardship bonus to Gatting's 1987 Pakistan tour party, now had another brainwave. He reasoned that England needed a strong figurehead in charge, someone whose reputation as a cricketer would leave no room for criticism, and a man with the kind of charisma and public persona that would send off the right signals in the world of cricket. So far so good. The problem was his choice: 'Lord' Ted Dexter.

The next the county chairmen heard of developments was at the winter Board meeting at Lord's in January 1989. They had gone there to discuss the Board's position with regard to overtures being made to England cricketers by Ali Bacher, the leading figure in South African cricket and later to become the head of the Unified Cricket Board.

Rumours had been circulating regarding a 'rebel tour' set up by Bacher and the chairmen discussed how the situation should be handled when push came to shove. At the end of the meeting Subba Row threw in, almost casually: 'By the way, gentlemen, I think we may have settled on the man we are looking for to chair the England committee. Ted Dexter.'

Chris Middleton, the controversial chairman of Derbyshire who, four years later, orchestrated the moves to oust Dexter, takes up the story. 'I knew very little about Dexter apart from the fact that he had been a marvellous Test batsman for England, but at the time we as county chairmen were happy to hear that one suggestion had at last been put forward. We were told by Subba Row that this had to be kept secret and that we should tell no one, and we all agreed. I didn't even tell my wife.

'Nothing more was said or heard on the subject for a couple of months. Then, one evening in late March, I was at home watching television and saw Raman Subba Row, his wife Anne and Ted and Susan Dexter dressed up for an evening out and heard Dexter announce that he had been appointed the new chairman of the England committee, the new chairman of selectors.'

Dexter had been installed, all right, but with absolutely no reference to the county chairmen. And the decision of Subba Row and Smith to present them with a *fait accompli* caused severe consternation. Many chairmen felt that Subba Row had overstepped the bounds of his authority and they never forgave him for it. They had thought that any firm proposal by the working party would be ratified by them before being allowed to take place. No such procedure took place. And that was not the only surprise in store.

The England committee was to comprise Dexter as chairman, Micky Stewart, the England coach, and the captain, whoever that may be.

And in a further move unbeknown to the chairmen at the time, Subba Row also decreed that the committee was to be joined and influenced by another figure, namely the chairman of the TCCB cricket committee, Ossie Wheatley, who was to have the veto over the committee's appointment of England captain.

Subba Row believed the Board needed this safeguard on the England selection panel because of what had happened the previous winter. Such an unholy mess had persuaded him that a man with a broader view of the whole picture should be included in the selection process.

But by effectively taking one of the primary functions of the England committee, namely the final say over the selection of the captain, out of their hands, Subba Row merely undermined their authority over the process. The potential for confusion was enormous.

And so it came to pass when Dexter was called upon to make his first decision as the new chairman of selectors – the choice of England captain. Three names were mentioned: David Gower, Mike Gatting and Graham Gooch. Dexter interviewed Gower and Gatting but not Gooch and it became clear quite quickly that the Essex man was never in the frame. Presumably he didn't fit into Dexter's idea of the required new style of leadership. Not surprising really as in his previous role as newspaper pundit Dexter had written in the *Sunday Mirror* that Gooch's captaincy at

The Oval Test against West Indies in 1988 had the effect on him of a 'slap in the face with a wet fish.'

Gooch had offered the perfectly reasonable assertion that 'a team is only as good as the players. Nobody can turn a bad team into a good one.'

Dexter thought better. This was his responese: 'No wonder the England team is in such a sorry state if the is the general atmosphere in the dressing room … A captain must make his men feel that everything is possible. The Gooch approach means that the West Indies were inevitably going to win at The Oval and that he was resigned to that result before the game began. Translate his theories on to the battlefield and there would never be a victory against the odds. David would never have killed Goliath because it wasn't worth a try.'

Steady on, Ted.

The full story of how Gower was chosen ahead of Gatting, and for that matter Gooch as well, did not come out until it was made public by the England committee at the end of the disastrous Ashes campaign of 1989, presumably in order to deflect some criticism away from the selectors over what had happened that summer.

According to the story it was Gatting rather than Gower who had been the first choice of Dexter and Stewart. Indeed, prior to the appointment the rumour-mill had gone into overdrive predicting that the Middlesex man had the job in the bag. Enter Ossie Wheatley.

Wheatley was a former captain and chairman of Glamorgan and a contemporary of Dexter's at Cambridge. But ninety-nine percent of county cricketers would not have known him had they fallen over him. Wheatley, it was said, had decided that the time was not yet right for Gatting to be reinstated because of the events that had happened during his previous term of office. Wheatley was ostensibly mainly concerned with Gatting's public row with the Pakistani umpire Shakoor Rana in the Faisalabad Test on the 1987-88 tour and other examples of poor behaviour.

It was never said publicly, however, but most of us were convinced that it wasn't only the behaviour of Gatting and his team during that winter that led to Wheatley employing his veto. Quite clearly, according to the story, the business involving Gatting and the barmaid at Rothley Court in the early part of the summer of 1988 had had a large bearing on Wheatley's decision.

Wheatley informed Dexter and Stewart that Gatting should not be considered and the new England committee turned instead to David Gower.

Not a great way for Dexter's 'Brave New World' to begin. And as the summer progressed many commentators were crying out for a return to the cowardly old one.

The explanation that Dexter had originally wanted Gatting ahead of Gower has always puzzled me. I never thought of Gatting as Dexter's type of captain. Clearly Micky Stewart would have wanted Gatt, as he was the captain on Stewart's and England's successful expedition to Australia in 1986-87. He was also captain when England reached the final of the 1987 World Cup. Stewart and Gatting were very similar in their approach to the game and got on well. On the other hand, Gower, all elegance, grace and style was much more Dexter's cup of tea. Perhaps Graeme Wright, then the editor of the *Wisden Almanack*, writing his notes in the 1989 edition, came closer to the truth than anyone thought at the time. He wrote, 'As much a surprise as the veto was the discovery that Dexter should have wanted Gatting as captain in the first place.

'In the three weeks before the new committee met to choose the captain, Gower was generally thought to be Dexter's favourite for the job; he was the one the new chairman singled out for mention. However, no decision was made at that meeting, which was said to have contained "detailed discussion". Five days elapsed before Gower was accorded a press conference at which Dexter announced that he was "the committee's choice" to captain England for the series.

'There was just a hint that he might not have been everyone's choice.

'The trouble, when things are kept secret, is that people start to look around for explanations other than the authorised version. I have always been one for conspiracy theories. For example if Dexter wanted Gower, and knew that his number two, Stewart, wanted Gatting, the veto could not have been more in Dexter's favour. It gave him the captain he wanted and prevented an initial disagreement with Stewart. The existence of the veto was known from the outset to the four men on the committee, and Dexter looked the sort who was at home walking the corridors of power. Of course it is equally possible that, sometime in March, Stewart persuaded Dexter that Gatting was the man for the job.'

As Wright suggests, it is equally possible that Dexter enlisted the help of Wheatley, his old Cambridge colleague, to do his dirty work for him.

Whatever the truth, all this was to remain secret, particularly to Gower, until the end of the summer, although the curly-haired one did get an inkling that all might not be well at the press conference to announce his appointment. Micky Stewart sat there quietly, with thunder in his face, barely uttering a word. Then when Dexter was asked whether the decision to appoint him had been unanimous, he answered somewhat mysteriously, 'After a long discussion, David was the committee's choice.'

At first the Gower-Dexter dream ticket did engender a certain amount of optimism and hope. And at that stage Allan Border's Australians offered little cause for alarm for the forthcoming 1989 summer Ashes series. Although the tourists made hay against the Duchess of Norfolk's XI in the traditional curtain raiser to the international season at Arundel, then against MCC at Lord's, they lost against Sussex in a one-day match and then lost their opening first-class match of the tour to Worcestershire by three wickets. They then got into their stride against Middlesex and Yorkshire, winning both matches easily, but with a Texaco trophy shared 1-1 and one game tied, the stage was set for a close and competitive Test series.

It turned out to be anything but.

England were not helped that summer by an extraordinary catalogue of injuries to key players, myself included, and the distractions caused by the recruitment of the South African rebel tourists. But the selectors did not help their cause by making the extraordinary decision to ditch Chris Broad after only two Test matches. Broad, who had scored four hundreds against Australia in the last five Tests including three during the 1986-87 Ashes series at the end of which he was named the Man of the Series and International Cricketer of the Year, was certain to be Graham Gooch's opening partner for the first Test at Headingley but, although he performed adequately there he was out on his ear by the time England contested the third match at Edgbaston. As he later signed up for the South African rebel tour, the second Test at Lord's was the last time he played for England.

By then, however, with Australia 2-0 up after two Tests, it was obvious that Border's team was a vastly different proposition to the one we had faced in 1986-87. Player for player there didn't seem to be all that much difference between the two squads. The greatest single factor in their supremacy, however, was an almost obsessive hunger for success brought to the Australian side by their captain.

It became clear quickly that Border and his coach Bobby Simpson had left nothing to chance in their preparation for this series. They had been on the wrong end of hammerings in 1985 and 1986-87 and they had spent the intervening two years developing a side full of players whose commitment and dedication to the cause was unquestioned. Furthermore, Border himself had undergone a transformation of character and approach.

Border had made himself unpopular with some of his team-mates by insisting that their wives would not be able to join them in the team hotels at any stage on tour, and each player was made fully aware of what was required on and off the field. Border himself set the tone for how he wanted his team to play and it was an inspiration to them.

I was not the only one of the England players who had forged a reasonably close friendship with AB over the years and it was his approach to me that led to my decision to sign up for his state Queensland during the winter of 1988. Throughout the 1985 summer series in England Border had been a frequent and welcome visitor to the England dressing room at the close of play, so often, in fact that his closeness to myself, Gower and Allan Lamb caused some ill-feeling inside the Aussie camp – fraternising with the enemy and all that nonsense.

After the 1986-87 series ended in another England victory Border was again criticised for what the Aussies back home perceived as an over-friendly relationship with the old enemy. The criticism stung this intensely patriotic Australian and this time round he had made a definite decision to become Captain Grumpy of a collection of players prepared to snarl, sledge and play dirty if necessary. His approach was not necessarily one I would have adopted, but the results spoke for themselves.

While Gower was displaying all the politeness and good manners that Dexter had wanted his team to show, Border just got on with the job of stuffing the Poms. Robin Smith the Hampshire batsman who had come into the side the previous summer against the West Indies, was clearly shocked by Border's ruthlessness on the field. It was not just the sledging he encouraged from bowlers like Merv Hughes and Geoff Lawson but the fact that Border went out of his way to be positively unpleasant to Smith and all the other batsmen at all times. No one minds a spot of sledging or winding up the opposition, but in my book they went too far and AB took them there.

Smith recounts the tale when, during a particularly hot and tense period of play during one of the Test matches, more out of courtesy than anything else he asked Border if it would be okay for our twelfth man to bring on a glass of water for him. Border's reply shocked Smith. 'What do you think this is, a f***ing tea party? No, you can't have a glass of water. You can f***ing wait like all the rest of us.'

When Gower quizzed his opposite number over the change in approach, Border told him, 'David, the last time we came here I was a nice guy who came last. I've been through all sorts of downs with my team, but this time I thought we had a bloody good chance to win and I was prepared to be as ruthless as it takes to stuff you. I didn't mind upsetting anyone, my own team-mates included, as long as we got the right result.'

In the face of such open hostility England needed to be at the top of their game. Planning and preparation and tactics needed to be spot on and the players all needed to be focused and pulling for each other. Above all we needed clear leadership and direction from the top.

What we got, from the first Test at Headingley to the last at The Oval was none of the above and the result was chaos.

At Headingley we were treated to the first example of Dexter's knack of making eccentric decisions when it really mattered. Quite apart from leaving out off-spinner John Emburey thus sending England into the match with an all-seam attack, Dexter persuaded Gower that if he won the toss he should send Australia in to bat first. The decision to field first was apparently based on Dexter's belief that an approaching build-up of cloud might allow movement through the air. No cloud came but there was movement through the air all right, generally from the middle of the bat to the boundary.

Furthermore, the decision to bat first came from the fact that while watching the weather forecast on breakfast television on the first morning of the match, Dexter had apparently seen enough to convince him that the match was going to turn out to be a rain-shortened three and a half day contest. In the event, of course, not a drop fell. England won the toss, put Australia in and on a belting batting track watched them score 601 for seven declared on their way to victory by 210 runs.

The tone was set for the series. And by the end of the third day of the second Test at Lord's the Ashes were as good as in Australia's hands. At that point, England, with Gooch, Broad and Barnett gone, needed another 184 runs to avoid an innings defeat. At the press conference afterwards Gower snapped when, after a question from former England colleague Phil Edmonds who suggested that Gower had put every single one of his bowlers on from the wrong end, the England captain stood up and hurriedly announced he had a taxi waiting. Gower got a flea in his ear from

Ted, followed by the notorious chairman's vote of confidence, but although he went out and scored a quite brilliant hundred on the Monday it was not enough to save the day. The series was only a third of the way through, but Gower realised the game was more or less up.

By the time I returned to the side after injury for the third Test at Edgbaston I could see there were problems inside the camp. Gower and Stewart were clearly rubbing each other up the wrong way, when, that is, they were bothering to speak to each other at all, Ted seemed to be in a world of his own and too many of the players appeared to have the upcoming announcement of the South African rebel tour on their minds to concentrate on the job in hand. While the Australians were all pulling in one direction, we were pulling ourselves apart.

Speculation had been rife all summer. And throughout that Old Trafford Test the dressing room resembled the headquarters of MI5. Whispered discussions over who had signed up and who hadn't and sudden silences dropping like a guillotine whenever a player not party to the skullduggery happened to enter the room – looking back on all the goings-on, the situation was absurd. I found it sad that England players did not have enough on their plate concerning themselves with events on the pitch. I've never known an atmosphere like it and if anyone needed any proof that some of the England players cared less about playing for their country than their Australian counterparts, this was it.

On the final morning of the fourth Test at Old Trafford the tension lifted when the party of sixteen players who had signed up on the rebel tour to South Africa that winter was finally announced, but I believe all the uncertainty created by the recruiting could easily have been avoided had Dexter and Stewart taken hold of events from the start.

What was inexcusable was that, as well as Gatting, who had already told Micky Stewart he would not be available for the winter tour to West Indies, presumably because he was going to be playing cricket elsewhere, the identities of several of those being targeted by the South Africans had been known to Stewart and Dexter for some time. Gower was convinced that they had an awful lot of information which they did not pass on to him. He could have done with it, if only to decide in his own mind who he was going to persevere with during the summer series. There was little point him playing some of the guys who were not going to be around for much longer and three of the players named in the South African squad were involved in that fourth Test – Tim Robinson, John Emburey and Neil

Foster. A fourth, Graham Dilley, had been selected to play but was unfit on the first morning, and five of the others in that sixteen-man party – Gatting, Chris Broad, Paul Jarvis, Phil DeFreitas, and Kim Barnett – had already played in the earlier Tests of 1989. The TCCB had been aware of what was going on and had asked players who were in line for selection for the winter tour to West Indies to indicate whether they would be available or not. Dexter and Stewart had known for some time the names of many of those who had signed up, yet they never uttered a word to the captain or even attempted to keep him in the picture.

Indeed, when Dexter handed Gower a sheet of paper with the names of the rebels on the first morning of the Old Trafford match, the captain was more flabbergasted by the fact that his chairman already knew the names in advance of their release by the South African organisers than at their identities. How long had Dexter known? And why didn't he let Gower know as soon as he found out?

When Gower found out just how much had been kept from him he was understandably bitter that the two men had not deemed it necessary to take him into their confidence. He pointed out that had he known everything that the chairman and manager had known there is no way he would have agreed to certain aspects of team selection, particularly the recall of Robinson, who was included for his first Test of the series in the full knowledge of Dexter and Stewart that it would be his last match for England.

Dexter himself later claimed that he had wanted to take decisive action, that he had wanted to put the players on long-term winter contracts to reduce the likelihood that they would make themselves available for the South African expedition. And after this bitter lesson the TCCB allowed him to go ahead with that plan. But there is no doubt in my mind that he should have let Gower know what was going on. Keeping quiet was unfair on Gower as he was always going to be the one who carried the can for England's poor performances on the field (as he later did, when Dexter and Stewart shoved it in his hands).

Perhaps Gower should have made more strenuous efforts to find out himself. But most of the time he probably had other things on his mind – most obviously trying to get England to play like an international cricket side.

Perhaps the saddest aspect of the end of the affair was that it overshadowed totally the contribution made by Jack Russell in that Test match, displaying fighting qualities sadly lacking in others and managing to concentrate on the task in hand of giving his all for the team when all around was a confused shambles.

Russell batted for 5 hours 51 minutes to make his maiden Test hundred of 128 not out, and in any other circumstances his example would have been an inspiration to his team-mates. Selected for the first Test at Headingley, he was given a torrid time by the Australian fast bowlers Merv Hughes and Geoff Lawson; so much so, in fact, that many commentators suggested he did not have the technique or the guts to play against short fast-pitched bowling. He noted the criticisms and, prior to the second Test at Lord's, decided to do something about it. The day before the match he spent hours in the nets sharpening his reflexes against groundstaff bowlers chucking orange practice balls at him, and the hard work paid off when he made 64 in England's first innings there.

Very much in the mould of my old mentor Ken Barrington, Russell had red white and blue coursing through his veins. It meant absolutely everything to him to play for England. As it did for the Middlesex bowler Angus Fraser, who made his debut at Edgbaston and while Robin Smith was not born in England, the native South African showed more pluck for the fight than many of his English colleagues. Yet all their efforts were obscured by the controversy surrounding players who decided to turn their back on England. Smith made another 100 in the fifth Test at Trent Bridge but it was to no avail as Australia won by an innings and 180 runs and although England improved to draw the last Test at The Oval, it was widely expected Gower would resign the captaincy.

All through the series the mood had fluctuated between despair and disbelief. Injury after injury meant that England were never able to pick their side from the squad originally selected. And the farce reached a spectacular climax at The Oval when England went into the final Test with a seam bowler, Alan Igglesden of Kent, who Stewart helpfully described as 'England's 17th choice.'

According to Gower, 'We replaced Moxon and Curtis with Hussain and Stevenson, but no sooner was the team released, than the usual business of people dropping out started up all over again. Malcolm's back went, Fraser did his knee, and DeFreitas, called in as a replacement having reversed his original decision to go to South Africa, pulled a hamstring. We replaced DeFreitas with Greg Thomas, who said, 'Sorry, I'm DeFreitas's replacement for South Africa'. Norman Cowans and Riccardo Ellcock were both contacted at Middlesex and both reported unfit, and Glamorgan's Steve Watkin was described as too jiggered to stand up for five days. I'm not sure whether I laughed or cried. We eventually ended up with two bowling places still to be filled the day before the game, and to add to the confusion, Ted, Micky and myself all came up with two different names. Eventually, through a combination of phone calls, and me handing over the final pick to Micky out of sheer exasperation, we settled on Derek Pringle and Alan Igglesden of Kent. This brought us up to 31 players for the series, and if there had been any plans for an end of term dinner, we would probably have had to cancel for the lack of a big enough restaurant. Morale, as you might have expected, was not exactly sky high.'

Dexter's brave new world had come crashing down around him. Perpetrator of a catastrophic misreading of conditions at Headingley, his policy of keeping Gower in the dark over the defections was equally misguided. And his habit of opening his mouth and walking straight into it had ensured that a man once considered merely an eccentric was developing a reputation for being dangerously out-of-touch.

After Devon Malcolm had made his debut in the fifth Test at Trent Bridge, Ted Dexter, having been asked for any plus points he could think of from the match, answered by saying, 'Who could forget Malcolm Devon?' Then, at the final press conference after the match Ted set the seal on an unhappy summer by insisting, 'I'm not aware of any errors we might have made.' The first of these Johnstonesque bloomers in dealing with the media were only a hint of things to come.

Gower was resigned to losing the captaincy at the end of that summer series. In fact, he had thought very seriously about chucking the job in himself. In the end he never got the chance to, because Dexter sacked him anyway. But neither he nor I was prepared for what happened next.

Micky Stewart had been discussing with me all summer long my availability for the winter tour to West Indies. I had been approached by the rebel agents who told me they were prepared to break the bank to sign me up. I was not keen to go, but the money on offer was staggering, so I decided to call their bluff by asking for £500,000 for a three-year deal, knowing full well that was way above what the others were getting and confident that they would not be able to come up with the goods. Furthermore in my heart of hearts I wanted to tour the West Indies. They were the one country against whom I still felt I had something to prove. And I told Micky very early on in the piece that I was more than ready to try. In fact we had already discussed plans for the winter strategy and Micky left me in no doubt that he wanted me there.

Dexter, apparently, had other ideas. Making a mockery of his earlier unflattering description of Gooch, Dexter decided that the 'wet fish' should lead the side in the West Indies. Neither David nor myself had cause to fear that this would have a negative impact on our chances of touring. Although Gower had been told by Dexter and Stewart at the end of the meeting when Gower was relieved of the captaincy that they believed a change of direction was necessary, he had no reason to believe he would not be taking the journey with them. And I was looking forward to doing all I could to help a new team develop.

But in a decision which smacked of dictatorship from the top rather than a partnership between the management committee and the captain, Gooch was instructed by Dexter that neither Gower nor myself were to be considered for the tour. Later I got the impression that Gooch might not have wanted me anyway. But I was convinced that Stewart had done. Why else would he have spent most of the summer trying to persuade me to make myself available?

What bothered me was that the subject was not open to discussion. Dexter had made his mind up, and that was that.

As far as Gower was concerned, losing his place in the team was something that had simply not occurred to him as a possibility. He accepted that the decision to replace him as captain was probably correct. In fact he had intended to resign before being sacked but there was no question in anyone's mind that Gower was worth his place in the side.

No question in anyone's mind, that is, except the minds of those who mattered.

THREE
'ONE MAN'S MEAT...'

'The problem as I saw it was that he [Gooch] didn't understand that one man's meat was another man's poison.'

G RAHAM Gooch's period as captain of the England side was not without its successes. Indeed on that first winter trip to the West Indies in 1989-90 they were unlucky to lose the series 2-1 to Viv Richards's side. Against all the odds England produced a wonderful performance to win the first Test at Sabina Park, Jamaica, and had the rain not fallen to wash out their hopes of victory in the third Test in Trinidad, they would have taken a 2-0 lead and earned at least a share of the series. In fact, victory at Port of Spain might have been decisive. Several of the players who had made West Indies such a great force in international cricket over the previous decade were coming towards the end of their careers. Gordon Greenidge and Malcolm Marshall were under particular pressure. And in certain quarters it was even being suggested that Richards would also have to make way for younger blood.

Had England won in Trinidad it is almost certain that big changes would have been made and I doubt whether West Indies would then have been able to turn things round in the way that they did, winning the last two Test matches at Barbados and Antigua to take the series. Even then England were only denied a share of the spoils by a magnificent spell of bowling from Curtly Ambrose in the fourth Test at Bridgetown.

England also had success in the 1990 summer series against India and New Zealand, winning both series against reasonable opposition by a single Test. Our 2-2 draw with the West Indies at home in 1991 which I had the pleasure of securing with the winning hit in the final Test at The Oval, the 2-0 victory over New Zealand on the winter tour of 1991-92 in New Zealand, and the second place we achieved in the 1992 World Cup were all positive results.

There was plenty to admire in the way Gooch went about things on a personal level. His ability to lead from the front was unquestioned. And his hundreds in the 1991 series against the West Indies may well have proved the difference between a successful and unsuccessful summer. I also marvelled at the fact that Gooch's batting seemed to get better with age. He had made the positive decision to try and prolong his career by getting himself as physically fit as he possibly could, and his intensive training routines worked well for him. No one could doubt his determination and commitment, not to mention his skill with the bat.

The problem as I saw it was that he didn't understand that one man's meat was another man's poison. And this led to a tension in the relationship between him and David Gower that was not only contrary to the best interests of the side, but which I believe ultimately cost him the respect of the cricketing public as well as the England captaincy.

Gooch's methods encapsulated a more scientific approach to preparation for tours, namely, rigorous fitness assessments at the Football Association's National Human Performance Centre at Lilleshall and programmes devised by the assessor John Brewer, designed to make England's players as fit at the end of a day's play as they would be at the start.

Gooch felt that these programmes would not only make the players physically stronger, they would also encourage them to be mentally tougher. But the issue was confused by the re-entry to Test cricket of David Gower during that summer of 1990 and later, by my return to the side at the end of the summer of 1991 prior to the World Cup trip.

When Gower was recalled for the first Test against India in 1990 after an absence of seven Test matches, he was very much on trial for his place on the 1990-91 tour to Australia. He did nothing out of the ordinary in the first two matches at Lord's and Old Trafford but he lit up the third match at The Oval with a sublime 157 not out in the second innings, and prepared to pack his bags.

Gooch and Gower were England's top run-makers on that unsuccessful 1990-91 Australia tour, but that apart they had very little in common throughout.

Having achieved a measure of success in the West Indies a year previously with his new fitness methods, Gooch was understandably keen to implement them for this particular trip as well. And when Gower turned up at Lilleshall for the pre-tour fitness assessments he came face to face for the first time with Gooch's fitness guru, a certain Colin Tomlin.

Tomlin had worked with Kent and Essex on an unofficial basis, and had a reputation for pushing players to their physical limits. He certainly did in Gower's case on this first occasion. For the workload he imposed on Gower left the laid-back one laid-out.

To my mind, having picked Gower for that winter tour to Australia, Gooch should have left it up to him to decide how he was going to go about things. Instead of relying on Gower to make sure he didn't let his immense talent down, Gooch tried to mould him into his idea of a 'team man'. But he totally misread the situation. One of David's terrific strengths is that he has always been an individualist. There is no way you could harness him and his talent by trying to boss him about. But that is exactly what Gooch and Stewart tried to do on that Australian tour. And on occasions they ended up treating Gower like a naughty schoolboy.

It had all been so different from the approach taken by Mike Gatting, Gooch's predecessor, on the 1986-87 tour to Australia. Then Gatt had allowed the senior players a certain amount of latitude. He wasn't concerned with what we got up to off the field and he certainly wasn't interested in having the whole team run around the outfield incessantly or spend hours and hours in meaningless fielding practice. Gower knew what was right for him. He didn't need Gatting, and certainly not Gooch, telling him how to run his life, or prepare for his cricket. What you saw is what you got with David and trying to alter his basic approach to the game was bound to end in disaster. In fact, Gower outbatted everyone on that tour with the possible exception of Gooch himself; his hundred in the second Test at Melbourne enabled England to make 352 and take a first innings lead. But the second innings collapse from 103 for one to 150 all out meant England got what they deserved, a beating by eight wickets. And his wonderful 123 at Sydney followed by some excellent bowling from Phil Tufnell and Eddie Hemmings put England in with a chance of actually winning that third Test.

Gower was doing the business at that stage but Gooch just couldn't leave well alone. Gower's refusal to turn himself into a robot for Gooch's pleasure and convenience left Gooch bewildered and angry. Backed up by Stewart, whose ambivalence toward Gower had turned into open and mutual animosity during the 1989 summer, Gooch made his displeasure at Gower's lack of co-operation quite obvious to public and players alike. And when Gower tried to lighten the mood in the now infamous 'Tiger Moth' incident at Carrara during the match between England and

Queensland, Gooch and Stewart quite rightly saw it as a massive two fingered salute to them.

Gower and his England colleague John Morris, who had made 132 in England's first innings, hired a pair of 1938 Tiger Moths and to greet a century by Robin Smith they persuaded the pilots to buzz the ground at low altitude. They were both fined £1,000. According to *Wisden*, 'For all their dereliction of duty in leaving without permission a game in which they were playing, it was a harsh penalty for an essentially light hearted prank, reflecting all too accurately the joyless nature of the tour.' Sadly Gooch, Stewart and tour manager Peter Lush suffered a collective sense of humour failure and it cannot be coincidence that Morris never played for England again.

The fact that Biggles and his mate had returned to the airfield after close of play and happily posed for photographs had not helped their cause, nor was Lush best pleased to realise that he had unwittingly lent Gower the money to hire the Tiger Moth in the first place. But such heavy-handedness was always only going to exacerbate the problem, raising Gower's resistance to what he saw as a far too regimented approach to the tour.

When the series ended in defeat at Perth, Gooch made no attempt to hide his dissatisfaction at Gower's contribution. He indicated that he was far from happy with the performances of some of his colleagues, and that many of them had a lot to reproach themselves for in terms of attitude, commitment and effort. In his book *Captaincy*, Gooch reflected: 'David Gower represents my biggest failure of man management since I've been England captain. I struggled to get through to him. I must bear a lot of responsibility for that, because I've always wanted us to be on the same wavelength ever since I became England captain. We are, after all, in the entertainment business and David Gower has been a fabulous entertainer since he first played for England. When you consider the free way he bats, his record at Test level is marvellous – all those beautiful centuries ... an average way over 40 (and a good deal better than mine). Who wouldn't want a guy like that in the side? Yet on that Australian tour, I had more meetings with the management about David than anyone else and I'm sad to say that I felt more at ease with him out of the England team in 1991. I was very keen to have him in Australian because of his class and experience and no one was happier than I was when his big hundred at the Oval against the Indians justified his inclusion... I still have total respect for him as a player. Yet we don't see eye to eye on what I expect from a senior player.

I need a lot more from him than just seeing his immense talent flower on occasions in a Test match … To me his lethargic attitude can rub off on some of the others, those who admired and respected him.'

Gower put his side of things in his autobiography: 'There were elements of truth in my feeling uncomfortable with the way the team was now being run, but in broad terms I was willing to fit in with almost anything to carry on playing Test cricket. I certainly felt under pressure when the tour party gathered at the initial fitness training, partly because I had not managed to drag myself onto the roads five times a day, and would not quite be up to the sort of gruelling routines I knew they had in mind, and partly because I felt that the hierarchy would be fascinated to see how I performed there. I didn't do too badly, without looking the picture of happiness throughout it all, and the gentleman appointed to put us through our paces did manage to get a certain amount of vomit from me on the football field. I blew up at him more than once, although this again could have been perceived wrongly in that I've always needed a certain amount of anger to drive me on through hard physical exercise. The mission down under did not get off to the best of starts, either in terms of performance or team morale. You can defend the work ethic in terms of what you put in, you tend to get out, and Graham is the best example I've ever played with who would leave nothing to chance, either physically or technically. It does not suit everyone, however, and there was a lot of early niggling about the way we were preparing. Days off appeared to be out of the question, and a non-playing day seemed to follow a regimented pattern; down to the training ground, a longish session of physical fitness training, followed by nets, middle practice, and back to the hotel some time in mid-afternoon. Where the build-up was going wrong was the management's attitude of telling everyone what to do. The more you relieve people of individual responsibility, the more master-slave the relationship becomes and the more resentment creeps in. The thing was being run like a puppet show. No one expects to be handed a questionnaire to fill in every morning. What would you like to do today? How do you want your eggs done? What time would you like a net, sir? I'm not saying that at all. There has to be a basic team discipline, and indeed conformity. But each touring side develops an atmosphere. Get the emphasis right, and it will be a good one; get it wrong, and it won't.'

There had to be some common ground, and Gower was worth making the extra effort for, but I simply don't believe Gooch did enough. Instead, he hid behind the parade-ground mentality that he and Micky Stewart had developed, and battered away at Gower until even after it became obvious it was a pointless and futile exercise.

What also did not help team morale was Gooch's insistence on referring back to the team spirit that he had engendered in the West Indies the previous winter. More than one player told me how much those who had not been in the Caribbean resented being told by those who had, how much better things had been there. This was the 'in my day' syndrome being taken to a ridiculous degree. After all the 'in my day' in question was less than 365 days previously. I believe Gooch became obsessed with the Gower situation and he allowed it to cloud his judgement in many issues. To him, there seemed to be a right way of doing things and a wrong way and nothing in-between. He was right, Gower was wrong and that was that.

Even when Gooch tried to have it out with Gower when the squad moved on to New Zealand for a series of one day internationals after the Ashes series was over, the tenor of their conversation was very much along the lines of how Gower had failed to give Gooch what he wanted. Gower couldn't really accept what he was hearing. After all he had given his captain two Test hundreds, as well as highest score in England's first Test match in Brisbane, 61 out of a paltry first innings of 194 and 27 out of an even more paltry 114 in the second.

Gooch was not helped on that tour by an injury to himself which meant he missed the first Test at the Gabba where defeat set the tone for the series. But I believe he would surely have had better success had he understood and accepted from the start that Gower was not going to be bossed around by him and that rather than trying to impose his will on the left handed batsman, he should accept him for what he was, and just let him play.

It's quite extraordinary to think now that Gower's record of 407 Test runs in five matches at an average of 45.22 including those two hundreds counted for nothing when Gooch started to consider his plans for the following summer series against the West Indies in 1991.

To my mind one explanation for Gooch's treatment of Gower lay in the captain's close relationship with a certain Geoffrey Boycott. Boycott had grown closer and closer to Gooch over the years. When Boycs shouted, Gooch jumped and he was grateful to the Yorshireman for his help in fine-tuning his batting technique. But their closeness extended to a distrust of Gower. Some observers believe that the real reason behind Boycott's negative attitude to Gower was that he feared for the safety of his Test batting record.

In fact, following England's return from Australia, Gower didn't play Test cricket again for more than a year, when he made his belated comeback at Old Trafford in July 1992, making his 115th Test appearance, passing Colin Cowdrey's England record, and then overhauling Boycott's record England aggregate of 8,114 Test runs with an exquisite cover drive to the boundary, a fitting shot to make him England's most prolific run scorer.

Gower made his comeback almost exactly eighteen months after that ill-fated Tiger Moth expedition. An awful lot of time in the wilderness and an awful waste of time. By that stage I had made my own return to the international arena, and had seen at first hand precisely the kind of things Gower was up against.

My dealings with the Gooch/Stewart regime left me about as impressed as Gower had been. Having been omitted from the party for the previous two winter tours and with no immediate prospects of a change of heart, I had decided to make my own arrangements for the winter of 1991-92, and this included a season of pantomime. I hadn't been one of those placed on a year's contract to secure my exclusive playing services and there had been no concrete commitment by the England selectors that I would be recalled, so I decided I had to be open to commercial offers for the sake of myself and my family rather than wait until September to see if I'd be picked for the tour.

Although I made a return to the Test side for the final match of the series against the West Indies at The Oval it was not until after the end of that match that Gooch indicated he wanted me on board for the 1992 World Cup the following February. Gooch said he wanted me in New Zealand for at least a part of the first section of England's winter plans, and after negotiations BBC television agreed to reschedule recording dates for a series of A Question of Sport programmes which would allow me to make it out there in time.

It was not envisaged that I would take part in the Test series against New Zealand although I eventually did as a result of injuries, but I needed no encouragement to get myself fit for the tournament. To give Gooch and Micky Stewart their due, we had at least come up with a plan for our World Cup strategy, something that was sadly lacking in 1996, namely, that I should be used in what later became known as the 'pinch-hitter' role. And Gooch and Micky, were sensible enough to give me a certain amount of leeway when it came to getting myself fit for the job in hand. But there's no doubt in my mind that England lost the World Cup that year because we simply ran out of steam.

Gooch's insistence on nets and physical training that Gower had come across in Australia on the tour of 1990-91 was very much in evidence when England toured New Zealand prior to the World Cup and this perpetual grind took its toll. What is more I don't recall a single day off in the entire tournament. As soon as the New Zealand series had been completed what we should have done was go off to the Gold coast or some other resort for a week of rest and relaxation in order to repair the minor injuries that had been collected against the Kiwis, recharge the batteries and take our minds off cricket.

Instead we all trolled over to Sydney for a week of nets and mickey-mouse practice matches against each other. By the time the crucial games came at the end of the tournament, although we were the best team on show, we were physically incapable of raising our game and this became obvious in our final defeat by Pakistan at the MCG.

Nevertheless, reaching the World Cup Final was an achievement that should not be underestimated and it was certainly the high point of our performance under Dexter, Stewart and Gooch.

Within a little over a year, however, all three had been replaced. And the common-link in their overthrow was Gower.

England's summer series against Pakistan in 1992 has passed into history as one of the most acrimonious on record. At the heart of the controversy lay the conviction of myself, Allan Lamb and several other England players, not to mention Micky Stewart, that the Pakistan bowlers Wasim Akram, Waqar Younis and Aqib Javed tampered with the ball throughout. I remain convinced to this day that all three of them cheated by contravening the laws of the game. I refer specifically to the laws of cricket 42.4 and 42.5 governing unfair play.

Law 42.4: Lifting the seam. A player shall not lift the seam of the ball for any reason. Should this be done, the umpire shall change the ball for one of similar condition to that in use prior to the contravention.

Law 42.5: Changing the condition of the ball. Any member of the fielding side may polish the ball providing that such polishing wastes no time and that no artificial substance is used. No one shall rub the ball on the ground or use any artificial substance or take any other action to alter the condition of the ball. In the event of the contravention of this law, the umpires, after consultation, shall change the ball for one of similar condition to that in use prior to the contravention. The law does not prevent a member of the fielding side from drying a wet ball, or removing mud from the ball.'

In my opinion the actions of Wasim, Waqar, and Aqib Javed were in clear and direct contravention of those laws. Using their fingernails they made such an unholy mess of the ball at times that a ball that had been in use for 40 or 50 overs looked as though a pack of dogs had chewed it. Although most of us in the England dressing room had complained privately about what was going on, the real facts did not start to emerge until the fourth Texaco trophy match against Pakistan at Lord's.

Lamb was a central figure in the controversy. In the end, by speaking out publicly over what happened, he made himself *persona non grata* as far as the England selectors and the TCCB were concerned. But it was not until more than a year later when a libel case brought against Lamb by the former Northamptonshire and Pakistan pace bowler Sarfraz Nawaz revealed publicly the real reason why the ball used in that Texaco trophy match had been changed, that Lamb and I were vindicated over the matter. Suffice to say, the acrimony and controversy overshadowed almost everything else that happened during that summer.

It also, at first, obscured the appalling treatment of David Gower by Gooch, Stewart and Ted Dexter.

On England's return from their winter tour to Australia in 1991 it was clear that Gower no longer figured in Gooch's long-term plans for England. Gooch stuck to his guns throughout the 1991 home series against West Indies and it was no surprise at all when Gower missed out on selection for the 1991-92 winter tour of New Zealand and the World Cup that followed. Gower just didn't fit into Gooch's idea of what was required by a team man, and the captain turned his back on one of the greatest talents the English game has ever seen.

It was not until halfway through the summer of 1992 that Gower was allowed back into the fold. Gooch had seen the way the wind was blowing during the first two Tests of the series. Although England had made 459 for seven declared in the drawn first Test at Edgbaston with fine centuries from Alec Stewart and Robin Smith they had done so on a belter of a pitch, and in the absence of Wasim Akram, Pakistan's most penetrative and dangerous bowler. But by the time England had finished the second Test at

Lord's, and lost by two wickets, it was clear to Gooch that England's batting was fragile. They managed just 255 in the first innings and 175 in the second and although England might have won had Wasim and Waqar not come together for the match clinching partnership in Pakistan's second innings, Gooch had seen for himself how devastating the Pakistan attack had become by this stage and he wanted Gower back to help deal with it.

Gooch had kept Gower out of the side for so long on what was basically a matter of principle. It's funny how principles can become blurred when the need arises. Gower was not complaining. He was delighted to be back, not only to be given the opportunity to overtake Boycott's record, but also to resurrect a career he believed could continue for at least a couple more years.

Gower needed to be at his very best at Old Trafford. Pakistan had racked up 505 for nine wickets declared in their first innings thanks to a double century from Aamir Sohail and England were 93 for three in reply when Gower strode to the crease. How ironic that he was welcomed there by the man who had kept him out of Test cricket for so long. The Manchester crowd had to wait until the Monday morning of the match to see the prodigal son return with a bat in his hand. And as *Wisden* reported, 'What followed was Gower in spades: a squeeze through slips, a superb cover drive, a delightful push through mid wicket, a head high chance to first slip, and finally, only 31 minutes after he arrived at the crease, a cover drive to the boundary, a fitting shot to make him England's most prolific scorer in his 200th Test innings.'

Gower went on to make 73, helping England to avoid the follow on, and although his effort was overshadowed by more aggro on the field involving the Pakistan acting captain Javed Miandad, the umpire Roy Palmer and Pakistan bowler Aqib Javed, nothing could dampen the delight of the English cricket public at seeing one of their favourite sons back where he belonged.

If Gower's contribution had been to enable England to avoid defeat at Old Trafford, his batting in the fourth Test at Leeds helped England win by six wickets and square the series. Gooch himself was magnificent in that match. England managed to bowl out Pakistan for only 197, then Gooch withstood everything a typical Headingley seamer's pitch and one of the most potent attacks in world cricket could produce, making 135 on the same ground as he had produced a majestic 150 to help England beat the West Indies the previous season. The value of his seven hour innings was put into perspective when, after he was bowled by Mushtaq Ahmed's last delivery before lunch, nine England batsmen fell for just fifty runs. As had happened so often before, a ball which had hardly deviated became a swinging hand grenade as England plummeted from 270 for one to 320 all out. Waqar Younis took all five of his wickets for 13 runs in just 38 balls, leaving Gower high and dry on 18 not out. More good bowling in Pakistan's second innings which produced just 221, meant England needed just 99 runs to win the match. And this is where Gower came into his own.

According to *Wisden*, 'England's supposedly simple task turned into a three-hour trial of skill, nerve and self control. Reduced to three front line bowlers by an injury to Aqib, the tourists remembered Imran Khan's famous entreaty to act like "cornered tigers". Waqar, Wasim and Mushtaq bowled with magnificent, legitimate hostility, backed by a fierce gale of appeals for this that and the other. Rejection by umpires Palmer and Kitchen brought several displays of theatrical astonishment by fielders, as well as three invasions by Pakistani spectators. The pressure increased when Atherton and Smith both fell to Waqar at 27 but, thanks to Palmer's unwitting help, Gooch clung on for two hours before he was caught at silly point off Mushtaq, soon to be followed by Stewart. Gower also stayed two hours, making an equally ice cool 31, after Latif's cap throwing act failed to convince either umpire he had been caught behind. With some late assistance from Ramprakash, Gower finally inched his way to the target which squared the series.'

By his standards Gower did not have a great match in the deciding Test at The Oval. And he did not paint the prettiest picture when, in England's second innings, he shouldered arms to a ball that came back off the seam from Waqar Younis and was bowled for one, leaving England 59 for four and still 114 short of avoiding an innings defeat.

Pakistan duly completed the job to win the match by 10 wickets and the series 2-1. Afterwards Micky Stewart added fuel to the fire of the ball-tampering controversy when he announced at a press conference, his last before retiring as manager to be succeeded by Keith Fletcher, that he knew how the Pakistani bowlers managed to swing an old ball more than a new one, but was not prepared to reveal the secret.

The reaction to that was nothing compared to the outrage that followed the announcement that Gower had been omitted from the winter party to tour India. In fact, the row over the absence of Gower, Jack Russell and Ian Salisbury rumbled on for months.

FOUR
THE DEMISE
OF DEXTER

*'It would amaze me if Dexter, even though in overall charge as
Chairman of Selectors, ever selected a player off his own bat
for England during his period in charge.'*

There is no doubt in my mind that Gooch's decision to leave Gower out of the 1993 winter tour to India and ri Lanka was the biggest mistake of his career as England captain.

Since Gower's return to the national side for that fourth Test against Pakistan at Old Trafford he had proved what England had been forced to miss for a year and a half due to Gooch's intransigence. Now Gooch added the final insult. The junking of Gower and the way it was done were an absolute disgrace.

Perhaps the worst aspect of the whole affair was how Gower first heard of his fate, not via a phone call from Gooch, the new coach Fletcher, or indeed the Chairman of Selectors Dexter. He read it in a newspaper.

The final Test had been completed on 9 August. The squads for the winter tours were not due to be announced until 7 September. Although the selectors, who by this time comprised Dexter as chairman, Fletcher as coach, and Gooch, did not finalise their plans until 4 September, the day before the NatWest Final between Leicestershire and Northamptonshire at Lord's, it was clear that Gooch had made his mind up some time in advance. He owed it to Gower to let him know, for he must have understood how his long-time team-mate and sometime friend would be devastated by the news.

Most observers were convinced that Gower would be selected. There was no reason to think otherwise. But as the date for the announcement of the squads approached a rumour started to develop that Gower's place was not as secure as it might have been. What is more those rumours also suggested that his place in the squad would be taken by, of all people, Mike Gatting.

At first this was dismissed as absurd. But on Sunday 6 September, the day after the NatWest Final, the *Mail on Sunday* ran a story stating categorically that Gower would not be going to India. Gower read it, held his breath, and hoped the story was wrong. He also waited for a phone call from Gooch or one of the other selectors to clarify the situation.

The call finally came on the following day, Monday 7 September. Sadly for Gower, it confirmed his worst fears. Not surprisingly, Gower went ballistic. And so did the national press. At a press conference to announce the squad, question after question was fired at Fletcher and Dexter and no sensible answer was forthcoming over Gower's omission. Fletcher tried to fob off the press with some excuse along the lines that Gower's inclusion alongside that of Gooch himself and Gatting would have meant too many batsmen in the squad in their mid-thirties. This inflamed the public opinion even more.

Gatting, who had signed up for the rebel tourists in 1989, had only recently become available for England again, having had his ban cut in half after South Africa's re-entry to the Test arena had encouraged a mood of reconciliation. What infuriated many was that Gower, who had refused any inducements to take the krugerrand and run during 1989 and had stayed loyal to England, was being ditched, while Gatting who had so obviously failed to put England first was being welcomed back with open arms to take Gower's place. Furthermore Gooch had also made room for John Emburey, his oldest and closest friend in the game who, as a member of Geoff Boycott's original rebel party in 1982, was the only cricketer to sign up for two rebel tours to South Africa.

Critics of the decision also highlighted Gooch's record in this respect. Between 1978-79 and 1986-87 Gower had gone on nine successive winter tours. The following year he asked for a break, understandably. And since that time he had made no conditions on his availability for England. As Matthew Engel, editor of *Wisden* commented, 'The contrast with Gooch – his decision to go to South Africa in 1981-82, his refusal, for family reasons, to tour Australia in 1986-87, his need to have Donald Carr fly out to Antigua in 1986 to persuade him to stay because some politician had criticised him, the fact that he planned to skip the abandoned India tour of 1988-89 until he was offered the captaincy, even his insistence on not going to Sri Lanka (Gooch had said in advance that although he was happy to captain in India, he would not do so in Sri Lanka) – is very stark.' Gooch, Fletcher and Dexter might have gained a modicum of credit during the episode if only they had come up with a straight answer to the straight question: Why? They failed to do so.

I believe they were embarrassed by the decision because they had no logical or reasonable grounds to make it. And the harder they were pressed, the clearer their only option became. It was to shut up and hope that the noise and fuss would die down. It never did, and for that we must thank a group of dissident members of the MCC. Led by a gentleman named Dennis Oliver, and against the strong opposition of the MCC committee, these MCC 'rebels' proposed a vote of no confidence in the England Test selectors over the omission of Gower, Jack Russell and Ian Salisbury. When the members met the rebels won by 715 to 412 votes on site. However, the postal vote went in favour of the selectors by 6,135 votes to 4,600. Never mind their defeat, the rebels had made their point.

By the end of the winter tour, which turned out to be an unmitigated disaster from England's and Gooch's point of view, the decision to omit Gower looked a sick joke. England became the first team ever to lose all their matches in a Test series in India, going down 3-0, each time by a huge margin. Then they lost to Sri Lanka in a Test match for the first time. And the anger that the MCC rebels had so eloquently displayed grew nationwide.

Gooch's first error of judgement, in my opinion, was to carry on as captain at the end of that summer series against Pakistan. I believe he was reluctant to tour India at all, and this should have been the moment when he called it a day as captain. Instead, the ten-wicket defeat by Pakistan at the final Test at The Oval began a sequence of seven defeats against four different countries which ran up to and included the Lord's Test against Australia in 1993 which was lost by an innings and 62 runs.

I believe Gooch would have gone, in fact, had Micky Stewart's replacement as England coach been anyone other than Keith Fletcher, Gooch's friend and mentor at Essex.

During that summer of 1992 Gooch had made various noises along the lines that he did not fancy touring the subcontinent in 1993, and although his annual procrastinations about touring were legendary, this time it appeared he was serious. Clearly, if he did not tour India in 1992-93, that would be the end of his captaincy. Fletcher had taken some prising away from his county job at Essex, and had negotiated a five-year contract with the Test and County Cricket Board executive committee, the length of which stunned and angered the county chairmen when they became aware of it later on.

Fletcher wanted Gooch alongside him for his first tour abroad as coach and persuaded him to change his mind.

Gooch later admitted that his decision to go was a grave error. On the day the England party arrived in India, it was announced that his marriage to his wife Brenda was over, which set the tone for his trip. On top of the criticism he was receiving back home over Gower's omission, he was never at ease with himself or physically well, and he batted badly.

Dexter, whose hold over affairs had become increasingly tenuous, did not help much either. After England lost the first Test of that series against India in Calcutta, strangely electing to play only one spinner in an otherwise all-seam attack on a spinner's wicket, Dexter announced that as a result of the continuing poor health of some of the England players, a study into air pollution levels in Indian cities had been commissioned. To this day we still await the results of that study.

And the offer of what was construed as a feeble excuse for dreadful performances produced predictable results in the national newspapers, one of whom suggested that, in future, any player fortunate enough to be selected for India should acclimatise by revving a car engine in a locked garage.

After the smog, came the prawn. According to *Wisden*, in the second Test match at Madras, 'England were well beaten by eleven men and a plate of prawns as India won the match – and with it the series – by an innings and 22 runs. The night before the match Gooch and Gatting had eaten in the Chinese restaurant at the team's hotel; their meal included an extra plate of prawns. Shortly before the start of play Gooch, complaining of sickness and dizziness, was forced to withdraw from the game. Later, after acting captain Stewart had lost the toss, Gatting and Smith, who had apparently eaten chicken in his room, both left the field feeling ill. There followed considerable debate as to whether the players had ignored the advice they were given about diet.'

And after defeat there, England became the first side to lose every game of a Test series in India when they went down by an innings and 15 runs in Bombay. By the time England, minus Gooch, had moved on to Sri Lanka, lost the Test match and two one-day internationals there, Dexter had turned his attention to the question of facial hair.

It would be hypocritical of me to join in the criticism of how the players looked on that tour. Sure, it is important for the team to look good on the field, but when it comes to stubble, no one could accuse me of attempting to boost the sales of razor blades.

But by now it was open season for the England team and management. And when a photograph of Bob Bennett, the tour manager, attending a press conference wearing a T-shirt and ill-fitting shorts appeared in the national papers back home, the latest in a long run of unflattering images, it only served to fuel the fire of those who had been so outraged at the original selection for the tour.

Criticism within and without the game had reached such a pitch that on 10 March 1993 while England were going down to their second defeat to Sri Lanka in a limited over international, and the TCCB was meeting at Lord's to discuss the England team's failure, there was widespread speculation that Dexter would be forced to resign.

While the nation waited for an explanation for England's poor showing, Dexter once again got the mood all wrong. He had declined to give any explanation for Gower's original omission, and stuck to that line throughout; nobody had been fooled by his attempt to introduce the Calcutta smog into the list of reasons why England failed in the first Test, and now he encouraged his critics to pile in once again with his comments over Gooch's beard.

'There is a modern fashion for designer stubble,' Dexter was quoted as saying, 'and some people believe it to be very attractive. But it is aggravating to others and we will be looking at the whole question of people's facial hair.'

He might have said that they would be looking at the whole question of why England had been thrashed 3-0 by India.

There is no doubt that England's cricketers wilted in the face of the Indian experience. As *Wisden* reported, 'In the bar at the team's hotel on New Year's Eve, one of the less experienced members of the party was in such distress that he was already longing for home a mere four days into the tour. The communal violence in the wake of the destruction of the temple at Ayodhya had resulted in hundreds of deaths all over India and created an unsettled atmosphere among the squad. Their fears were heightened when the first international match, due to be played in Ahmedabad, was cancelled because the safety of the players could not be guaranteed. As a result of this and crowd disturbances at games that did take place, some of the party simply gave up trying to come to terms with a country that, at the best of times, can be quite overwhelming.' True, the schedule of matches and the constant travelling demanded was hardly conducive to allowing the players to concentrate on their cricket first and foremost. But without any clear leadership from Fletcher or Gooch the spirit in the squad visibly flagged. England's players should have been mentally tough enough to deal with everything that was thrown at them, but they clearly weren't. Gooch, who is not a great fan of touring the subcontinent at the best of times, withdrew further and further into his shell. All the time, nagging away in the back of his mind was the fact that he had been persuaded to carry on as captain for that winter tour against his better judgement. And his air of fatalism spread throughout the party.

The players had also been let down in terms of their technical preparation.

As the tour did not start until the beginning of January, England had had three full months to prepare following the end of the English domestic season. Fletcher had organised regular get-togethers at Lilleshall, but he had totally misread the conditions England would be facing and consequently organised exactly the wrong type of practice for batsmen and bowlers. India had formulated a plan in advance to get the best out of their spinners on wickets designed for them and they carried it out to perfection. The batsmen spent many hours of intensive practice facing the England spinners on artificial surfaces known as spin mats. These took spin but they were also quick and bouncy. The wickets England actually had to play on in India were dry and dusty, taking prodigious spin but with hardly any bounce or pace. Therefore when England's batsmen lined up against Anil Kumble the leg spinner, Venkatapathy Raju the left-armer, and Rajesh Chauhan the offspinner, the batsmen were bamboozled. All the batsmen had been used to waiting until the last minute before playing the ball off the back foot, and the bowlers got into a rhythm in conditions which bore no resemblance to what they would actually encounter when they faced the real thing. Their technique was all wrong.

This wasn't Fletcher's only mistake. After having returned from a spying mission to Johannesburg to watch India play in South Africa, Fletcher delivered his verdict on Kumble saying, 'He didn't turn a single ball from leg to off. We will not have much problem with him.'

Kumble finished up taking 21 wickets in a three-match series, Raju took 16 and Chauhan 9, and the Indian spinners took 46 of the 58 England wickets to fall in the series.

It was not an auspicious start for Fletcher in his new role as coach. But as he'd only just taken up the reins, the major criticism following the end of the tour was pointed in the direction of Dexter and Gooch and on England's return it was only a matter of time before both men had to go.

The lack of a sensible plan for the succession to the England captaincy now took its toll. Gatting's return to the fold had created speculation that he was now in line to regain the job he had lost five years previously, while Alec Stewart, who had captained the side in Sri Lanka in Gooch's absence was Gooch's preferred choice and odds-on favourite, particularly as the outsider in the race, Mike Atherton, had found himself out of favour in India.

England would probably have been thoroughly beaten by Australia in the summer of 1993 anyway, for among their number was a young leg spinner who exploded into the consciousness of England batsmen during that summer and stayed there ever since. Shane Warne set the tone for the series when he produced the 'Ball from Hell' to Mike Gatting in that first Test at Old Trafford, a delivery which spun from way outside leg stump and clipped Gatting's off bail. Gatt wasn't the only one to be flabbergasted by the amount of turn that Warne had extracted from the pitch and the ball did huge psychological damage for the series ahead.

But by now Dexter and Gooch were both beginning to lose the plot. Fletcher, meanwhile, just seemed out of his depth. As the summer wore on, England's policy, or lack of it, over Gooch's position and the actual selection of the side, became more and more muddled. Gooch, who had gone against his instincts in agreeing to captain the side in India, was again persuaded by Dexter and Fletcher to stand as captain at the start of the Ashes series. Once he had made his decision to comply with their request, Gooch had wanted to be appointed for the whole series to send out a message of solidarity and purpose to Allan Border's Australians.

Should things go badly he did not want speculation over his position to be constantly undermining the team's efforts and he was not happy when Dexter made the decision to appoint him for three Tests only.

By the second Texaco trophy match at Birmingham it was clear to me that Gooch was losing his way badly. England had lost the first one-day international at Manchester by four runs, but when Robin Smith lit up Edgbaston with his extraordinary innings of 167 not out, the highest score for England in a one-day international and the fifth highest in all, enabling them to reach 277 for five in their 55 overs, Gooch was presented with an obvious opportunity to rekindle confidence and enthusiasm. Australia set about chasing their target in a reasonably sedate manner, and when Mark Waugh and Allan Border came together in a partnership which ultimately proved decisive, Gooch, as fielding captain, looked all too satisfied with a policy of containment. In fact Waugh and Border hardly played a shot in anger, as they collected slowly but surely and reached their target with ease. Ian Chappell describes Gooch's performance that day as reminding him of a rabbit caught in headlights. England's all seam attack looked inadequate and their fielding became ragged. Not only did Australia win by six wickets, they overhauled England large total with two and a half overs to spare.

Gooch found some batting form in the first Test at Manchester making 65 in the first innings and 133 in the second before being given out handled the ball, but defeat there made up Gooch's mind that as soon as the Ashes were gone he was going too. Perversely however, this was the moment when Dexter decided to accede to Gooch's original request, and offered to appoint him for the remainder of the series.

Just prior to the second Test at Lord's, Dexter had a meeting with Gooch and put the proposition to him. Gooch, against his better judgement, agreed, but offered this rider to Dexter: 'I'll do it as long as I can begin to motivate the side to be more competitive.' What happened instead was that, after Australia had won the toss, Taylor and Michael Slater put on 260 for the first wicket. By a quarter to twelve on the third morning of the match Allan Border was able to declare at 632 for four.

England capitulated meekly, bowled out for 205 and 365 with only Mike Atherton who made 80 in the first innings and was run out for 99 in the second, producing a blameless performance, which was to stand him in good stead later when the captaincy issue was finally resolved in his favour.

The Test was lost, by an innings, before tea on the final day – before, indeed, the Queen had arrived for the traditional presentation of the teams. Gooch, who before the second Test at Lord's had criticised his players for not showing the correct 'mental fibre' and had taken on the responsibility of captaining England for the remainder of the series on condition that they perform better than they had done at Old Trafford, searched his soul again and found no reason to continue. Once again, however, he was persuaded out of making that decision by Dexter and Fletcher. And it was at this point that Dexter once again demonstrated that he was clearly out of touch with the public mood. At the press conference after the match Dexter sought to introduce a note of levity into the proceedings. In the circumstances it was exactly what was not was required. The reporters wanted answers to the questions cricket supporters all over the country were asking themselves.

There was a certain amount of residual anger over the Gower saga; he was still out of the frame for selection and yet those who had been picked were proving themselves clearly not up to the job. Mike Gatting, in particular, who many saw as the villain of the piece for being selected ahead of Gower for India, had managed just 4 and 23 in the first Test at Old Trafford and five in the first innings at Lord's. Although he made 59 in the second, some blamed him for running out Atherton when on 99, and many were now fed up with what they saw as Gooch's obsession of keeping Gower out of the side.

Dexter's first offering was feeble enough. When asked how much blame he himself took for all the bad selections Dexter replied, 'How long is a piece of string?' The mood inside the room where the press conference was held became more hostile but the longer it went on the more Dexter appeared blithely unconcerned. When asked for some serious observations about why England were underperforming Dexter responded with his idea of a joke. He said, 'We may be in the wrong sign … Venus may be in the wrong juxtaposition with somewhere else.'

Dexter said afterwards that he had been harpooned and lampooned by the press. It seemed to me that he had given them a target that even they could not miss.

Dexter's supporters point out, quite rightly, that their man's heart was in the right place. He was a great batsman for England, and, on occasions an inspirational figure as captain. And he had a theory for every occasion. Some of them may have been quite unintelligible to the majority of his fellow cricketers, but many players who represented England during his tenure at the job of Chairman of Selectors had been grateful to him for a spot of technical advice from time to time. When he took over the job in 1989 he stated that everything in his life had prepared him for that moment. Certainly he saw himself as a crusader and his mission to improve the fortunes of English cricket. He was, by all accounts, tireless in his efforts to improve the game at domestic level. And it is largely down to him that the counties agreed to change from three-day championship cricket to a four day competition. By the time Dexter set his plan in motion, playing conditions were loaded so much in favour of batsmen, what with flat batting tracks and low seamed balls for the bowlers to use, that it was almost impossible to achieve a result in a three-day match, assuming good weather throughout, without contrivance. That is not how the game should be played, but it was certainly how the game was being played for a period during the late 1980s and early 1990s.

Ted also made a conscious decision throughout his time as chairman to put some distance between himself and the players. Often this had hilarious results. On seeing a young player he didn't quite recognise bringing his cricket case into the England dressing room at Trent Bridge before a Test match, he paused, looked up and offered his best wishes to the player concerned for the match ahead. Unfortunately for Ted, the young cricketer in question was a member of the Nottinghamshire ground staff.

The whimsical side of his nature became graphically clear to me when on the eve of the third Test against Australia in 1989, he handed out his version of 'Onward Christian Soldiers' to the England players and invited them to sing it in the bath at the top of their voices that evening. It read 'Onward Gower's cricketers, striving for a score. With our bats uplifted, We want more and more...' You get the picture.

But this detachment had negative results. He certainly should have let Gower into his confidence over the identity of those who had signed up for the rebel tour to South Africa in 1989, and if only he had come forward with a credible reason for Gower's omission from the winter tour party to India in 1992-93, even his sternest critics might have laid off when things went so badly wrong in the subcontinent.

Furthermore, it seemed to me that his grasp over selection had become more and more tenuous. Once it became clear that the team that had lost so narrowly in the World Cup final to Pakistan had needed to be dismantled, it was imperative that Dexter came up with a solid, consistent and forward-thinking selection policy. Instead for the next year or so, England teams were picked along the traditional lines of lottery, hunches and guesswork, characterised mainly by Gooch's personal preference. Why else would Gatting have returned ahead of Gower for that India series, or John Emburey been included in the first place at the age of 40, or why would Neil Foster, Gooch's county team-mate at Essex for so long, have been selected for that second Test of the Ashes series in 1993 at Lord's?

It would amaze me if Dexter, even though in overall charge as Chairman of Selectors, ever selected a player off his own bat for England during his period in charge.

Apart from decreeing that myself and Gower should not be considered for the 1989 West Indies tour, which was a negative deselection rather than a positive selection, I got the impression that he was happy to leave everything in the hands of Gooch and Micky Stewart thereafter.

But what frustrated most observers towards the end of Dexter's reign was that detachment had turned into aloofness, even arrogance. And that manifested itself strongly in the events that surrounded the end of Gooch's captaincy.

The story of Gooch's final days in charge revealed what was, to my mind, Dexter's greatest failings, an inability to communicate, and poor man management.

Gooch had made it quite clear to Dexter and all concerned that once the Ashes were gone he would resign. Although the third Test at Trent Bridge had produced an improved performance by England, who managed a draw and might even have won had the bowlers managed to capitalise on the work of Graham Thorpe, who made an excellent debut century, and Gooch himself who made 120 in England's second innings, when the teams moved on to Leeds it was back to the same old story. Australia won the fourth Test by an innings and 148 runs. Now was the time for Gooch to be as good as his word. But Dexter managed to make what was a difficult experience for Gooch a bitter one.

The outcome of the fourth Test at Leeds became clear from very early on. Gooch had gone into the match believing it would be played on a traditional Headingley strip whose lateral movement encouraged the English type of seam bowling. Sadly, for him at least, following bad reports from umpires Ken Palmer and Mervyn Kitchen the year before, Yorkshire, fearful that another pitch scandal would cost them their place on the Test rota, felt obliged to dig up the pitch. The new strip, laid five years previously and used for only one first-class match, was an unknown quantity. Having selected the appropriate squad for a seamers' paradise, namely one exclusively reliant on seam, Gooch was dismayed when, having left out the off-spinner Peter Such, he lost the toss and watched while Australia built a huge 653 for four declared.

England were not helped when Martin McCague of Kent was forced to pull out of the attack on the second day with an injury later diagnosed as a stress fracture of the back. But in an innings lasting nearly fourteen hours, the Australian batsmen helped themselves. In response, England simply shrank. They made just 200 in their first innings, and although they made a better fist of things in the second, scoring 305, when the final day of the match dawned Gooch realised it was to be his last as England captain.

He telephoned Dexter, who was not present on that final day, and told him of his intention to resign that evening at the press conference after the match. Dexter then tried to persuade Gooch to delay his announcement for a day. Not because of any reasons of PR or that he felt the timing of the announcement would be detrimental. But because he was stuck on the golf course with clients. Gooch tried hard to persuade Dexter to cancel his game of golf. Dexter claimed the engagement was one he simply could not get out of. At this point Gooch, unsure of the effect of making his announcement in Dexter's absence, telephoned his friend David Norrie, the *News of the World* cricket correspondent. Gooch explained the situation to Norrie, who told him that if Gooch delayed the announcement he would look ridiculous. He had made clear repeatedly that if England's performances did not improve he would resign the moment Australia's grip on the old urn was confirmed. That moment had arrived and Norrie told him that if Gooch left Leeds that night without having resigned, he would be hammered, and rightly so.

Gooch decided to go ahead with the announcement. In an emotional press conference he explained, 'It is the best way forward ... The team might benefit from fresh ideas, a fresh approach, someone else to look up to.'

Gooch's departure was inevitable, as this was England's eighth defeat in their last nine matches. But this was a sad end to his period in charge. Despite largely critical reaction to his treatment of David Gower since he took over the captaincy from him in 1989, Gooch had enjoyed success, notably by leading his team to the final of the World Cup competition in 1992. Had he obeyed his instincts, and not allowed himself to be persuaded by Keith Fletcher to captain the side in India on the following winter, Gooch could have stepped down with good grace and with a creditable record.

This way, due to the prevarication of those in charge, lack of clear thinking and direction from Dexter at the top, Gooch's reign as captain ended in sour disappointment.

Within a fortnight, Dexter had gone as well, in similarly sad circumstances.

Just before midday on Monday 9 August 1993, the final day of the fifth Test at Edgbaston, an announcement on behalf of the Test and County Cricket Board was made by their media relations officer Ken Lawrence. He delivered a brief statement to the press and broadcasting boxes at the ground, and a few minutes later Jonathan Agnew revealed its contents on BBC Radio's 'Test Match Special'.

As he did so, a spontaneous outburst of applause echoed round the ground. The reaction of those listening to the commentary through earpieces told its own story. The resignation of Ted Dexter as Chairman of Selectors was greeted with almost unanimous approval. Six months before his five year term officially ended, Dexter had decided enough was enough.

The Lord's spin-doctors soon got to work, claiming that Dexter had intended to resign at the end of the summer anyway, but there is no doubt that he brought forward the timing of his resignation so that he could jump before he was pushed by the county chairmen.

A group of them, led by the Derbyshire chairman Chris Middleton, had become increasingly disgruntled as the summer wore on. Middleton and his supporters believed that the mess over Gower's omission from the party to tour India, and later his increasingly bizarre public utterances had made the chairman and the Board a laughing stock. Perhaps the final nail in his coffin was the reaction to his botched announcement of Mike Atherton as Gooch's successor as England captain.

This should have been a straightforward affair. Once Gooch had carried out his intention to resign on the final day of the Headingley Test, the England committee comprising Dexter, Ossie Wheatley, Micky Stewart, Keith Fletcher and A C Smith, took little time in deciding that of the available candidates, Atherton, Mike Gatting and Alec Stewart, the Lancashire batsman was their man.

On the Wednesday of that week a press conference was called at the Hilton Hotel opposite the Lord's ground where the reporters were informed as to how the decision was made.

'We were unanimous,' said Dexter, 'except for Dad.'

Micky Stewart, whose son Alec had been passed over, was not present at the press conference, but when he was informed of Dexter's remarks, he went apoplectic.

The former England coach had gone to extraordinary lengths during his time in charge to outlaw the word 'Dad' along with the words 'son' and 'nepotism' inside and outside the England dressing room ever since Alec was first selected for England for the West Indies tour in 1989. He was, quite rightly, livid at the suggestion that his loyalty to his son might have affected his judgement over whether Alec or Atherton should be elevated to the position of England captain.

Dexter later apologised, but the damage had been done. He claimed later that this was an off the cuff, jokey remark intended to demonstrate Micky's entirely natural loyalty to Alec. Stewart was forced to ring Atherton and explain himself. Atherton took the phone call and Stewart's explanation in good spirit.

But once again Dexter had opened his mouth and jumped in. And, for some, this for some was the last straw.

Middleton was the instrumental figure in the removal of Dexter. For some time he had been losing patience with Dexter and had taken soundings from his fellow county chairmen. He met, spoke to or telephoned all of them for their views.

According to Middleton: 'With the possible exception of M J K Smith of Warwickshire, the chairmen were, to a greater or lesser degree, universally hacked off with Dexter. All summer long I heard the same things; he's out of touch and he makes too many gaffes. I had had first hand knowledge of one in particular. Quite early on in his reign as chairman, he was interviewed on a Midlands radio programme and asked where our next fast bowlers were coming from. He referred to a recent Derbyshire match, saying: "What chance do we have of producing new pace talent when a county like Derbyshire go into a match with an attack comprising a West Indian, a South African and a Dutchman?"

'It was bad enough that he had given a new nationality to Ole Mortensen from Denmark, but Alan Warner and Simon Base were flabbergasted. The next day I went into the dressing room to discover that the players, who had read Dexter's comments reprinted in a national newspaper, were going loopy. Our 'West Indian', Warner was born in Birmingham and our 'South African' was Base from Maidstone in Kent.

'Simon was understandably upset. He said: "What chance have I got when the Chairman of the England Selectors thinks I'm a Springbok?"

'Whenever I spoke to one of my fellow county chairman about Dexter the main complaint was that none of them ever saw him. The general feeling was that he had no interest in county cricket whatsoever. My message to them was that instead of moaning about him we should take action and, if the general consensus was that he should go, we should get rid of him. It seemed clear that he was intending to stay on until the winter tour to West Indies. But with the normal August board meeting coming up I wrote to all the county chairmen suggesting that we had to take the opportunity to remove him there and then.'

Halfway through the Edgbaston Test, Dexter got wind of what was to happen at the Board meeting, made his excuses and left.

Atherton, who was captaining England for the first time, was not the only one who was surprised that Dexter had not informed him of his decision beforehand. Several members of the TCCB's own executive committee only found out when they heard about it on radio or television or through increasingly frantic telephone calls.

Through their chief executive A C Smith, the Board attempted to put a rather different complexion on affairs. In their statement announcing Dexter's resignation, they said: 'Mr Dexter had already informed the Chairman and senior officers of the Board prior to start of the current Test series that he was not seeking re-election after March 1994. Furthermore, Mr Dexter had previously volunteered to finish in the autumn of 1993 to give a new chairman more time to settle in before the next home season. It is this suggestion that the Board has now adopted.'

In fact this was news to almost all the members of the executive committee and quite clearly neither Middleton nor the majority of his county chairmen, if any, had been let in on the secret.

Had they known earlier that Dexter was intending to stand down, it is almost certain that his critics would have allowed him to go quietly and with dignity. By keeping the lid on over his intentions, Dexter and the Board had left themselves exposed. No one should be surprised that they did, however. By now most observers had long since given up attempting to understand the mysteries of Lord Ted and Lord's.

FIVE
ILLY'S CHANGE OF PLAN

*'What chiefly annoyed, depressed and irritated me about the
Illingworth years was not that one man had the responsibility, but
that the man given the responsibility was the wrong man.'*

A FUNNY thing happened in March 1997. The English cricket
authorities put the responsibility for selecting their Test team in the
hands of people who still paid full fare on the buses.

Twelve months on from the leadership contest he would almost
certainly have won but was prevented from entering, there were no such
problems for David Graveney this time.

Graveney, the overwhelming choice of the counties, was elected
unopposed as Chairman of the Selectors only a week or so after England
arrived back from their 1996-97 winter tour to Zimbabwe and New
Zealand. The ECB management committee then demonstrated how much
they'd learned from the Illingworth regime (and those of Ted Dexter and
Peter May before him) about appointing selectors who had quit playing
the game between twenty and one hundred and twenty years beforehand,
by inviting two current players, Graham Gooch and Mike Gatting, to join
Graveney on the selection committee.

Some observers found it strange to say the least that three men who so
obviously and publicly turned their back on English cricket when signing
up for the rebel tours to South Africa (Graveney had been the manager of
Gatting's 1990 tourists), should now be entrusted with the responsibility
of picking England's Test side. While I can sympathize with those who
believe that those who walked away from English cricket in search of the
krugerrand may have been welcomed back too quickly and too readily into
the mainstream of English cricket, there is no doubt that on purely
cricketing grounds, the three men possessed the kind of knowledge and

experience of the modern game I consider absolutely vital. The most amazing aspect of all this, of course, is that it took so long for those running English cricket to realise the necessity of having current although senior players involved in the selection of the national side. At the end of a decade during which the ultimate responsibility for the picking of England sides was in the hands of men whose first instinct was to complain that things were not like they were in their day, such a move meant that players now knew that they were to be judged by men who spoke the same language and played the same game.

I still don't believe this new system is perfect. I would far rather the final responsibility for the selection and discipline of the England side be put in the hands of one man, a 'supremo' if you like, adequately paid for being the person who takes the pat-on-the-back when things go right, and the knives in the back when things go wrong. One of the very few things on which I agreed with Illingworth is that the chairman of selectors should be the man in front of whom the buck stops. Apart from the fact that in his case he only adhered to the theory behind this principle rather than the practice of it, what chiefly annoyed, depressed and irritated me about the Illingworth years was not that one man had the responsibility, but that the man given the responsibility was the wrong man.

Ray Illingworth was appointed Chairman of Selectors in March 1994. From that time until the time when he officially retired after presiding over the selection of the England winter tour parties to Zimbabwe and New Zealand in September 1996, Illingworth was just the kind of high-profile chairman the Board had wanted. In fact he was rarely out of the newspapers, either justifying his latest unilateral selection policy or slagging-off players like Devon Malcolm, Angus Fraser, Robin Smith, Alec Stewart, and even the captain Mike Atherton. As time passed Illingworth became so voluble in his criticism of them, that the prevailing feeling towards him of many of the England players was that they couldn't trust him as far as they could throw him.

More than one player told me that Illingworth would often say one thing to their faces and another behind their backs. In the end, most of them couldn't wait to see his back moving through the exit door.

His battles with the captain Mike Atherton were the constant theme, or some might say running joke of his chairmanship. And even after he had finally disappeared from view at the end of the summer of 1996, he still wouldn't give it or Atherton a rest. Atherton must have been feeling bad enough at England's failure to convert obvious supremacy into victory in the first Test of the 1997 winter series in New Zealand at Auckland. He expected to take criticism for the fact that having got the Kiwis on the ropes they couldn't deliver the knockout blow and he was prepared for it. What he wouldn't have been ready for (who would?) was direct criticism from the man who was still nominally chairman of selectors.

Cue Raymond, bursting into print in his column in the *Daily Express* the day after the match had ended in a draw, laying the blame for the shortcomings of England's attack fairly and squarely at the door of the England captain. He wrote, 'Mike Atherton must take much of the blame for England's unbelievable failure to beat New Zealand. His lacklustre, unimaginative captaincy and some awful bowling, lay at the heart of another alarming debacle.

'It is a sadness to say so,' continued Illingworth, 'having worked so closely with Mike over the past few years, but if this carries on, there will be no alternative to replacing him as England captain.'

If such a direct attack carried out in the pages of the national press sounds faintly familiar, it should. Perhaps the most extraordinary episode took place just before and just after England left for their three-month tour of South Africa in the winter of 1995.

A week before the team departed each player received a letter from Tim Lamb, then the Cricket Secretary of the Test and County Cricket Board and number two to Chief Executive A C Smith. It informed the players of Illingworth's stipulations over what would and would not be acceptable in terms of public comment through the media. Where a simple 'mind your language' would have sufficed, the players were issued with something that sounded like a directive from George Orwell's 'Thought Police' It read: 'I would emphasize to you that from the date of receipt of this letter you must not make or concur or directly or indirectly assist in making any public statement whatsoever regarding the tour or any members of the tour party without the prior consent of the Board's PR manager Richard Little.

'*Public statement* means writing a book, writing for the press, public speaking, broadcasting, or giving an interview of any kind.

'Ray has stipulated that no player will be permitted to write any national or local newspaper article of any sort, including any diary piece either prior to or during the tour.'

Yet within days the players came up against Illingworth's habit of enforcing one rule for them and another, completely contradictory one for himself. On the day before Atherton and his men were due to leave for South Africa, the *Sun* newspaper printed the first of three articles entitled 'The Boycott and Illingworth Tapes'.

In them, Illingworth revealed confidential information concerning Atherton, including his likes and dislikes among the current England players.

The headline above the first piece read, 'ATHERTON IS SO STUBBORN, INFLEXIBLE AND NARROW-MINDED.' In it, with remarkable prescience, Illingworth discussed what was later to become a major issue, the action of fast bowler Devon Malcolm. He said to Boycott, 'The ideal is to get him (Devon Malcolm) to be more consistent without losing his pace.

'Before The Oval, we had Devon in the nets bowling off a shorter run. He was bowling at Graham Thorpe, and Thorpe said, "Bloody Hell, he was at me all the time." There wasn't much difference in pace from normal.

'I said to Michael Atherton that Devon's action is much better when he uses that short run. "For goodness sake, try it," I told Michael. Devon was happy to give it a go. He wasn't worried about no balls or anything and the West Indies were scoring millions.

'But he's stubborn you know, is Michael. He didn't try it. He can be inflexible.'

On another part of the double-page spread, under the headline 'IT WAS DAFF-T TO AXE PHILLIP' Illingworth revealed why Atherton did not want Phillip DeFreitas in his side:

Boycott to Illingworth: 'What about Phillip DeFreitas? He's become the invisible man. He was England's best bowler last year (1994 against South Africa and New Zealand).'

Illingworth: 'Yes.'

Boycott: 'He played in the first Test this year and disappeared. He's not going to South Africa and he's not in the configuration for the World Cup.'

Illingworth: 'We've had discussions about Phillip and feel he's better in England than overseas. But he's not ruled out of the World Cup. DeFreitas has a problem – Mike (Atherton) and him didn't get on well at Lancashire.'

So there we had it. Atherton didn't want DeFreitas in the side because he didn't like him.

The next day's offering was even more revealing. Under the headline 'TUFNELL? HE'S SIMPLY TOO MUCH TROUBLE FOR ATHERTON', Illingworth revealed the reasons why Phil Tufnell, the talented but mercurial left arm spinner, had been left out of the squad for the tour to South Africa. Readers would have been left in no doubt that Atherton's decision not to include Tufnell was based on the fact that he didn't trust him to behave himself on or off the field. Whether this was true or not, what gave Illingworth the right to speak on behalf of his captain over such a sensitive issue? And what effect did that have on future relationships between Atherton and Tufnell? Not surprisingly Tufnell was extremely upset to discover that Atherton felt this way about him; and Atherton was simply stunned that Illingworth should be so indiscreet.

I saw this as blatant undermining of Atherton's position as captain of the side. And the same message was contained in Illingworth's words, widely quoted in the national press the day before England departed for South Africa, regarding the picking of teams in South Africa. Illingworth announced that the selection committee, formed by the combined brains of the team and tour managers, captain and vice-captain, would no longer be utilized. He would do the job himself. Having announced that he was going to have full and final say over who played and who did not, Illingworth justified his actions by harking back to what he perceived as Atherton's selectorial errors during the previous summer. He said, 'I have been in the game a long time and would back my judgement of players against anyone's. Against the West Indies last summer there were a couple of times when I felt I was persuaded not to follow my gut reaction. For instance, I wanted to play leg-spinner Ian Salisbury at Old Trafford, and I was not happy using Robin Smith as an opener. I don't think I will make those mistakes again.'

In other words, the mistakes over selections only happened because Illingworth was persuaded to go along with those decisions against his better judgement. How must Atherton have felt about that?

As usual, A C Smith, the Chief Executive of the Test and County Cricket Board, reacted swiftly – by saying and doing precisely nothing. In fact, when one journalist contacted Smith for his views over what Illingworth had said, and the possible consequences for team unity, A C Smith replied, 'Oh, Atherton has seen those articles and laughed.'

That same journalist tracked down Atherton and asked him to share the joke. When Atherton was shown those pictures by a reporter at the

Wanderers Ground in Johannesburg on the first day of training he uttered one word: 'Diabolical'. Hilarious.

Illingworth could not even hide behind the convenient and often employed device of being misquoted or having his views misrepresented by the newspaper. I know he was sent copies of all of those articles expressly for his approval. If he had wanted a single word taken out it would have been. What's more he made sure there was plenty of supper on the table before he started singing, taking a fee of £1000 for the pieces.

How ironic that when Jack Russell made his views on Illingworth known in his autobiography Illingworth claimed Jack was only being critical in order to make a fast buck.

And what was that about Ray's stipulations over what the players could or couldn't say to the newspapers? It seemed what he really meant was that *he* could say what he liked about any of them but *they* were obliged to say nothing.

Throughout Illingworth's reign as chairman of selectors the Board attempted to convince the cricketing public that he and Atherton worked together as bosom buddies. The truth is rather different, and the strain caused by Illingworth's attempt to dictate to his captain rather than work with him seriously undermined England's performances during the period in question.

Any discussion of the relationship between Illingworth and Atherton must begin at the beginning, not the moment when Illingworth was appointed in the spring of 1994, but the moment Atherton was appointed captain in the summer of 1993.

When Atherton succeeded Graham Gooch after the latter's resignation in the Ashes summer of 1993, the Lancashire opener was given a mandate for change with a promise that no matter how bad the results were in the period immediately following his appointment, he would be given time to carry through his ideas. When England won the final Test of that Australian series at The Oval the plans seemed to be working. Three Tests later, or to be more precise, three defeats at the hands of West Indies later, on the winter tour of 1994-95, and it was all change.

It had been the intention of the Test and County Cricket Board's executive committee to appoint M J K Smith, who travelled to the Caribbean with England in the role of tour manager, as Dexter's successor before the end of the 1993 season. In fact their plan to do so was sufficiently advanced for them to have agreed with Smith that the announcement could be made along those lines. Enter various county chairmen. Enter Illingworth.

Many of the chairmen had been annoyed, aggravated, and determined to take action over the fact that over a period of years the executive committee, and individual Board members for that matter, had been making executive decisions without reference to them; Raman Subba Row's 'hardship' bonus to the players on Mike Gatting's 1987 Pakistan tour had raised a few hackles, but the terms and conditions negotiated by Keith Fletcher when he agreed to take over from Micky Stewart, a five-year contract at £40,000 per annum, when they were eventually made known to them left some county chairmen steaming with rage. Many chairmen also recalled their resentment at the fact that the appointment of Dexter as chairman of selectors back in 1989 had been rushed through by Subba Row before they knew it. They saw the same pattern emerging this time, with Smith lined up to take over from Dexter after a cooling-off period following the latter's removal/resignation.

Consequently A C Smith was instructed to defer any announcement until the full Board, that is to say all the county chairmen, had met. MJK's appointment was put on hold, a four-man working party comprising A C Smith, Ossie Wheatley, and two county chairmen, Worcestershire's Duncan Fearnley and David Acfield of Essex, was set up draw up a shortlist and the leadership contest was begun.

Meanwhile out in the West Indies, the young players who had been sent out with Michael Atherton to sink or swim, were finding the water rough and deep.

The vision of England batsmen being rolled over for 46 in quick succession by Ambrose certainly concentrated the minds of those county chairmen who saw Illingworth as the answer and, coincidentally, of course, stories of M J K Smith's ineptitude as tour manager began to circulate.

I don't know how many current players the working party discussed Illingworth's position with. I do know that, had they taken the trouble to ask they may not have liked what they heard. For my money, Illingworth was out of touch with the modern game. Even though he was a regular commentator for the BBC Test match team and in that capacity had watched Test cricket as a critic for the last ten years, what did he actually know about what went on in the field and in the dressing room? And how could he possibly relate to the modern players who were at least twenty if not thirty years younger than him – in the case of someone like John Crawley, young enough to be his grandson?

Furthermore, for a man who always purported to care passionately about the fortunes of English cricket, it struck me as a little strange that Illingworth only became available once he had been told by the BBC that they would not be using him as a commentator for the second half of the summer of 1994.

Once the Trinidad tornado had blown away Atherton and his team, the appointment of Illingworth became a foregone conclusion. With his gruff 'call-a-spade-a-shovel' professional Yorkshireman image, he was exactly what the more reactionary county chairmen wanted. What is more, with his contacts in the media, they felt he could be guaranteed to say the right thing at the right time to the right people. That way, if things failed to improve at least they had a barrier between themselves and the press.

The problems were two-fold. First, in appointing someone as chairman of selectors who wanted to run the show himself, only a matter of months after appointing a captain they expressly told would be able to do just that, the Board were inviting disaster.

Secondly Illingworth's appointment sent out all the wrong 'in my day' signals to the world of cricket.

As it turned out, within seven months of his accession, the plan for youth had been torn to pieces. For when England arrived in Australia for the winter tour of 1994-95 they included in their ranks Graham Gooch and Mike Gatting – a masterpiece of forward-thinking by any standards. It was their selections that caused the Atherton/Illingworth conflict to come to a head.

SIX
THE FINAL SAY

'Bolus, Titmus and Illingworth were all fine players in their day … but their first-hand experience of cricket was experience of cricket in the past.'

ACCORDING to Ray Illingworth, 'I asked for, and got, an assurance I would have the final say (over selection), and that was the most important thing of all to me. If I do a job, I want to do it well, and it is vital that I am in charge. It is not a matter of an ego trip, rather that I have always been keen for responsibility, and everyone then knows where the buck stops. I don't hide from anything or anybody, and I told the Working Party that I was quite prepared to be judged on results.'

Three-nil down to the West Indies after three Tests, had England under Mike Atherton lost the final two matches of the 1994 winter series in Barbados and Antigua, the way would have been clear for Illingworth to impose himself, his personality, his ideas and his authority over the running of the England side. As it happened, the corpse jumped out of the coffin.

Thanks to Alec Stewart who made 118 and 143, Angus Fraser, who took eight for 75 in the West Indies first innings and Andrew Caddick, who took five for 63 in their second, England pulled off an amazing victory in the fourth Test at the Kensington Oval in Bridgetown by 208 runs, becoming the first visiting Test team to succeed there since R E S Wyatt's England team fifty-nine years earlier, and only the second ever. Alan Lee, writing in *Wisden*, observed, 'Cricket's aptitude for producing the inexplicable has seldom been so convincingly demonstrated. And yet it was no fluke. England dictated the game and won on merit, eight minutes after the scheduled tea interval on the final day.'

Should anyone believe that the West Indies had taken their foot off the pedal having already won the series, they should take note of Curtly Ambrose's reaction to being the last man out. After having his stumps re-arranged, he demolished them with an angry swing of the bat, an act which cost him a £1,000 fine from the match referee.

The final Test in Antigua was dominated by Brian Lara. His 375, which beat by ten runs the record individual score in Test cricket created thirty-six years earlier by Sir Garfield Sobers, was an unforgettable performance. It ensured West Indies made an intimidating and potentially match-winning total of 593 for five declared.

An England team not worth bothering about would have capitulated in the remaining two days and lost heavily. Under Atherton, this one responded very differently. He and Robin Smith both made hundreds in a third wicket partnership of 303. Jack Russell, Chris Lewis, and Caddick all made valuable contributions as England made the same score to ensure a well merited draw.

Back home, instead of congratulating England on their huge improvement in the last two Test matches, the newly-appointed chairman started as he meant to go on. He rubbished them.

First, in a questionnaire he completed for the *Cricketer* magazine, he replied to a question concerning which current players he admired with the answer, 'None'. Then he made it quite plain that no fewer than five of the players on the winter tour would be lucky to survive when he came to selecting it. He nominated Graeme Hick, Robin Smith, Angus Fraser, Chris Lewis and Jack Russell as ripe for the chop.

As far as Atherton's own vision of the future was concerned, Illingworth's arrival and input muddied the waters. Had he been able to back his judgement and his instinct with support from a chairman not determined to stamp his own authority on proceedings, Atherton would have stuck with those players that came through for him in the West Indies; players like Graham Thorpe, who had started the tour disastrously but through application and hard work had improved sufficiently to score 86 in the third Test in Trinidad and 84 in England's second innings in Barbados to help establish their winning position. Instead, for the first Test of that summer of 1994 against New Zealand, and as a sign of things to come, Thorpe was pushed out, and Graham Gooch, in the year of his 41st birthday, pulled back in.

As many of us feared, the recall of Gooch, who had made himself unavailable for the tour to West Indies, and was only finally considered for selection on the understanding that he would definitely be available to tour Australia the following winter of 1994-95, turned out to be a calamitous error of judgement.

Viv Richards had seen England battle through after a poor start in the Caribbean and he was impressed by their recovery. At the end of the tour he asked: 'The big question facing Mike Atherton as he settles down to analyse the progress made by his team is this: "What am I going to do about Graham Gooch?" He went on: 'Based on ability alone, Gooch would win a place in almost every Test side in world cricket and there is no doubt that he would still be valuable to England. But if I were Atherton I would stick with the guys who have come through what has been a very arduous tour even though that would mean the end of Gooch's international career.'

I know Atherton was unsure in his own mind which way to go. Illingworth, however, was not. In my opinion he was not interested in the long-term view. He wanted instant success to justify his appointment as Chairman of Selectors.

At first Illingworth's plans worked. Helped by Gooch's double-century against a poor Kiwi attack England smashed the tourists by an innings and 90 runs and, for the time being at least, this success obscured the problems bubbling beneath the surface.

The heart of the dilemma was who should pick the side – the captain, who had to lead the team on that field and had to have a hundred percent confidence in the ability of every single one of those players, or the Chairman of Selectors? One of the problems in the early part of this relationship was the massive difference in age, not only between the captain and chairman, but also between the captain and the other two selectors that the chairman had recruited, albeit by the vote of county chairmen now firmly in his pocket, Brian Bolus and Fred Titmus.

Bolus, Titmus and Illingworth were all fine players, and Titmus and Illingworth in particular, excellent ones, but their first-hand experience of cricket was an experience of cricket in the past. Their ideal team contained five specialist batsmen, an all rounder, and two spinners. In fact, just about everybody's ideal team did, provided the players required were available. Atherton, on the other hand, mindful of the ability of current players at his disposal, took a far more pragmatic approach. He always maintained that the priority was to score enough runs to take yourself out of danger of losing a match before you could strike for victory. In his eyes at least that meant playing six specialist batsmen at most, if not all times.

Atherton often pointed to the example of Australia and West Indies who respectively selected Allan Border and Viv Richards or Clive Lloyd or Gus Logie in the No.6 batting position. For sure he would have been delighted to have had an all-rounder, a batting and bowling specialist at number six like myself for instance, but one look around the county scene told him there simply wasn't that animal available at the time. Furthermore, his attitude to his bowling attack was simply this: if four bowlers weren't good enough to dismiss a side, very rarely were five going to do it for you.

Illingworth's solution to the problem beggared belief.

Craig White had made his debut for Yorkshire in 1990 as a batsman who could bowl off-breaks. In his eight championship matches in that season he made a total of 166 runs at an average of 13.25 and bowled 122 overs of spin, taking nine wickets. He didn't play at all in the Championship for Yorkshire in 1991. In 1992 he came second in the batting averages, scoring 859 at an average of 47.72 but his bowling had become almost non-existent. He sent down three overs in the entire Championship season.

Two years later, however, he was making his Test debut as an England all-rounder. And what form was it that persuaded Illingworth that here was a man to fill one of the biggest holes in the English Test side? During 1993 Craig White played seventeen championship matches for Yorkshire, making 816 runs at an average of 37.09. But the big difference, apparently, concerned his bowling.

Having decided to junk his off breaks for medium pace, he topped Yorkshire's bowling averages. Not with a hundred wickets, however. Not with eighty wickets. Not with fifty. In total, Craig White sent down 120 overs of his new style bowling ... taking twelve wickets. In effect White had won his chance to represent England in Test cricket as a result of one hundred and twenty overs of medium paced bowling. Not in a month, not in a season, *but in a career*.

White's was not the only selection that caused Atherton to scratch his head in bewilderment. For the second Test against New Zealand at Lord's, instead of sticking with a winning side Illingworth decided that Devon Malcolm had to go.

In came Paul Taylor, the Northamptonshire left arm swing bowler. Paul is a great trier. He earned his opportunity to tour India in 1993 as a result of steady and competent performances in the Championship over a number of seasons. But by his own admission he had struggled, and showed little sign of being able to make the jump from good county professional to Test-class bowler. Atherton had seen him at first hand in India and knew exactly what his shortcomings were. Yet Illingworth decided to pick him for that Lord's Test, and the result was embarrassing. Not for Taylor who tried his best but simply wasn't up to it, but for Atherton himself. In New Zealand's first innings, of 476, England clearly missed Malcolm's extra pace. As third seamer, Taylor bowled twenty overs, taking one for 64. By the time New Zealand batted again in their second innings, it was clear that Atherton had seen enough. He allowed Taylor just six overs. The fact was that Atherton had not rated Taylor from the start. And by using him so sparingly in the match, he proved it.

Atherton and Illingworth disagreed about other players throughout that summer. After the New Zealanders had left and South Africa replaced them as opponents in a three-Test series for the second half of the summer, those disagreements came to a head.

Atherton had felt for some time that Robin Smith was not batting as he himself would have liked and although the combative Smith wouldn't hear of it, it was probably right that he should have a rest now. The argument was over who should replace him. Graham Thorpe, who had made significant progress in the West Indies, was the obvious choice. Atherton, however, was desperate for John Crawley to be given a chance that the England captain felt his Lancashire colleague's ability warranted. Had he had six batting places available, I'm certain both Crawley and Thorpe would have played. But with Graham Gooch filling one of those five specialist batting places, and Craig White the sixth in his position as all-rounder, there was only room for one of these young talented batsmen. On the night the selectors met to pick the side, Saturday 16 July, at the Copthorne Hotel in Manchester, the first stalemate of the Atherton/Illingworth regime took place.

Bolus, Titmus and Illingworth, on the one hand, were adamant they wanted Thorpe. Mike Atherton and Keith Fletcher the team manager were equally insistent Crawley must play. Strangely, rather than put his foot down as he was entitled to do, having secured the final say over the selection, Illingworth decided to back down and let the captain have his way.

In his book *One-Man Committee* Illingworth spells out his position over Crawley. He said, 'I know Mike (Atherton) had seen much more of Crawley than the three of us put together (Illingworth, Bolus and Titmus), and you have to say that anyone who scores big double hundreds must have something.' Illingworth went on, 'I was not sold yet, because I watched him early in the season at Lord's for the A side, and again at Old Trafford against Yorkshire, and he got out playing balls towards leg, which I would rather have seen him play straighter.

'It is all very well being strong one side of the wicket, but top bowlers in Test cricket soon work that out and make you play somewhere else.' [Like they did with Viv Richards, I suppose.]

Sorry, I don't get it. Illingworth clearly didn't want Crawley. He'd made great play of the fact that his was going to be the final voice over selection. So why didn't he use it?

Another thing bothers me about Illingworth's comments. The selection committee comprised Illingworth as chairman, Mike Atherton the captain, Keith Fletcher the coach, Brian Bolus and Fred Titmus. When he said that Mike Atherton had seen much more of Crawley than 'the three of us put together', which *three* was he referring to? Presumably himself, Brian Bolus and Fred Titmus. Why didn't he say 'the four of us, Bolus, Illingworth, Titmus and Fletcher?'

Perhaps in his own mind he always saw the selection committee as a question of 'them' and 'us' – Fletcher and Atherton being 'them', and Bolus, Titmus and himself being 'us' – or maybe even at this early stage he had such scant regard for Fletcher's opinion that he merely ignored it.

Then we come to his explanation over how he allowed Atherton to win the day. He said, 'So it went on, Crawley v Thorpe, until I called for a vote to see if anyone had changed their minds. No, two-two, so it was down to me. I could prove my point to the press by overruling the captain, or I could go with him on a wider principle. That is what I did because I did not think that was the issue to get heavy about – not if it meant denying the captain a batsman he clearly wanted. That was not compromising my views, either on the individual concerned or my declared intention to have the final say in selection. It was more a matter of common sense, and does not mean that I shall not overrule in the future. The plain fact is that it is written into my contract that, not only do I get the final say, I have a veto about any player except the captain, and that is held by the chairman of the Board.'

I'm sorry, Raymond, but if you really felt Thorpe was the better man to select in the interests of the side, why on earth didn't you put your foot down? And what was all that about proving your point to the press? Surely the most important thing was to select the best side in your opinion.

Illingworth's comments do not add up. Forgive me for what some might call a flight of fancy, but it's just possible that Illingworth was giving his young captain enough rope to hang himself with. Illingworth knew there would be a largely hostile reaction to the omission of Thorpe; conspiracy theorists might argue that he let Atherton and Fletcher have their way over Crawley so that he could afterwards say 'I told you so' if Crawley failed. Far-fetched? Maybe, but not so far-fetched as some of the ideas Raymond came up with during his time in charge.

In any case, Illingworth did not have to wait long for the England captain to place himself firmly in the chairman's pocket.

SEVEN
A DIRTY BUSINESS

'Illingworth's main concern appeared to be what he thought the newspapers might write. There is no mention here of what was right for cricket, right for England, or right for Atherton.'

THE events of Saturday 23 July 1994, the third day of England's first Test against South Africa for the best part of thirty years, will long remain in the memory of all the protagonists after one of the most controversial incidents in modern cricket history.

Matthew Engel recorded the events in *Wisden* as follows: 'The Atherton affair took over all discussion of the match, and the genuinely historic outcome – a devastating South African victory – was all but forgotten amid the fuss.

'Normally, England being bowled out for 99 on a sound wicket might have caused a great deal of anguish. However, everyone was preoccupied by the fact that Atherton, fielding on Saturday afternoon, was seen by the television cameras taking his hand out of his pocket and rubbing it across the ball before passing it back to the bowler. He was called before the referee, Peter Burge, to explain what the official statement called his 'unfamiliar action' and answer suspicions that he had broken Law 42.5 by using an artificial substance to alter the condition of the ball. Burge said he had accepted Atherton's explanation without saying what it was. But the following day, after further television pictures were shown that looked even more sinister, and England's batsmen had crumbled to a humiliating four-day defeat, Atherton admitted publicly that he had not told Burge the truth by saying that he had nothing in his pocket. In fact, he said, he had some dirt there that he'd picked up to keep his hands dry and prevent moisture getting on the ball while Darren Gough was trying to reverse swing it; the second set of pictures clearly showed some of the dirt falling off it.'

In my opinion Atherton was at fault for more than one reason. Team-mates at Lancashire and Atherton himself explained how, when he was bowling leg-breaks in county cricket before his back injury prevented him from continuing, he would often carry dust in his pocket to keep his fingers dry and help him grip the ball. Darren Gough, the Yorkshire quick bowler who had made such an impression since making his debut in the first one-day international of the summer, clearly needed the ball to be a dry as possible in order for him to gain reverse swing, that is to say, swinging the ball in the opposite direction from the way it would normally go. But with all the controversy surrounding the actions of the Pakistan fast bowlers Wasim Akram, Waqar Younis and Aqib Javed during the Test series of 1992, Atherton knew that all actions in this regard had to be whiter than white and beyond reproach. The slightest suggestion of doing something illegal with the ball was bound to lead to enormous controversy, even more so if the perpetrator was the captain.

Atherton's own thoughts on the subject of ball-tampering were clear. As he said later in his book *A Test of Cricket*, 'I am not alone in thinking that the Laws should be changed to allow certain action which the players tacitly accept as part and parcel of the game.'

But I'm afraid in this instance those views were beside the point. Ball-tampering was illegal in 1994 and it still is today, and everyone is watching for it.

My other complaint about his behaviour concerns what he said to the match referee Peter Burge. Atherton has frequently admitted that his major regret over what happened that day was that he did not tell Burge the whole truth over what was in his pocket at the crucial moments. He said this: 'I have expressed my full apologies to the match referee for my foolishness in not telling him of the dirt in my pocket. Thinking back to that meeting, I gave my response without considering the consequences and believing that I had done nothing improper, but not wishing to raise any suspicions about my actions. I cannot turn the clock back but I fully accept that on this occasion I was thoughtless and should have given him the full picture.' Correct. And if he had done the fuss would have been over before it had begun.

Illingworth's performance, on the other hand, was little short of extraordinary.

Illingworth states that he first heard about what had been going on from Mike Procter, the South African coach, shortly before the tea interval on that Saturday. At this point he was told by the Board's media liaison officer Richard Little that he had a video of the incidents in question in his office. Illingworth went to see it straight away. It was at this point that Illingworth got a message to Atherton via Graham Gooch that he should come to see Illingworth during the tea break. According to Illingworth, 'I asked him (Atherton) to turn his pockets out and I saw what looked like dry dust. He told me he often did it to stop sweat getting onto the ball when he bowled and did not see anything wrong as it was simply to soak up the sweat on his hands.' Illingworth then, fully apprised of the whole situation, settled back to watch the last period of the match. He was obviously so confident that nothing untoward had happened, that instead of talking to Atherton again at the end of the match or hanging around to make sure that no action was going to be taken, at the close of play he went straight to the Cornhill sponsor's hospitality tent at the Nursery End at Lord's. This was common practice, a chance for Illingworth and the players to unwind after the day's play and chat with sponsors and their guests.

But while Illingworth was there he received a message from Peter Burge that he wanted to see Atherton and Keith Fletcher.

What happened next defies belief. From the very fact that Peter Burge had sent a message to the tent saying that he wanted to see the England captain and the England coach, Illingworth must have been aware that trouble was brewing. He knew Burge would have had access to all the available television footage. He'd seen how the pictures looked. And what did he do? He left the ground. At eight o'clock. Right slap bang in the middle of Burge's interrogation of Atherton and Fletcher. He says, 'I chatted about it (with Mike Procter in the Cornhill tent) and did not have a clue when I left the ground at about 8 pm that the thing was still dragging on in the pavilion.' But Illingworth had been told that Burge wanted to see Atherton and Fletcher. He claims that when he left the ground he was unaware that they were still being questioned. 'I did not have a clue', he insisted.

He might have hung around to find out. He might even have talked to the press with whom he had such a wonderful working relationship to find out exactly what was going to appear in their papers the following morning, or even to comment on Burge's statement.

Later, according to Illingworth, 'It was only by chance that I ran into Burge back in the hotel opposite Lord's at around 10 pm. He told me that he had issued a statement saying he accepted Atherton's explanation. I must admit, I did not dream that the press would make so much of it next morning.'

From this point the affair becomes ever more curious. According to Burge the matter was closed on that Saturday evening. He had questioned Atherton over what he called 'unfamiliar action' with the ball and had said that he accepted Atherton's explanation. Thank you and goodnight.

And although one or two of the Sunday morning papers, notably the *Mail on Sunday* and the *News of the World*, raised the question over whether Burge's action went far enough, and even suggested there might have been some cover-up over what happened, it is probable that the whole issue would then simply have disappeared. Although Illingworth later claimed that Burge was a hard liner and prepared to take action over any indiscretion, his subsequent record after these incidents proved otherwise. For instance his performance during and after the first Test between England and New Zealand in Wellington on the 1997 tour there hardly smacked of hard-line treatment.

Paul Allott, my co-commentator on Sky TV, highlighted a problem with the New Zealand fast bowler Geoff Allott who, as the television pictures clearly showed, was picking the seam.

This direct contravention of Law 42.5 brought the following comment from Paul: 'It's illegal. He shouldn't be doing it. He's naive.' Burge had access once again to all the television footage available. He watched it. Yet he chose to do absolutely nothing. It is not beyond the bounds of possibility that, left to his own devices, Burge would have followed precisely the same course of action at Lord's in 1994.

In any case and for reasons that are hard to fathom, Illingworth decided he could not leave well alone. Whereas on the Saturday evening he had been satisfied that the matter was closed, a couple of headlines in the morning papers had sent him into a frenzy. He recalls: 'I got to the ground at 9.30 am and saw Atherton immediately. I told him we simply had to do something, otherwise the heavy mob of the Monday morning press would crucify him and everyone else.' Once again Illingworth's main concern appeared to be what he thought the newspapers might write. There is no mention here of what was right for cricket, right for England, or right for Atherton. Only the possible response of the national newspapers.

Atherton himself had seen A C Smith and Doug Insole of the TCCB executive committee the previous evening after the official hearing and been told that he mustn't make any further comment. He said, 'I will not be making a statement nor do I anticipate making one in the future.' And if Burge was satisfied and the umpires were satisfied that there had been no offence against the laws of the game, what was the point of pursuing the matter?

Now Atherton became little more than a bystander in the drama that unfolded.

While he and the rest of the England team were collapsing for 99 to lose the match by the huge margin of 356 runs, Illingworth was working himself to a standstill behind the scenes. He decided that a statement must be prepared for Atherton to read out and that there would be a press conference in order for him to do so. As the day wore on the mood became more and more ugly. England were getting thrashed on the field. Off the field rumour fought with counter rumour among a press corps eager to milk whatever story was about to emerge for all it was worth. Finally, the long-awaited press conference took place.

Illingworth read his statement first, told the press that he did not believe Atherton had done anything illegal and then informed them that he was fining him the maximum he could, £2,000 in total for two so-called transgressions: £1,000 for having the dirt in his pocket, and £1,000 for not telling the whole truth to Burge. The second fine was probably fair enough. The first didn't make any sense at all. If Atherton hadn't done anything wrong, as Illingworth insisted, why fine him? It could only have been a PR exercise to placate what Illingworth had previously named the 'heavy mob of the Monday morning press' and in that case it was wholly unsuccessful.

The matter didn't end there. In fact it dragged on for another couple of weeks, until the circus moved on to Headingley for the second Test. In the intervening period, everyone from bishops to headmasters to cab drivers to chat show hosts, came forward with their own opinion of what Illingworth, by his actions, had turned into the major sports story of the year.

On more than one occasion thereafter when Illingworth recounted the episode he made great play of his claim that by taking the action he did he had saved Atherton's captaincy. That if he had not done so Burge would have taken strong action which might have forced Atherton's removal as captain. The question must be asked, however: Was this Illingworth's way of finally establishing his authority?

The events at Lord's did strengthen Atherton's position in one respect. Finally, the evidence of England's second innings capitulation was enough to persuade Illingworth that his plan for a team containing only five specialist batsmen and an all-rounder was not working. For the first time in the summer, Illingworth accepted the principle that England should play six specialist batsmen at Headingley. And with a batting order of Gooch and Atherton to open, Graeme Hick at three, Graham Thorpe four, Alec Stewart five and John Crawley six, England made 477 for nine declared in their first innings, enough to make sure the match was drawn. Atherton's own response with the bat, falling one run short of what in the circumstances would have been a famous hundred, an innings lasting three-hundred and twenty minutes of sheer bloody-minded guts and determination that spoke volumes about his reserves of resilience.

England's performance in the final Test of the summer at The Oval, the strategy behind it and the motivation imparted on his team by Atherton gave a further demonstration, should any be required, that Atherton deserved to be given more control over the selection and running of the side than Illingworth wanted to give him.

England went into the last match of the series with four seam bowlers and no specialist spinner. The attack which caused consternation among cricket purists was Devon Malcolm, Joey Benjamin, Darren Gough and Phil DeFreitas. The selection of such a side was clearly against Illingworth's basic cricket principles. But one look at The Oval pitch on the morning of the match had persuaded Atherton that a spinner would be no more than a passenger. He insisted he wanted his four front-line pacemen even though such a move had to constitute a gamble, with Benjamin, the Surrey seamer, playing his first match and Darren Gough and Devon Malcolm both capable of going for plenty if their pace was slightly misdirected. Many observers were amazed that Illingworth had not put his foot down and insisted on a spinner being included. In the end the policy worked in perfectly, and Illingworth was happy to claim the credit for this master stroke of strategy. As he said in *One-Man Committee*: 'It looked defensive, it looked all wrong, yet we honestly did it as our best way to win the game and halve the series.'

Anyone who had overheard a conversation he had in the press box of The Oval on the second morning of the match would have gained a rather different impression of Illingworth's role in the whole affair. Illingworth was not a regular visitor to the press box during Test matches, certainly not during the hours of play, but on this occasion he felt a trip up the stairs from the England dressing room was well warranted. In that morning's *Times*,

Alan Lee, their cricket correspondent, had railed over England's omission of a spinner, making it quite clear he thought the selectors had made an enormous blunder, and that the very idea of going into a Test match on the flat bouncy wicket at The Oval without the spin option was just plain daft. Illingworth had obviously read the piece for it was Lee that he had come to see. Interestingly he did not take Lee to task, rather, he sought to give him the impression that the final decision was one that he didn't agree with from the start. Lee was not the only one who was confused by this. For a man who asked for and got an assurance that he would have the final say on selection, Illingworth was making a habit of keeping very quiet in selection meetings when push came to shove.

Funny what tricks a win can play on the memory.

To my mind the difference was that Atherton, having finally got his way over the team he wanted, had led them with confidence and assurance. And in the case of the match-winner Devon Malcolm, he personally had got more out of the erratic fast bowler than anyone before or since.

Malcolm had started just as his captain had wanted him to. Bowling fast, if not always in the right place, he castled the South African opener Peter Kirsten for 16, and followed that up by cracking Jonty Rhodes a fearful blow on the head, sending the South African number six to hospital, and forcing him to retire hurt.

So far so good. But Malcolm's bowling with the second new ball was so innocuous that it sent Atherton into a fury. At the end of the day's play the England captain even ignored the usual protocol of allowing the South African batsmen to leave the field first, when, having gestured his intention to do so to the batsmen in question, he ran off the field ahead of them. No one knew it at the time, but he was preparing himself to deliver a few well chosen words to his errant fast bowler, and when Malcolm finally got back to the dressing room Atherton took him to one side and did just that. Atherton tore into Malcolm, leaving him in no doubt as to the consequences of a repeat performance. The squad for the winter tour to Australia was due to be announced within the next ten days and Malcolm was made aware that his seat on the plane was by no means booked.

The second day of that final Test was dominated once again by Atherton and Burge. Burge, who had responded to what he considered to be having the wool pulled over his eyes in the first Test at Lord's by announcing at Headingley that, should Atherton 'sneeze at breakfast he'll have double pneumonia by tea-time', at last got his revenge at The Oval. After watching

South Africa make 332 in their first innings, Atherton was lbw for nought at the start of England's reply. He clearly felt he had hit the ball, and on the slow march back to the dressing room gave a couple of glances at the edge of his bat. It's an old trick and everyone's done it. You might feel, and you would probably be right, that Atherton would have been better advised to keep his eyes firmly fixed on the route to the dressing room and follow it. Human nature being what it is, however, Atherton couldn't resist letting everyone know how he felt about the decision. It was a misjudgement and it cost him £1250, half his match fee. Burge, prompted by the third umpire Alan Whitehead, a man with whom I never got on during my playing career as I found him too concerned with the letter of the law rather than the spirit, swung into action once again. Whitehead, looking at the television pictures of Atherton's exit, turned to the ICC match referee and said, 'That's dissent'. Burge, no doubt fuelled by righteous indignation, decided to act.

As if Atherton hadn't enough on his plate trying to win the Test match, this latest visit to Dr Burge's surgery might have caused a lesser man to crack. While Atherton was attending the disciplinary hearing, Gooch was hard at work on his behalf. Gooch saw the pressure Atherton had been under during the previous four weeks both from inside and outside the camp and took it upon himself to deliver to his England colleagues a rousing message to get behind their captain. If nothing else it demonstrated forcefully whose side the players were on.

The following day, thanks to Malcolm, England began the process of putting together a performance that would cement Atherton's position as leader of the side for the Ashes tour. Malcolm, fired up by Atherton's warning, went to war. He finished with nine for 57, the sixth best innings analysis in all Test history, and the best ever at The Oval.

Victory helped blow away all doubts that Atherton should lead the side down under and, bearing in mind how right he had been over the balance of the side for that final Test it should have been enough to enable the captain to have his way over who accompanied him. As events turned out, it was not.

EIGHT
DAD'S ARMY

'As the [1994-95] tour wore on it became clear that the selection of Gooch and Gatting was a massive error of judgement.'

ENGLAND'S squad for the 1994-95 Ashes tour turned out to be a selectorial disaster, not only for those included but also for one notable omission.

Twelve months on from selecting a youthful party to sink or swim against the West Indies, Atherton's instincts and judgement were largely ignored. Instead, presumably applying the principle of mixing youth and experience, Illingworth masterminded the selection of a squad that simply made no sense.

Not only was Gooch retained for a trip he later described as his 'tour too far', but he was joined in the senior citizens' enclosure by Mike Gatting, the 37-year-old Middlesex captain whose previous tour, to India in 1993, had been a personal nightmare.

In his book *One-Man Committee* Illingworth devoted three lines to the crux of the matter. He wrote: 'The captain said we should identify a group of young players and stick with them. I asked him to name a few, but there was not a great deal forthcoming.'

So that was it.

As the tour wore on it became clear that the selection of Gooch and Gatting was a massive error of judgement. There are those who blame Atherton for allowing the situation to develop, and for not sticking to his guns over younger players. It's very difficult to see how he could have done, without risking his position as captain. In the long run Illingworth always had the ultimate sanction over non-co-operation from his captain.

There are also those who believe Illingworth was working to a hidden agenda. He had never made any secret of his admiration for Gatting's captaincy. Indeed, at the height of the 'dirt in the pocket' controversy at Lord's, the strong word was that, had Atherton not survived the furore, the Middlesex skipper was lined up to replace him.

The position over Gooch also requires scrutiny. After being persuaded against his will to tour India as captain in 1993, Gooch had vowed that that was to be his last overseas action. At first, he was as good as his word. On the basis of picking a squad of young talented players with a license to fail, Atherton was happy to go to the Caribbean without Gooch. The situation developed when, halfway through that tour, Atherton made it known that he would not consider Gooch for the upcoming summer series against New Zealand and South Africa, unless he made a commitment to tour again the following winter in Australia. Atherton had realised that his policy required loyalty from him as well as commitment from others. As far as he could, when England returned home at the end of the Caribbean tour, Atherton wanted to stick with those in whom he had put his faith in the first place. If Gooch came in ahead of any one of them, even though he was not prepared to tour the following winter, how could Atherton in all conscience demand and expect loyalty?

Gooch responded to Atherton's move by saying, 'It looks as though the door could be closed. As far as I'm concerned the decision I made at the end of last summer not to tour again was final.

'Mike believes the only way forward is to pick players who are going to be available all year round.'

Had both men stuck to their guns, that would have been the end of it.

But it was Gooch who gave way, announced he'd be available for the winter tour to Australia and enabled Illingworth to rush him back into the fray, without any concern for the long-term consequences. Surely, for instance, it would have been more beneficial for England's chances in Australia at the end of the year to have given younger men like Thorpe and Crawley a chance to develop against the Kiwis and South Africans before the upcoming Ashes tour.

Gooch did make a double century in the first Test against New Zealand at Trent Bridge. But as the season wore on, and he struggled for form, his confidence suffered as well. Indeed by the final innings of the final Test against South Africa at The Oval Gooch was close to jacking it all in.

After his double hundred, Gooch's run of Test scores read: 13, 0, 20, 28, 23, 27 and 8. Even before he went out to bat following Devon Malcolm's dramatic burst an incident occurred that almost persuaded Gooch to retire from international cricket on the spot. After Devon had struck his first blow, firing out Gary Kirsten and his brother Peter and Hansie Cronje to leave the South Africans one for 3, Kepler Wessels, the captain, and Darryl Cullinan managed to put up some kind of resistance. But when Wessels was out at 73 for four, caught behind by Steve Rhodes off Malcolm, England were poised to wrap things up.

Brian McMillan top-edged a hook towards Gooch, positioned on the fine leg boundary. He merely had to move ten yards to his left and wait for the ball to drop into his hands. It was a stone cold sitter. But Gooch miscalculated and the ball hit his hands before dropping to the floor. As Gooch himself said, 'Not having been a regular fielder anywhere near the boundary all through my career, I cannot remember such a loud collective groan from a packed crowd. Miserable? I felt worse than miserable. I was stunned with depression. That's it, I decided, I should pack in Test cricket here and now. My fielding had dropped to unacceptable standards. I was a forty-one-year-old liability.'

In fact Gooch sought out Keith Fletcher and Illingworth that night and told them that he had decided he was going to retire from Test cricket. They told him to sleep on it but later he sought out Atherton in the bar at the Conrad Hotel in Chelsea Harbour, where the players were staying. Displaying characteristic loyalty, Atherton told his predecessor as captain, 'Don't make any hasty decisions.'

Looking back, I believe Gooch put Atherton in an impossible position. Clearly Gooch had this conversation with Atherton because he wanted to be persuaded out of retiring. Even if Atherton felt that was the right course of action, what could he have said? 'Yes Goochie, you're dead right. You dropped a sitter. You're over the hill. Now bugger off'. By the end of the Ashes tour, the following February, he probably wished he had done after all.

Gooch was always going to be, at best, a reluctant tourist. He had stated his reasons for not wanting to do so again, after the 1993 tour of India and Sri Lanka, *ad infinitum*. Gooch is dedicated to his children and, following the break-up of his marriage, was determined to spend more time with them, particularly during the winter months. He also is somewhat of a home boy. There's nothing he likes better than a couple of pints down the local, or watching his beloved West Ham play at Upton Park, and good luck to him. He has, of course, done his utmost to stay in peak physical condition to deal with the demands of Test cricket. But it was obvious to everyone concerned that if he struggled for form in the same way that he had done that summer against New Zealand and South Africa, home would seem a lot further away for him than for most of the others. In that respect there had to be a huge danger in selecting both Gatting and Gooch because their 'seen it all before experience' could just as well become a negative as a positive.

Gooch was not the only one to put pressure on Atherton in this respect. Again in his book *One-Man Committee*, Illingworth reveals that he had tried to force the issue over Atherton's age concerns. After the final selection meeting Illingworth had one final task to complete his first summer in charge as England's Chairman of Selectors, the writing of his report to the Board detailing his version of events that summer. He wanted to place on record Atherton's opinion of himself, Bolus and Titmus as selectors. He wrote, 'Therefore, I asked the captain if he had any reservations about the three of us. When he said no, I also told him I proposed to put that into my report for the Board.'

What did Illingworth expect Atherton to say? 'I'm sorry Raymond but I consider you, Brian and Fred to be out of touch with the modern game. I was elected as captain on the promise of being able to put into operation a plan to put faith in young players. I also confidently expected to have the final say in the selection of them. What's happened since you took over the job in April is that my authority over the selection of the side has been undermined, and the original plan has been junked. I wanted six batsmen in the side all summer long and you've only recently let me have them. I've expressly told you that I think we should go for young players and you've ignored me. Now you ask me if I have any reservations about the three of you?'

As I've said there's only going to be one winner of that little game.

Quite apart from the selection of Gooch and Gatting, the omission of Angus Fraser was possibly the most contentious issue of the entire relationship between Illingworth and Atherton.

Fraser and Atherton were good friends, having begun their England careers the same summer, during the 1989 series against Australia. They are both Lancashire born, both fiercely ambitious and patriotic, both fuelled by desire to do well and for England to do well, and both nearly always convinced they were right.

Atherton had been the man responsible for bringing Fraser back into Test cricket after injury had disrupted his career. When Atherton took over the captaincy from Graham Gooch in 1993, one of the first things he did was to enquire from Fraser about his form and fitness. Fraser told him he

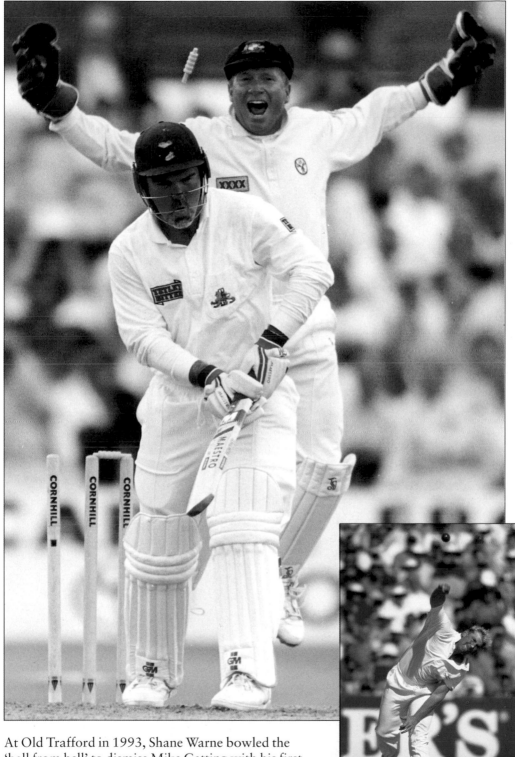

At Old Trafford in 1993, Shane Warne bowled the 'ball from hell' to dismiss Mike Gatting with his first delivery in an Ashes series. Four years later England devised a plan to counter his threat, then saw the Australian seamers cash in.

Left: TCCB secretary Donald Carr, who backed down over his decision not to allow players' wives on tours.

Below left: A C Smith, the long-standing chief executive of the Test and County Cricket Board. He knew much but said little.

Below: M J K Smith, a favourite to succeed Ted Dexter as Chairman of Selectors, until Illingworth showed up.

Above: Graham Dilley, my Worcestershire and England team-mate. He went into hospital for minor surgery but tests revealed liver damage – the result of overuse of painkillers to help him get through a day's play.

Above: Helping to win the World Cup in Australia in 1992 would have been one of my greatest achievements. Sadly the effects of over-training and preparation took their toll.

Below: Forever being accused of a lack of athleticism in the field, the 1995 England tour party to South Africa were determined to put things right, regardless of how ridiculous they looked…

Above: Ted Dexter and Micky Stewart face the press in the Long Room at Lord's to announce David Gower's appointment as England captain for the 1989 Ashes series. The strained expressions might be explained by the fact that Gower was not Stewart's first choice for the job. Was he Dexter's?

Below: Dennis Silk, former chairman of the TCCB. His heart was in the right place, but when he spoke out over the failings of the English game the reactionary counties disposed of him.

Below: Keith Fletcher, England's coach from 1993 to 1995. When Ray Illingworth was appointed chairman of selectors in the spring of 1994, Fletcher's days were numbered.

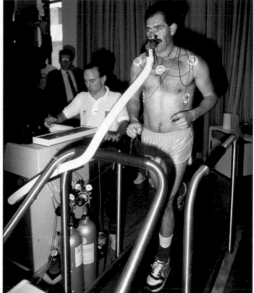

Above: 'We will not have much of a problem with him.' Anil Kumble shoved Ted Dexter's words back down his throat with 21 wickets in the 1992–93 Test series.

Above: Graham Gooch made the most of his talent by pushing his body to the limits. But he couldn't understand that one man's meat was David Gower's poison – and mine.

Below: Waqar Younis is one of the greatest bowlers in world cricket. But the events on and of the field that dominated England's 1992 series with Pakistan cast a giant shadow of suspicion over the methods he and others used to achieve their success.

Dennis Lillee, the greatest fast bowler I ever faced. Sponsor Patrick Whittingdale wanted to make his coaching skills available to England fast bowlers. The TCCB didn't want to know.

Below: Rodney Marsh, the great Aussie wicket-keeper was the driving force behind the Australian Cricket Academy. The ambition of Dennis Silk, the TCCB chairman, to set up such a facility in England was scuppered by the county clubs.

Below: Mark Nicholas, the former Hampshire and England A captain who moved smoothly into a career in the media following his retirement from the game. His plans to revitalise cricket were strangled at birth.

The three stooges … or Bolly, Illy and who? Ray Illingworth, Fred Titmus and Brian Bolus were the England selectors who made Mike Atherton's captaincy a misery. At various stages all three wanted him out of the job. According to Titmus, the fact that Atherton broke Peter May's record for captaining England was a 'travesty'.

Above: In a crowded and heated press conference at Lord's in 1994, Mike Atherton explains his 'unfamiliar actions' with the cricket ball during the first Test between England and South Africa. The dirt-in-the-pocket affair might have cost the England captain his job; Ray Illingworth claims his prompt action saved Atherton. It probably caused more problems than it solved.

Below: Robin Smith, one of the bravest England batsman in modern times. Illingworth so infuriated him during the 1995–96 tour to South Africa that he considered puling out of the World Cup squad.

was sure he could still do a job for him and most crucially for the team. After England had been soundly beaten in Atherton's first match in charge by eight wickets, the captain spoke to Fraser again, this time to tell him that he would be playing in the final Test at The Oval. Fraser paid Atherton back in spades, taking five for 87 in Australia's first innings and following up with three for 44 in the second to help England to memorable victory by 161 runs.

Thereafter, Fraser's form in the West Indies fully justified Atherton's decision to recall him. He really came into his own in the fourth Test in Barbados, taking eight for 75 in the West Indies first innings as England established a winning position. With Caddick and Stewart he was instrumental in West Indies first defeat at Bridgetown for 59 years.

Imagine his delight, then, when word reached him that Illingworth, the new Chairman of Selectors, was somewhat dismissive of his efforts. Illingworth believed that Fraser's undoubted ability to put the ball in the right area on a nagging length was not enough . He wanted Fraser to start swinging the ball and he said so.

I believe that the pressure Illingworth put on Fraser to reinvent himself was one of the main reasons why, during the 1994 summer series against New Zealand and South Africa, he struggled to find his best form. I am convinced that part of Fraser's problem that season was trying to live up to Illingworth's idea of what the chairman felt he should be rather than what he was. No wonder Fraser struggled. And the harder he tried, the less effective he became.

Despite this, Atherton retained faith in Fraser at all times. He knew he could always rely on him for a hundred percent effort and was confident that once in Australia for the 1994-95 Ashes tour he could guarantee his bowler the right balance of rest and practice to get him primed for the Test matches. Although Fraser was left out of the final Test against South Africa, at The Oval, as far as the captain was concerned Fraser would be on the plane for Australia come what may.

The other selectors, however, were clearly not of the same mind. I first heard of the rumours that Fraser's position was under threat around August. The message seeping out from within the selection committee was that Fraser had lost his penetration, not temporarily, but for good, and that, whatever the captain felt, Illingworth would not have him down under at any price.

Perversely, having seen how Atherton galvanised his side to victory at

The Oval, this was the moment Illingworth chose to put his foot down and crush Fraser's chances of selection.

Illingworth made great play throughout his tenure as Chairman of Selectors over the fact that the approach to the England team and their preparation would now be more professional than ever. Illingworth supporters claimed that he'd forgotten more about Test cricket than many of the young generation ever knew. And now he proved just how much he had forgotten.

His bright idea for England's best chance of winning the Ashes in Australia that winter was to pick an attack to take wickets on the fast bouncy pitches on which the series would undoubtedly be contested. The theory was perfect but, sadly, more than twenty years out of date.

The fact is that as anyone who had played Test cricket in the previous two decades would have told Illingworth, Australian pitches were now very different in character from the ones that he played on when leading England to Ashes victory in 1970-71. The pitch at Brisbane normally encourages slow movement off the seam, and if a fast bowler manages to get the ball above waist-high at Melbourne and Sydney he is doing a superhuman job. Adelaide is flat and full of runs and Perth, the only one of the five Test match pitches which actually encourages some pace and bounce, quite often has too much of the latter so that out and out fast bowlers simply cannot control how far over the wicket keeper's head the ball will sail.

Illingworth's philosophy was based on an outdated theory. He sacrificed the accuracy and control Fraser would supply for the raw pace of Kent's Martin McCague. As Illingworth freely admits he twisted Atherton's arm over the selection of McCague ahead of Fraser.

There was nothing sentimental in Atherton's reasoning. He knew that it was likely to be a long hard winter, and that he wanted bowlers he could trust to keep batsmen in check. He certainly did not go along with Illingworth's idea that England were going to blast anyone out. He didn't want Fraser in his squad because he was a mate. He wanted him in his squad because he considered him the best bowler at England's disposal and an absolutely vital component of any attack that he might choose.

Eventually Atherton was proved right and Illingworth wrong. McCague froze when asked the big question on the first morning of the first Test in Brisbane and later had to be sent home through injury. Fraser replaced him and proved what England had been missing with a magnificent display in Sydney. But had Illingworth had his way, the

Middlesex paceman would not even have had the chance to make that belated contribution.

A couple of days after the announcement of the squad an article appeared in the *News of the World* under the headline 'YOU'RE GUTLESS'. It purported to represent Fraser's views of Atherton and Illingworth when neither the chairman or captain rang him to let him know he was not going to Australia that winter. Fraser, who wears his heart on his sleeve at the best of times, was understandably upset at being left out. He did not, however, in the article or anywhere else describe Atherton or Illingworth as gutless. But as a result of some headline writer's over-enthusiasm, Fraser was fined £2,000 by Illingworth. The same amount, incidentally, that he fined Atherton for his so-called misdemeanours at Lord's. Over the top? Maybe, but not as much as what he tried to do next. Fraser had been placed on standby by the selectors in case of injury or illness. Not only did Illingworth fine Fraser, he actually wanted him taken off the list of standby players, as a result of what he'd said. In essence, Illingworth was prepared to deprive himself and England of the performances of a bowler who might yet play a significant part in the series, should one of his main squad bowlers be injured or ill, merely because he was upset that the bowler dared to question his judgement or authority. Pathetic.

Another of Illingworth's blind spots in selection concerned the abandonment of Essex off spinner Peter Such. Such had been England's leading wicket-taker during the 1993 series against Australia in England, when he removed the Australian captain Mark Taylor four times, and Mark Slater and Allan Border three times. After missing the tour to the Caribbean, no doubt on the grounds that only one spinner was required and the best spinner was still considered to be Philip Tufnell, Such was recalled for the series against New Zealand at the start of 1994. He played in the first three Test matches and although not at his best bowled adequately – well enough, in any case to be persevered with. Furthermore, two of the selectors, Illingworth and Titmus were acknowledged expert off spinners in their time.

Rather than simply cut him off, why didn't they set to work to help Such improve? Halfway through the summer of 1994, my information was that Illingworth simply didn't rate Such as a bloke, that he thought him weak, soft, and lacking the 'moral fibre' that he wanted to see in his England players. Quite where he got that idea from, I've no idea. But Illingworth himself confirmed that impression in an interview he gave halfway through England's tour of South Africa in 1995-96. He said, 'Although Such probably bowls offspin as well as anyone, we felt basically he was a very soft person. While I wouldn't argue that he might have done a reasonable job as a bowler he is frightened to death when he bats against quick bowling.'

By the time the first Test took place in Brisbane, Illingworth had damaged England's cause even further, this time using his favourite weapon, the biggest mouth in cricket. The players were finding it hard enough to get into any kind of form, and their early preparation had been disrupted when Phil Tufnell temporarily lost his marbles, trashed a hotel room in Perth and ended up booked in for bed and breakfast at the local psychiatric unit. Thankfully that particular crisis had passed but the team could surely have done without the storm of controversy created by Illingworth's ill-timed and ill-judged comments to a group of journalists at a Sports Writer's Association lunch in London just days before the first Test was due to start.

First he criticised Atherton for not ringing him up to discuss selection issues and said, 'I saved his neck last year when I fined him £2,000 for the alleged ball-tampering incident at Lord's and this is how he repays me.

'If I hadn't fined him he would have been banned for two matches and he wouldn't be England captain now. The least I expected was a phone call to let me know how things were going. He had all my numbers in Spain and elsewhere and he has chosen not to use them.'

All very well, but if Illingworth was so distressed why didn't he ring Atherton? In fact as Chairman of Selectors, surely it was his duty to do so.

Next, when questioned over the possible call-up of Fraser for the Brisbane Test in view of illness and injuries to Malcolm and Benjamin, this is how Illingworth reacted: 'Fraser did bugger all last summer. I can't believe there is serious talk from the captain about drafting him in. If he is suggesting that Fraser plays in the first Test I will be on the phone to him like a rocket.

'We agreed before the party left that Fraser never looked up to it. He struggled in the West Indies and, although Atherton wanted him to go, he just wasn't the man for the job.'

Surely this was an example of Illingworth letting his fluster and bluster get in the way of the facts. It was only according to him that Fraser had struggled in the West Indies. Those who saw him produce a match winning performance in Barbados begged to differ And as for his assertion that 'we agreed before the party left that Fraser never looked up to it', try telling that to the captain.

Then Illingworth turned his attention to manager Keith Fletcher. When asked about Fletcher's role he turned to the person next to him at the lunch and said, 'He's team manager, isn't he? He nicks a few catches in practice.'

Obviously, in Illingworth's view of man management and motivation this represented just the kind of morale boosting message of support they all needed. What on earth was Illingworth up to? He claimed later that his remarks were taken out of context by a group of journalists eager to splash him all over the back pages. According to one or two of the journalists who were present at the lunch that I spoke to he was more than happy to oblige. He knew exactly what he was saying and how it would be reported. After all prior to taking up his position as Chairman of Selectors, he was employed as a columnist for many years by the *Daily Express*, not averse to stirring up a bit of controversy in his own words, not reported by others, but written by him.

No wonder the players he was now in charge of as Chairman of Selectors didn't know whether they were coming or going with Illingworth. He very rarely knew himself.

By the time Illingworth arrived in Australia, just prior to the second Test in Melbourne, the morale within the England camp had degenerated severely.

During that first dismal month and a half England's performances had been abject, and they deserved to be 3-0 down in the Tests. It was during this period that the depth of the misjudgement over selecting both Graham Gooch and Mike Gatting for the tour became obvious.

Once things started to go badly, Gooch very quickly retreated into his shell. As each day went by, he became more and more convinced that he had been wrong to make himself available. He found little in common with many of those around him. He was missing home more and more as each day passed. And try as he might he was finding it impossible to shrug off the depression that had descended on him after he had given his wicket away to Shane Warne in the second innings of the first Test with an uncharacteristically loose shot.

Gatting, strangely for him, had also became somewhat reclusive. A naturally gregarious man and a hearty competitor, he became more and more of a peripheral figure as the tour went on. If you could ever call Gatting's figure peripheral that is. Their diffidence, allied to coach Keith

Fletcher's usual quiet approach and growing unease in Atherton over the resources at his disposal meant that the squad as a whole was prone to be downbeat and negative in outlook. This was reflected in their preparation as well as their performances.

Whereas the Australians bubbled with vibrancy, competitiveness and commitment in their intense net sessions, England's players largely appeared to be going through the motions. Indeed their practice sessions were the subject of much merriment in the Australian papers. Greg Baum of *The Age* began his preview to the second Test in Melbourne by writing, 'England trained and grass grew at the MCG yesterday, two activities virtually indistinguishable from one another in tempo, but each with its own fascination.'

Perhaps England's most significant performances came in the two matches they contested against the Australian Cricket Academy at the North Sydney Oval towards the end of 1994. Against a team of young, enthusiastic and determined cricketers schooled in the arts and crafts of winning by their coach Rod Marsh, the former Aussie wicket-keeper and an infectious enthusiast who believes that winning is not everything but the only thing, England on the other hand, were pedestrian, ponderous, pathetic and while they were losing the second of two matches against the academy, a plane appeared in the sky and wrote the word 'Why?' with its vapour trail.

The question related to the building of Sydney Airport's new runway, not to English cricket and its obvious failings. According to Matthew Engel writing in *Wisden*, 'Invisibly, it hung there all tour, even after the victory in Adelaide.'

Even the chairman admitted, 'It's amazing to me in two or three months how things have drifted. It's very disappointing.' I wonder if he reflected on how team morale might have been affected by his pre-Brisbane rantings from 10,000 miles away?

Clearly there was no comparison in the team spirit among the England touring party at that stage to that so evident in the players who had fought back from being 3-0 down in West Indies the previous winter. To my mind the fact that the inclusion of Gooch and Gatting had raised the average age substantially was no coincidence. Never more obviously were Atherton's gut-feelings over younger players proved right than when England fielded. With the two old men parading the outfield, England looked embarrassing at times. I'm not criticising Gatting or Gooch here. They tried their hardest to get as fit as possible but there's a limit to how mobile the body can be at their age. Added to their lumbering, players like McCague and Tufnell hardly had a spring in their step either. And when Malcolm came in for the second Test in Melbourne, the picture was complete. What made them look so ghastly was the brilliance of the Australians. And it was around this time, the second Test at the MCG, that I believe Gooch finally realised the truth, that he was simply past it at the highest level.

Indeed, after allowing himself a reasonable period of reflection, this time he finally made up his mind. On the eve of the fourth Test at the Adelaide Oval, at the end of January, Gooch announced his retirement from Test cricket as of the end of the tour. Shortly afterwards, when the squad arrived in Perth for the final Test, Gatting followed suit.

No doubt Illingworth will put the improvement in England's performance, a draw at the Sydney cricket ground, and then victory at the Adelaide Oval in the fourth Test, down to his influence.

There are those who believe, on the other hand, that it was the presence of Fraser rather than Illingworth which might have had something to do with it. Finally drafted in for the third Test at Sydney, he played his full part in a three-man pace attack with Malcolm and Gough that rattled out Australia for 116 in their reply to England's 309, then bowled England within a whisker of what would have been a dramatic victory, taking five for 73 in Australia's second innings and in all probability only being prevented from finishing the job by rain and bad light.

By the end of the tour the message contained in England's final performances had become clear. In Adelaide, after Gatting had finally produced an innings of substance John Crawley made a huge contribution and Chris Lewis, another man not originally wanted on the voyage, came in and helped England win. In the final Test in Perth, the lion's share of England's runs came from Graham Thorpe and Mark Ramprakash, the men Atherton had originally selected for the previous winter tour to West Indies, but who had found themselves out of favour with Illingworth.

Although Gatting's hundred at Adelaide had helped England win there, that innings was very much the exception that proved the rule. In Perth normal service was resumed. Both he and Gooch failed with the bat and, more crucially, were part of an abject fielding performance that allowed Australia to get off the hook as eleven catches were put down.

The first, by Gooch off Malcolm in the very first over of the match, set the tone.

Michael Slater, the dashing right-handed opener, chased after a quick ball from Malcolm and edged it fast but catchable towards Gooch at second slip. Gooch got to the ball, but not quick enough. It went to ground. Slater went on to make a to make 124 out of Australia's 402 all out, a total which virtually killed the game and England's hopes stone dead. Thorpe's hundred was just reward for a solid tour; Mark Ramprakash, drafted in as a result of injuries to Graeme Hick and Alec Stewart, made his highest Test score, 72 and followed that up with 42 in the second innings to prove what might have been had England trusted in his undoubted talent at the end of the previous winter's tour to West Indies rather than letting him stew back in county cricket. But Australia, ruthless in these situations, pressed home the advantage to win by a massive margin of 329 runs.

It was at this point, after the series had been decided 3-1 in Australia's favour, that Atherton decided to put on record in detail his views over what went wrong on that tour and over how England should proceed in future.

In front of a crowded press room at the WACA ground in Perth, Atherton spoke clearly and deliberately from a prepared speech. At first when he shuffled the notes in front of him, many of the assembled press corps thought he was going to resign.

Far from it. Instead he reiterated his belief that England required younger selectors and younger players. He thanked Gooch and Gatting for their contribution to the tour and paid tribute to their service to England over the years. But he insisted, 'The message is clear. England need a young mobile and refreshing team to remove the memories of tired defeatism. It needs people with character and spunk, players of fiery egos and burning desires. Patience must be shown, for there will surely be some dark hours. What we require are selectors who are more in touch with the dynamics of the modern game, ideally former recently retired Test players who are able to communicate with current players more effectively because they have played the same game and talked the same language.'

It was hardly necessary to read between the lines to understand the message Atherton was communicating about his Chairman of Selectors.

By so publicly drawing attention to his concerns over how the England team should be run, Atherton was taking a huge risk. It took courage and conviction for the England captain to lay his cards on the table so obviously. But he felt the message had to be delivered and he did so.

It very nearly cost him his job.

NINE
ILLY TAKES CHARGE

*'What he [Fletcher] lacked was the charisma to motivate
players to play out of their skins.'*

IT was inevitable that heads would roll after England returned from that
1994-95 Ashes tour of Australia. Although the team's performances had
improved substantially once Angus Fraser arrived, the draw in Sydney
and victory in Adelaide would be forgotten alongside a scoreline which read
'lost 3-1', particularly in view of the fact that in the World Series Challenge,
the normally triangular tournament between three Test playing nations
which the Australian Cricket Board used to spice up their winter tours,
England were not only outplayed by Australia and, in Sydney, Zimbabwe,
but also by Australia A, the host nation's second XI hastily drafted into the
competition presumably to give the first team a proper game.

Now remind me, Raymond, just where did that buck stop again?
Apparently not in front of Illingworth, according to him and the county
chairmen. Miraculously not only did the man at the top survive, but his
power was actually enhanced.

When the axe finally fell it was team manager Keith Fletcher who felt its
blow.

Fletcher had been appointed in September 1992 to succeed Micky
Stewart, and at the time no one was arguing. Although I believe he did
England a disservice by persuading Gooch to captain the side in India in
1993 against his better judgement and his part in Gower's omission
reflected no credit on him, the 'gnome', as he was known in county cricket,
was an astute technician whose one-to-one coaching with individual
players was highly-valued.

It was he more than anyone who had persevered with Graham Thorpe
and it was he who had first identified the huge potential of Darren Gough.

What he lacked was the charisma to motivate players to play out of their skins. As coach of a collective group of players he was too inclined to trust them to work out their problems for themselves. And it was this hands off approach that probably led to his downfall.

Illingworth had hardly gone out of his way to support Fletcher, with his public remarks about him being the coach who 'nicks a few catches', and whatever story Illingworth peddled privately about what had gone on in Australia, the chairmen of the county clubs bought it.

When the press assembled at Lord's on 8 March 1995 to hear the results of a review of the Australian tour by the executive committee of the Board, most were expecting some criticism of Illingworth. None expected Fletcher to be sacked.

A C Smith, the Chief Executive of the Board, read out a prepared statement which said, 'Keith Fletcher has been team manager since September 1992 and during this period England have played against India and Sri Lanka, Australia at home and in Australia, West Indies, New Zealand and South Africa. In a total of twenty-six Tests we have won five, drawn six and lost fifteen. Keith has carried out his duties conscientiously and has contributed to the development of many members of the team with his professional expertise in coaching and ancillary matters. But his lack of success has led to a loss of confidence in his abilities, and there has been little progress in the development of the England team.

'We believe that we have to look elsewhere for a man to rekindle the pride and passion in playing for England, a motivator, who is also an expert cricketer, somebody who will raise team spirit and get the best out of individual players and the team as a whole. Our choice is Raymond Illingworth.

'Raymond will continue as Chairman of Selectors, take on full responsibility for the England team and be accountable for its performance. This appointment is for this summer against the West Indies and next winter in South Africa and for the World Cup in India and Pakistan. At the end of this period his performance will be reviewed.

'What happens now and during this year is also very important and that is why we have taken the decision to put Raymond Illingworth in charge of both selection and effectively management of the team for the next twelve months. Ray has the total support of the whole Board and we know that he will draw on his vast experience and use his exceptional man management skills to develop a successful England Test team.'

Smith added to the prepared statement, 'We have no intention of minimising or reducing the role of captain. Indeed, Ray has been asked to forge a partnership with the captain to produce between them the best results and performances. In the normal way the three selectors will appoint the captain when they're ready. Ray's two fellow selectors for 1995 will be Fred Titmus and David Graveney.'

Fletcher's departure was probably inevitable from the moment that Illingworth took over. Some journalists, analysing the comings and goings around that time, believed that Graveney's arrival and Fletcher's departure was more than coincidence. Prior to the executive committee review of the reports on that Monday it was believed that Fletcher would survive. It was also widely understood that Brian Bolus was certain to make way for David Graveney. In that case the selection committee would have comprised Illingworth as Chairman, Fletcher as team manager, Atherton as captain, Fred Titmus and Graveney. Generally speaking, Graveney and Fletcher would have been expected to support Atherton over tight decisions. That meant that if it came to any split votes, Atherton would carry the day with the support of Graveney and Fletcher.

In other words, Illingworth, deprived of Bolus and with only Titmus to count on for full support, would have been in the minority when push came to shove. Had that situation been allowed to occur by the TCCB executive committee, the final say Illingworth demanded when they appointed him in 1994 would, in effect, no longer have been his. In the event Fletcher was sacked. Illingworth, meanwhile, was given full and unprecedented power as Chairman of Selectors and coach rolled into one.

Brilliant. Did the powers-that-be ever stop to consider what message they were sending out to the world of cricket by squeezing a sixty-two-year old into an England tracksuit and calling him 'boss'?

They could not have offered Atherton a more humiliating response to his plea for the introduction of younger selectors into the process of developing the England side.

What on earth would Illingworth have in common with the young players? Born at different times in different ages and from different cultures, they simply didn't speak a common language. What England players wanted was to be motivated by a vibrant vital new driving force. What they got was a bloke whose attitude to modern day cricketers was that none of them were fit to lace the boots of the proper cricketers he played with in his day.

Not all the blame should be laid at Illingworth's door. The biggest error of judgement was made by those who selected him in the first place. For them he was a comfortable, conservative option. What's more they understood that his popularity with some sections of the media with whom he had been working as a colleague for the past ten years, and the fact that he would more often than not do their job for them with a well-timed quote, meant that any discussion over the serious problems afflicting the English domestic game was liable to be overshadowed by the daily soap opera he would provide them. In many ways Illingworth was an ideal choice for them. If he succeeded they could take the credit for their perspicacity. If he failed it was always going to be he who failed and not them.

In the second paragraph of Smith's prepared statement which read: 'Raymond will continue as Chairman of Selectors, take on full responsibility for the England team and be accountable for its performance', the TCCB washed their hands of the whole affair. Now everything was up to him. Of course that was what he wanted, but it also meant that they could hide behind him if things went wrong.

Unfortunately it also meant that the tension that had existed between Atherton and Illingworth was bound to continue.

Illingworth was mightily peeved by Atherton's comments over younger selectors and younger players made during and at the end of the England tour that winter. Now Illingworth seemed determined to make Atherton pay for speaking out of turn.

Illingworth claims that Fred Titmus was the strongest voice in opposition to Atherton, that Titmus had been most upset by Atherton's comments and that he was in favour of replacing him but do the facts support this? What would have quashed all the speculation before it began would have been a quick meeting between the new selection committee, Illingworth, Titmus and Graveney, and a firm and definite decision over who the new captain would be. Instead, Illingworth did not arrange the first meeting of the selection committee until Tuesday 18 April, some six weeks after the date of 8 March when the new committee had been formed. The new meeting, which Illingworth arranged, was due to take place during the first main match of the season, between the England A team and The Rest at Edgbaston. Illingworth had in fact told the national press guys that that was when the captaincy would be decided.

Imagine their reaction when they turned up at Edgbaston to be told that any decision over the captaincy would be delayed at least ten days. The announcement would now be made on the Sunday of the one-day match between Yorkshire and Lancashire at Headingley. Obviously the media took that to mean that the selectors were not unanimous over Atherton's reappointment. And they were right. It wasn't just Titmus who'd voiced his concerns, either. Illingworth had made it clear that he had been angered by Atherton's pronouncements in Australia and I'm convinced that without the presence of David Graveney, the new selector, Atherton would have been sacked.

Had Brian Bolus still been there instead of David Graveney, there would have been no one to speak up in Atherton's defence. As it was, Graveney insisted Atherton must retain the captaincy. And he persuaded Illingworth to talk to Atherton about their differences and try and resolve them as quickly as possible. A meeting was duly arranged to take place during the Benson & Hedges match at Old Trafford between Lancashire and Leicestershire. It turned out to be nothing less than a showdown between the Chairman of Selectors and the captain. Once again Illingworth went on and on about Atherton's public pronouncements over the age of the selectors and the need to bring in younger players. Atherton responded by complaining about what Illingworth had said at that sportswriters' lunch prior to the first Test in Brisbane. The row went on for some time and Graveney felt the atmosphere was very hostile. Titmus also had his tuppenny worth, and the meeting was going nowhere fast until Graveney stopped the proceedings by asking the two men, 'Do you both think you can work together?' It stopped all arguments in their tracks. And Atherton's response probably saved his captaincy. What choice did he have? He might have wanted to say, 'No, of course I can't work with this old bugger'. He might have wanted to say, 'I want final authority over who should be in the side I take onto the field'. He might have wanted to say, 'Let's clear the decks and develop a strategy for the next three or four years'. He might have said, 'Let's identify the young players we think have the guts and technique to survive at the top level and stick with them'. He might have wanted to say, 'Unless you let me have all this I won't continue as captain'. If he had done he would have lost the job, I'm absolutely certain of that. Some may say he should have taken a stand. But the England captaincy is a huge job to give away. I know, I did it myself, and I never got another chance to prove that I could captain England.

In the end Atherton chose pragmatism. He still wanted the captaincy and still felt he could make a difference. So he bit the bullet and bit his tongue.

As events turned out, the summer of 1995, which for England meant a six-Test series against the West Indies after three one-day internationals, was again full of the kind of controversy that characterised Illingworth's time in charge.

Angus Fraser, the man Illingworth didn't want in Australia, again found himself unwanted for the first Test at Headingley and he watched from the sidelines just as aghast as everyone else when, after England had made 199 in their first innings, West Indies cashed in on some woeful early bowling, racking up 282, a lead of 83. Then after England had made 208 in their second innings West Indies rattled off the 120-odd required for the loss of just one wicket. Then came the second Test at Lord's, and more controversy and confusion as Illingworth unilaterally decided, without reference to the other selectors or captain, that Stewart should keep wicket and not Steve Rhodes, who had originally been picked to do the job. Thanks to Fraser's return and a wonderful debut by Dominic Cork who took 7-43 in West Indies' second innings, England pulled off a victory that seemed to justify Illingworth's decision. But the rumblings of dissatisfaction over Illingworth's brazen dictatorship and the embarrassment encouraged some in high places to begin to doubt the wisdom of investing him with so much power.

Those doubts were heightened by events at Edgbaston, the venue for the third Test.

There have been a multitude of claims and counter-claims over who was responsible for the pitch that scuppered England's chances. What was not in doubt was that it was tailor-made for the Windies attack. The first ball from Curtly Ambrose pitched on a good length and sailed over Atherton and wide of the wicket-keeper for four wides. The final ball of the match was bowled at 12.18 pm on the third day. The game lasted only 172.2 overs and West Indies won by an innings and 64 runs. The pitch was lethal, a disgrace, and dangerous. But hadn't Illingworth insisted that he would be responsible for making sure pitches would help rather than hinder England's chances?

If so, why hadn't he bothered to take the trouble himself to take a look at the pitch prior to his arrival at Edgbaston the day before the match? Illingworth claimed that one selector had seen the pitch in advance, namely Fred Titmus, and wasted no time in laying the blame squarely at his door when he said that his fellow selector had merely said the pitch looked 'a bit funny'.

When Illingworth did finally turn up at Edgbaston he was as horrified as everyone else by what he saw. The pitch had tufts of thick grass all over it. It was hard and bouncy all right, along the lines of Illingworth's directive to the groundsman, but bouncy as in bouncing bomb. When Illingworth and his supporters spoke of the new professionalism he would bring to proceedings I don't suppose they envisaged the sight of grown men crawling around the Edgbaston Test pitch on their hands knees trying to cut the lushest areas of grass with pairs of scissors.

The Warwickshire public were livid at being short-changed by such a truncated and one-sided match. Afterwards one or two of the members jostled Atherton and Illingworth and the captain was openly critical. He was right to be disappointed. At Lord's, inspired by Cork and Fraser, his side won a marvellous victory to square the series 1-1. And now all their efforts were undermined by a terrible pitch, the result of carelessness and lack of attention to detail on the part of the Chairman.

This extraordinary series twisted again at Old Trafford where England won by six wickets thanks once again to the bowling of Angus Fraser and an all round performance by Dominic Cork. After Graham Thorpe had made 94 in England's first innings Cork chipped in with an unbeaten 56 batting at number nine. And he followed that up by taking a hat-trick in West Indies' second innings to remove Richie Richardson, Junior Murray and Carl Hooper and become only the eighth England bowler to do the trick.

After that, however, the series petered out rather tamely with two draws on batting belters at Trent Bridge and The Oval, the chief feature of which was the seemingly endless batting of Lara.

Ray Illingworth's first summer in total charge of the affairs of the England team had not been unsuccessful. Their 2-2 draw was a creditable result and even though this West Indies side was clearly at war with itself with constant squabbling between Richie Richardson, Lara and Ambrose which continued throughout the summer, England's all round performances suggested they might enjoy a happy return to South Africa, a country they were about to visit for the first time on an official basis since 1964-65.

In the event England ended their winter journey in dire disappointment. Inadvertently perhaps, but undoubtedly in fact, Illingworth set the tone for what was to follow with his articles in the *Sun* newspaper on the eve of their departure, where he openly criticised the captain and called his character and temperament into question.

If the England players thought this was a strange way to demonstrate what the Test and County Cricket Board had called Illingworth's man management and motivational skills, they hadn't seen anything yet.

TEN
DISARMING DEVON

'Lever and Illingworth used the press as a stick with which to beat Malcolm, knowing full well that Malcolm could not respond to those criticisms publicly.'

THE most obvious casualty of England's 1995-96 tour to South Africa was Devon Malcolm. There are many words I could use to describe Illingworth's treatment of Malcolm on that trip, perhaps the most appropriate is simply 'bullying'. Illingworth maintains that throughout his trials and tribulations with the England paceman, the change he was trying to make in Malcolm's bowling action was so slight as to be almost negligible. The plan Illingworth had fostered with his bowling coach Peter Lever was to make Devon run in straighter and after releasing the ball run down the pitch straighter, creating a delivery action which would enable the ball to be propelled fast and also to swing. Fair enough in principle, but it ain't what you do it's the way that you do it, that's what gets results.

The danger signs were flashing as early as the first week of the tour. One of the media crew, John Thicknesse of the *Evening Standard*, had been informed by the management off the record that there were problems brewing with Malcolm. Lever insisted that Malcolm was refusing to listen to any possibility of change, and that he was being stubborn and bloody minded. The fact is that in the early part of that tour Malcolm was endeavouring to return to full fitness after an operation on his knee to remove fluid. If he was running in gingerly in those early sessions and early matches it was only to be expected. But Lever and Illingworth misread the situation and accused him of sheer laziness and as the tour went on tension grew.

What Illingworth and Lever appeared to have forgotten amongst all this was the psychological effect that the mere presence of Malcolm had as far as the South Africans were concerned. Only a year earlier in that final Test of the 1994 summer, Malcolm destroyed South Africa at The Oval with one of the greatest displays of fast bowling ever seen. Malcolm took nine for 57 in South Africa's second innings enabling England to win the match by eight wickets and square the series. The legend goes that after Malcolm had been hit on the helmet by Fanie de Villiers, he reacted by staring back at the fielders who had gathered round and saying, 'You guys are going to pay for this. You guys are history'.

None of the South African batsmen who were preparing to face Malcolm in the Test series that winter would have forgotten his bowling that day. He made them look frightened. And some of them were.

But instead of building Malcolm up as the potential match winner he so obviously was, the England management spent the first two or three weeks of the tour trying to get him to change his action. What message did that send out to the South Africans? Not that Malcolm was a bowler in whom England had full confidence and South Africa needed to fear, but that there was something fundamentally wrong with the most potent weapon in their fast bowling armoury. Good thinking.

The situation boiled over when England played their first first-class match of the tour against a South African invitation XI at Soweto. This was clearly a huge moment in the history of South African cricket. Soweto is the emotive heartland of black South Africa. Here hundreds of human beings crushed by the apartheid regime found an expression and an outlet for their rebellion. For the South African cricket board to be able to stage a first class cricket match here proved just how far the country had come in attempting to normalise political relations. And the arrival of President Nelson Mandela by helicopter put an emotional seal on the proceedings. When he arrived midway through that first morning session, Mandela made a point of singling out Malcolm, the only black man in the England party. He said, 'I recognise you, you're the destroyer'.

Malcolm said afterwards that Mandela's words had made him feel ten feet tall. And that is exactly what Illingworth and Lever should have been trying to do as well. Within 72 hours, however, they managed to make him feel ten inches small, as they took the unprecedented step of withdrawing him from the match. With the South African invitation XI still batting on that Sunday morning, Malcolm was sent off to nets at the Test ground at Centurion Park, a 45 minute drive up the road.

When asked by a journalist who had travelled to the nets to find out what was going on and why Malcolm wasn't playing at Soweto he shrugged his shoulders and replied, 'Don't ask me.'

The same journalist went up to England batsman Graham Thorpe who was facing Malcolm in the nets and asked what was happening. Thorpe answered, 'I don't see what the fuss is about. He tried to bowl the way they wanted him to bowl and hit the side of the net. At gnat's pace. He could hardly pitch it on the cut strip. Then he went back to bowling his old style and he bowled fast and swung it.'

Malcolm found the pressman and said simply: 'I'm keen to put my side of the story but I can't. If I talk I'll say things I shouldn't. And they will hammer me.' Perhaps he already had said too much. In an interview in the previous week's *Independent on Sunday* he had said, 'They don't pick me all summer and then suddenly it's win us a Test match, Devon. People expect me to do it every time. If I don't, I'm dropped. It does seem I'm singled out.' And later at Centurion Park he told Peter Hayter of the *Mail on Sunday*, 'When I had that net this morning I tried to do what they wanted me to do for ten minutes. It was hopeless. I can't. Malcolm Marshall did not have a perfect action yet no one tried to change him. I know what's best for me. I'm recovering from injury and I have to take it at my pace. I honestly did try to do what they were asking me to do but I couldn't do it. When I was bowling well in the old style in the nets no one said a word to me. I had all the batsmen in trouble and there was not a single word from John Edrich, the batting coach, who was watching. I know what they want me to do but I don't feel comfortable. It's not broke, so why try and fix it? It's not me. I've taken a hundred Test wickets bowling the way I know how to bowl. If people had caught catches in Perth on last winter's Australian tour, I might have won the match and helped square the series. Why are they singling me out? If they didn't want me the way I am why did they pick me in the first place?

'Now I am cornered. If I fail they'll say they tried to help me but it was no good because I wouldn't listen. If I succeed they'll say they put a rocket up my arse and it worked. They'll take the credit if it goes well. I'll take the blame if it doesn't.'

The following day the England management made their position quite clear. Lever and Illingworth went to extraordinary lengths to inform the English press of their disappointment and anger at Malcolm's attitude. The day after the match at Soweto had ended, a contingent of English journalists had gone to the England team hotel to seek out Atherton for a ten minute chat prior to England's next match against Border. They spoke to Atherton and had some quotes neatly tucked away with which to write their preview pieces. Then they bumped into Peter Lever in the hotel foyer. Lever said to them that if they hung on a few minutes he might have something for them. Meaning he might have a story for them. Lever then disappeared into the lift and went up, and after about ten minutes returned with Illingworth and Edrich. They came out of the lift and walked towards the hotel pool and the English press men dutifully followed them.

What was said around the hotel pool that morning left none of the English press men in any doubt as to who the management believed was the villain of the piece. According to Peter Deeley in the *Daily Telegraph* it went like this: 'The consequences of Devon Malcolm's failure to respond to attempts by the tour management to change his bowling action came to a head yesterday when Ray Illingworth virtually ruled him out as England's chief strike bowler in the Test series against South Africa.'

Bowling coach Peter Lever who has been working with Malcolm, commented, 'He has just one asset – pace. That apart he is a nonentity in cricketing terms'. He explained that Malcolm's left arm fell away at the moment of delivery. 'I have tried to straighten Devon out, but I just can't do it.'

Back home the reaction was almost universally condemnatory of the England management's position. According to Neil Foster, former England and Essex bowler, 'If they've picked him they should show some belief in him. Sure he is one of six bowlers in the party but you can't start knocking him before the series has started.' E W Swanton, the veteran and revered *Telegraph* columnist, said, 'This bright spotlight on Devon Malcolm's action is a great pity from the viewpoint of team spirit. I can quite understand if he resents all this public criticism from the team management. His position as the only black man in the team out there makes his situation an unduly sensitive one in itself.'

Kim Barnett, his Derbyshire captain, went further. 'The last two years have been Devon's best with close to seventy first-class wickets each season and a nine-for in a Test match. To me that suggests he's a better bowler now than ever before so why tinker with something which is working well? They should accept him for what he is, a potential match winner, and allow him to be the best judge of what works best for him.

'What I find particularly iffy is the fact that something which should be dealt with, if at all, as a private matter between Devon and the management has been turned into a big public issue.'

These were not the only voices raised in criticism. Mike Atherton was similarly distressed at the treatment of his fast bowler and in particular the abandonment of him by Illingworth and Lever. After Lever had had his say around that hotel pool, Illingworth supported the bowling coach by saying, 'At the moment he wouldn't frighten you lot, let alone them.' When Atherton was told of what had been going on by Hayter, he replied, 'I hope when they write that the management has washed their hands of Devon they don't mean me. I'm on his side.'

There are several elements of this that I find particularly disturbing.

Sure, if Peter Lever felt that Devon's action needed some work he was duty bound to try and carry it out. But anyone who knows Devon at all knows that the way to get the best out of him is to convince him that you are on his side. He does not respond well to the big stick. And it was inevitable that he would view being pulled out of that historic match at Soweto as a humiliation.

Even then Malcolm might have responded had Lever and Illingworth kept the problem in-house. To my mind what was unpardonable in their action was to make the whole thing so public and to go out of their way to do so. It was clearly a case of setting Malcolm up in advance should things go wrong.

Once again the message being broadcast to the other players was that things that should have been kept within the confines of the dressing rooms or at least the nets, were liable to be made known to all and sundry. Lever and Illingworth used the press as a stick with which to beat Malcolm, knowing full well that Malcolm could not respond to those criticisms publicly. They had that in black and white in Tim Lamb's letter to them on the eve of departure. In it, you will recall, Illingworth stipulated that no player would be allowed to make public comment no matter how far they were provoked by a member of the England management team. It was ironic that in a country whose oppressed black majority had for so long fought and finally won the right to freedom of speech, here were the England cricket team management denying their players that basic right.

In the circumstances it was a major achievement that England managed to arrive at the final Test in Capetown still enjoying equality in the Test series. The first Test at Centurion had been washed out, as eventually was the third in Durban. England had a brief chance to win the fourth Test in Port Elizabeth but ended up hanging on for the draw and, of course, who could forget that magnificent contribution by Atherton in the second Test at the Wanderer's Ground in Johannesburg when the England captain batted 643 minutes to make 185 not out and, with the help of Jack Russell who made a battling 29, saved the Test match they had looked bound to lose.

In Capetown, however, Malcolm's earlier prediction came chillingly true. On the fastest pitch of the series England chose to bat first having picked only five specialist batsmen. Presumably they thought the pitch was due to deteriorate and selected the extra bowler in order to exploit that. What happened is that they were blown away for 153 in 68.1 overs. Importantly in view of what was to happen after the match, Robin Smith was the only England batsman to put up a real fight. He batted for more than four hours, defying everything that South Africa could throw at him including the left arm 'frog in a blender' spin of Paul Adams, the eighteen-year-old who had become South Africa's youngest Test player in the fourth match at Port Elizabeth.

The game and the series hinged on a passage of play on the second afternoon. Adams, in only his second Test, shared a last wicket stand of 73 with Dave Richardson to turn the contest on its head. When Adams came to the crease South Africa were 171 for nine, a mere eighteen ahead of England. Atherton threw the ball to Malcolm, confident that his big fast bowler would be able to blast his way to a breakthrough he and they so desperately needed.

An hour later Adams and Richardson had effectively set up a winning position for South Africa. Malcolm had in fact caused Adams huge problems when the young spinner first came to the crease. He first survived a streaky Chinese cut for four, and with Malcolm pitching the ball well up in order to try and york the batsman, eight leg byes resulted followed by four overthrows, when Dominic Cork, Malcolm's Derbyshire team-mate, tried to pull off a run-out that was never on. Thereafter Malcolm's bowling became more ragged. He tried for extra pace but, not surprisingly, since he hadn't bowled in a match for nearly a month, lost his direction and his confidence.

What is more I don't really think people understood how much pressure Devon felt he was under. There is enough on a guy playing in Test cricket as it is, but when he actually goes out there thinking that the chairman is gunning for him, it is very difficult for him to relax and settle into the game.

When the South African bowlers routed England for a second time for only 157 in the second innings then Gary Kirsten and Andrew Hudson knocked off the seventy required to win, it was Malcolm who felt the full force of Illingworth's anger.

In the England dressing room, in front of all Malcolm's colleagues, Illingworth snapped.

In an extraordinary five minute period which left the England players speechless, Illingworth first announced he had agreed with the local authorities to play a one day match against a Western Province XI the following Saturday.

It was the last thing they wanted to hear. They had been embarrassed and shattered by their crushing defeat particularly as it had taken place in front of thousands of England supporters who had travelled to South Africa and seen them lose the match and the series in just three days, but while Atherton, Stewart and the other players were on the field taking part in the post-match presentations, Illingworth had been busy behind the scenes negotiating a fee of twenty-five thousand rand for the players to play in this unscheduled match. When they arrived in the dressing room they expressed their irritation and puzzlement. They were furious that Illingworth had made a decision like this without reference to them. The atmosphere in the dressing room was tense. And it exploded when Illingworth turned to Malcolm and said 'You bowled crap and probably cost us the Test match'. If I had been in Malcolm's shoes then, I'm not sure I would have been able to contain myself. To my mind Illingworth was lucky to get away without physical damage, for Malcolm would have been quite entitled to chin him on the spot. Not only was Illingworth completely out of order to bawl out a player like that in front of the others, his criticism was also plainly unfair. What about the England batsmen who'd managed to be bowled out for 153 and 157 in the match? I would have thought some blame for England's defeat might have been attached to them.

Illingworth saw it differently. He needed a scapegoat and Malcolm was an easy target. He wasn't the last, however. In the immediate aftermath of defeat at Capetown Illingworth made his feelings on the future development of the England side plain to Hayter. 'Perhaps now I'll be the one going out for younger players and not Mike', he told him. A couple of days later, Hayter invited Illingworth to go on the record with his views. In the lobby of the team's hotel in Capetown, Illingworth spelled them out to Hayter and fellow Sunday paper journalist David Norrie of the *News of the World*. During a half-hour interview Illingworth volunteered the names of those most at risk. They included vice-captain Stewart, Robin

Smith, Angus Fraser, Richard Illingworth and Mark Ramprakash, as well as Devon Malcolm.

Both newspapers carried stories outlining Illingworth's hit list on Sunday 7 January. By midway through the following week the stories had filtered back to South Africa and Smith, on hearing that his neck was on Illingworth's block, came to see me. I had known that there had been problems between Smith and Illingworth all through the tour. But as far as Robin was concerned this was the last straw. By the time England had moved to Bloemfontein for the second one-day international on 11 January Smith was ready to quit the tour altogether.

He told me, 'I've heard what Illingworth said about me and I'm shattered. The man has not exchanged two words to me throughout the entire time we've been in South Africa. I just don't know where I am with him. I don't know if I'm coming or going. If he wants me out I wish he'd tell me himself. In the Test match in Capetown I made the highest score on either side, 66. If I hadn't had to hit out because I was losing partners in the first innings I could have carried on and got a handy little not out for myself. But because I was playing for the side first and not myself I went down firing. You know the kind of bloke I am, I'm nervous about my game, I lack confidence. I need someone to build me up, to tell me that I'm good enough. What I don't need is the Chairman of Selectors undermining my confidence in this way by publicly doubting whether I've got a future at Test level. The way I'm feeling now, I may as well just pack my bags and go home. I know that would mean pulling myself out of the World Cup squad but I just can't see any way that I can work with that man.'

Smith meant every word he said. He was baffled by the fact that Illingworth had given him the cold shoulder throughout the tour and so was I. Another example of Illingworth's man management? A funny way to run a railway. I managed to talk Smith out of quitting by reminding him that not too many cricketers get the chance to play in a World Cup and that, in any case, the best place to answer Illingworth was on the pitch.

As for Stewart I believe Illingworth misread the situation totally. Alec himself admitted that he had had problems with his footwork all tour. But his 81 in the second innings at Port Elizabeth had certainly saved the match for England. Illingworth's comments could not have come at a worse time for him personally. At the same time as the Capetown Test was being fought out at Newlands, his mother Sheila was seriously ill in hospital back home. Fortunately, she was able to make a full recovery after an operation to remove a brain tumour, but at the time all those comments must have hit hard. I believe Illingworth was deadly serious about wanting Alec out of the frame. And hindsight reveals what a shocking decision that would have been. For in the calendar year following the Capetown Test match Stewart scored more runs in Test cricket than anyone else on the planet and finished it not only England's Player of The Year but also their highest-ranked batsman in the world ratings.

Indeed Stewart was left out of the squad for the first Test of the 1996 summer against India at Edgbaston and only returned to the side for the second Test at Lord's when Nick Knight, the Warwickshire opener selected to succeed him as Mike Atherton's opening partner, was ruled out through injury. Having been given a reprieve he made the most of it, scoring a wonderful century against Pakistan at Headingley and a finish in the tour to Zimbabwe and New Zealand firmly established as England's wicket-keeper/batsman all-rounder.

But Illingworth was as good as his word with the other players nominated for departure from the Test arena. For, following England's dismal performance in the World Cup in India and Pakistan, Stewart was the only one of the chairman's dirty half dozen to play for England again during the remainder of 1996, in the Test series against India and Pakistan, and only then by default, and the only one to win selection for the 1997 winter tour to Zimbabwe and New Zealand.

Before that was to happen we had the little matter of the World Cup.

ELEVEN
END OF THE WORLD

'England were, to put it mildly, dreadful in the [1996] World Cup.'

THE 1996 World Cup was a cockeyed tournament from the start. Quite apart from the troubles Australia and West Indies had rousing themselves to play against Sri Lanka in Sri Lanka – and their final decision to withdraw on the grounds of safety, although predictable, was fairly gutless – the qualifying period which took nearly a month was largely meaningless. Its whole purpose was to whittle down the twelve competing nations including three associate members (Kenya, United Arab Emirates and Holland) and Zimbabwe, to eight quarter-finalists. Guess who didn't qualify?

The imbalance in the qualifying groups meant that England reached the quarter final stages even though they lost to the three Test playing nations they encountered, South Africa, Pakistan and New Zealand and only because they were better than United Arab Emirates and Holland.

And they weren't all that much better than the Dutch as it turned out. Graeme Hick scored an unbeaten hundred as England reached 279, but Holland were always in the game, especially when van Noortwijk and the 18-year-old Zuiderent added 114 in twenty-seven overs. England were only in the clear once van Noortwijk, trying for a third six, was caught in the deep by Darren Gough off Peter Martin for 64. England ran out winners by 49 runs but against a team of part-timers that included in its ranks three forty year olds and a couple of students, this was hardly the performance of a premier Test playing nation.

Indeed it was after this match that Dennis Silk, the chairman of the TCCB, found he could contain himself no longer. He said, 'I would think we might come about seventh in the rankings of international cricket. It was salutory to see how well Holland played against us and to think that with their limited resources they were not that far away in terms of performance.

'We have to compare ourselves with the best and the fact is we do not appear to be making any progress. Rather, we are dropping further behind those with whom we are competing.

'We have no batsmen currently ranked in the top five in world cricket, no bowler in the top ten, and no world class spinner. That is not a fluke but it is a worry when you consider we have the only fully professional cricket structure in world cricket.

'We used to have pairs of fast bowlers like Trueman and Statham or more recently Willis and Botham, who would petrify opposing batsmen. Where are their kind now? And when was the last time we saw an eighteen year old playing Test cricket for England?

'Everything will depend on how seriously people are prepared to believe we are being left behind. We can carry on having a cosy game amongst ourselves in domestic cricket, which might please some. But it is not going to do us any good at all in terms of international cricket.

'The standard of county cricket is perhaps lower than it has been in most people's memories.'

This was an extraordinary condemnation of our domestic game, coming as it did in the middle of the World Cup campaign. But Silk, like many of us, had seen enough. And when England finally departed from the competition, beaten by Sri Lanka by five wickets in Faisalabad, the wailing and gnashing of teeth started in earnest. The headlines that followed were predictable.

The *Sunday Mirror* said, 'END OF THE WORLD FOR PATHETIC ENGLAND'. The *Independent on Sunday* said, 'HAPLESS, HOPELESS, HUMILIATED'. Christopher Martin-Jenkins in the *Daily Telegraph*, echoing Silk's words, said, 'The England team and the system which produces it is a heavy lorry in the slow lane being passed by a succession of sports cars'. And Peter Johnson in the *Daily Mail* neatly summed up the stalemate in which English cricket found itself. He wrote, 'Annihilation by that mighty cricketing nation Sri Lanka – one of the most predictable results of the World Cup – brought the usual demands for mass sackings, promises of fresh starts and threats of revolution. We have heard them all before – and seeing English cricket plod on, blind to the rest of the world, still running and playing the game for the benefit of the pensioners who take their thermos flasks and marmite sandwiches to our barren county grounds.'

England were, to put it mildly, dreadful in the World Cup. From the first match at Ahmedabad on 14 February when they were beaten by New Zealand by eleven runs they struggled not only to find out what their best team was, but to work out how they should play. Sri Lanka, meanwhile, had worked out a precise formula to deal with the fielding restrictions of the first fifteen overs. They used their opening batsmen as 'pinch-hitters'. Sanath Jayasuriya, and Ramesh Kaluwitharana were the trend-setters in this new technique, blazing shots all around the wicket and hitting over the in-fielders to get their team off to flying starts. By the time they faced India in Delhi in their penultimate qualifying match, Sri Lanka had the business down to a fine art. They made chasing a target of 272 to win seem simple. The two openers hit 42 runs in the first three overs, and had passed 50 in only five overs when Kaluwitharana, looking for his seventh four, was out for 26. Such a brilliant start meant they were able to shrug off Sachin Tendulkar's 137 for India, recover from a mini-collapse, and win the match with eight balls to spare.

Although England possessed the perfect answer in Robin Smith, he didn't even get a game until their last qualifying match against Pakistan. And I found the fact that they ignored him totally baffling. No one who was at Edgbaston on 21 May 1993 to witness England's one day international against Australia will ever forget the power and majesty of Smith's innings. *Wisden* called it 'one of the greatest innings ever seen in limited overs cricket'. Smith scored 167 not out, the highest score for England in a one-day international, and the fifth highest in all. *Wisden* said, 'Smith hit seventeen fours and three sixes in 163 balls. It was an innings of physical strength allied to magnificent technique and was still the talk of the ground when the Australians batted.' Yet when England played New Zealand, the United Arab Emirates, Holland and South Africa, Smith was nowhere to be seen. England did employ someone called Smith as a pinch-hitter, Warwickshire's off spinning all-rounder Neil Smith, who had some success against the UAE and Holland, scoring a debut 27 before retiring ill and then 31. But when it came to the real stuff against South Africa in Rawalpindi he managed just 11 runs. Finally England woke up to the possibility of using Robin Smith in that role against Pakistan in Karachi with predictably successful results. He and Mike Atherton put on 147 for England's first wicket in twenty-eight overs, the best for any wicket against Pakistan in limited-over internationals by England. England cited Smith's groin strain, suffered in the ten-day warm-up period they enjoyed in Karachi, as the reason for his absence from those earlier matches, but Smith himself was adamant that he was fit to play had anyone bothered to ask him.

England's other major selection howler concerned Jack Russell. Russell had had a magnificent tour of South Africa and was rightly England's man of the tour. He took 27 catches behind the stumps and had England's batsmen given their bowlers something to aim at in the second innings at Capetown there is every possibility he would have beaten Rod Marsh's world record of 28 in a series. His battling support of Mike Atherton in the drawn Test at the Wanderers was everything you'd expect and more from this gritty determined character. Yet Jack was clearly surplus to requirements in the World Cup and Alec Stewart should have kept wicket in the competition. Russell's presence merely unbalanced the side, and left England short in the bowling department. I sense even Jack believed he shouldn't have been there.

But the most depressing sight of all was Illingworth, who spent the entire campaign moaning about a travel itinerary that was, admittedly, daunting, practice facilities that were practically non-existent, and generally giving the impression that he couldn't wait to get home. Just when England needed to be at their most vibrant, their most positive and their most committed, the message that 63-year-old Illingworth was giving out was, 'What the hell am I doing here?'

He wasn't the only one asking that question.

TWELVE
THE GRAVENEY FIASCO

'As the Board knew, had I been elected [to sit on the selection committee], there would have been fireworks...'

AFTER the disaster of England's pathetic World Cup performance and the disappointment of their defeat in the Test series in South Africa, the spring of 1996 should have been a time for a fresh start. When Ray Illingworth agreed to become England coach as well as Chairman of Selectors a year previously he had been happy to accept full responsibility for the team's performance and be accountable for it. England's performance was shocking in the World Cup. He was accountable. He should have gone.

As his tenure in the job was at an end an election was called. Predictably, however, Illingworth decided to stand again.

There was a large ground swell of opinion around the country and among the county chairmen that the time had come for Illingworth to ride off into the sunset. He wouldn't hear of it, of course. In another case of the disappearing buck, Illingworth had made sure that everyone else was to blame for England's poor winter tour but him. And his comments to that effect in his book *One-Man Committee* were part of an ongoing saga which involved him, the TCCB disciplinary committee and Devon Malcolm and dragged on all summer. The dissatisfaction of some of the counties manifested itself when Warwickshire and Surrey approached David Graveney, the chief executive of the Professional Cricketer's Association and persuaded him to stand in opposition to Illingworth for the job. As much as promoting Graveney, their actions were founded on the conviction that Illingworth had by now become an embarrassment, and they were spot on.

Graveney was unsure whether to stand or not at first, bearing in mind the potential conflicts of interest which might arise as a result of his role with the PCA, particularly in the area of player discipline, but his backers had no reservations that those bridges could and would be crossed when he came to them. After receiving what he believed were assurances from his employers at the PCA, he decided to stand. Once he had done so, support for him grew steadily.

The TCCB announced that a postal ballot would be held and a new Chairman of Selectors would be picked before the end of March.

By that time Graveney was confident he would win. On the plane journey to visit his father Ken in America, Graveney counted the votes he knew he was due to receive. The figures added up. As far as he was concerned, barring any last minute hitch, the job was his.

The last minute hitch came in the shape of a telephone conversation Graveney had with Dennis Silk, the Chairman of the Board.

Silk is a man of many qualities. He was one of few within the shadowy corridors of power who understood fully the depth of the crisis in which English cricket currently found itself. He was known to be in favour of taking action over the English domestic structure, he was a fervent supporter of the idea of a national cricket academy and was broadly in favour of England players being contracted to the Board rather than their counties. He had a lifelong passion for the game, and it distressed him to see how far England had fallen behind the rest of the world. He was tireless, energetic and forward thinking. But he had blind spots and one of them concerned Ray Illingworth.

Silk had been the driving force behind the move to invest Illingworth with unique, unlimited and unprecedented powers as Chairman of Selectors and coach rolled into one. He respected and admired Illingworth's undoubted commitment, but also, as chairman of the executive committee who appointed Illingworth, he clearly had a lot to lose if Illingworth was perceived to be a failure in the job. His reputation and his judgement were on the line over Illingworth and he was determined to give him the benefit of the doubt at all times.

Sadly, the other side of this loyalty meant that he was not prepared to listen to the will of the majority of the counties. From the moment Warwickshire and Surrey had nominated Graveney, it was clear that the vote was going to be tight. As it became obvious that it would almost certainly turn out to be in Graveney's favour, Silk and his colleagues on the executive committee understood that they needed to take action if they were to preserve Illingworth's position. So they did.

Publicly it was the voice of the PCA that was heard to instruct Graveney to withdraw. Behind the scenes, however, Illingworth's supporters on the executive committee led by Silk were busy attempting to preserve the status quo.

And the matter came to a head in sinister fashion.

Graveney arrived at his father's home in the States to be told that Silk had been on the phone and wanted to speak to him. By the time their subsequent conversation had finished Graveney decided he had no option but to withdraw from the contest.

Exactly what words passed between them over the transatlantic connection is, of course, known only to Graveney and Silk. Suffice to say that Silk made Graveney aware in no uncertain terms that if he went ahead with his campaign he might find that his salaried job as General Secretary of the PCA would be under threat.

How did he know? Well, the fact that the PCA is directly funded by the TCCB might just have had something to do with it.

Graveney got the message and, for the sake of his and his family's financial well-being, stood down, embarrassed and frustrated.

His supporters were furious. For not only was their man out of the race, the lateness of his withdrawal meant that there was no time for them to put up an alternative candidate. Coincidence? Pull the other one. Illingworth was duly appointed unopposed by default.

Less than twenty-four hours after the 43-year-old Graveney had been confirmed as Illingworth's only challenger, he had pulled out of the fight.

The official reasons given concerned conflict of interest; that, as General Secretary of the PCA Graveney would have been put in impossible positions should he need to discipline players in his role of Chairman of Selectors. I believe this was merely a convenient excuse. Any such potential conflicts could easily have been circumnavigated. The Warwickshire officials who supported Graveney in the first place insisted all along that Graveney's union responsibilities would not affect the way he would run the England set-up.

In any event, the association's president Jack Bannister (who just happens to have been the man who helped Illingworth write *One-Man Committee* – what was that about conflict of interests?) and chairman Tim Curtis, announced that it was they who had given Graveney an ultimatum to decide between the two jobs.

The PCA statement explaining their change of heart was transparent. It read: 'Having supported David Graveney's selection as an England selector last year, the officers of the association, chairman Tim Curtis and President Jack Bannister, gave further consideration to his nomination as Chairman of Selectors and decided that, if successful, there would be unacceptable difficulties for the association.'

Graveney was made to look weak and could only say, 'As a paid employee of the Cricketer's Association I accept the instruction of the President and the Chairman. I would like to take this opportunity of thanking Warwickshire and Surrey for nominating me and to any other counties who might have supported me. I apologise for any distress this decision may have caused to them or any other party. It has always been my wish to serve the game to the best of my ability and I shall continue to do this in the future.'

The question remains: Was the ultimatum delivered to Graveney by the PCA theirs or someone else's? For if this was indeed their decision and theirs alone why on earth should they have left it until the fifty-ninth minute of the eleventh hour to make it? Were they not aware that Graveney's campaign had been up and running for the best part of a month?

Graveney's manifesto may well have scared the living daylights out of Silk and his executive committee. On the eve of England's abysmal World Cup quarter-final defeat at the hands of Sri Lanka, the TCCB announced the result of their deliberations at their spring meeting. Along with such hard hitting and far-reaching items as point 3, the timing of the tea interval, the Board announced that a working party would be set up to review all aspects relating to the administration, selection and management of England teams at home and abroad, and 'all-encompassing reviews that will look at all areas that have a bearing on the performance of our national teams.' This working party was to be chaired by David Acfield, the Essex chairman and former off spinner, and would make their recommendations to the executive committee and then to the Board before the end of that 1996 season. Yet here was Graveney coming up with his own plan as to how the England team should be selected and then run before that working party had even met for the first time.

Graveney's vision of the future was radical. It was full of big names and big ideas. He saw an overseeing role for himself as chairman, he was keen on the appointment of a team manager/administrator. He was keen to engage a certain I T Botham to help in motivation. He wanted to recruit men like David Lloyd and Mike Gatting as coaches and he envisaged the creation of a much larger management and backup team. He was also keen to explore areas such as sports psychology, diet, fitness and technical preparation that by now had been fully integrated into other top sports, but were still to the majority of those in charge of English cricket regarded with suspicion and cynicism. In short, Graveney was keen to pursue a far wider brief than that of merely picking the side.

No wonder the executive committee blanched. For they saw their thunder being stolen.

Yet they had no right to interfere with the democratic process. If a majority of the county chairmen wanted change quickly then they should have had it. Or at least been able to vote for it. Instead huge pressure was put on Graveney to throw in the towel before the first bell had even rung. Talk about match fixing. The whole thing was a shambles and made English cricket look ridiculous in the eyes of world sport.

What it did prove once and for all was that Illingworth was now a lame duck as Chairman of Selectors.

One year earlier, according to the press release which announced Illingworth's elevation to supreme power, Illingworth 'had the total support of the whole Board.' Now, not only did he know he had nothing like it, but he also understood that at least two of them, Warwickshire and Surrey, could not wait to see the back of him.

Faced with such incontrovertible evidence of lack of support in the Chairman of Selectors and team manager, the executive committee and Illingworth realised that his position in the latter role was untenable. A few days after he had been confirmed as chairman of the selectors, Illingworth announced that he was no longer to continue as team manager, saying, 'I have stepped down as manager for two reasons: the first, the public perception of the tour to South Africa, and of the World Cup campaign was that they (presumably England) were not as successful as should be expected. Second, I felt that it was time to allow a younger man to be in charge of all aspects of coaching, which I hope will be a benefit to everyone, especially the players, who always have been, and will remain, my priority.' Oh, so Illingworth felt it was time to *allow* a younger man to be in charge. How kind of him. Who the hell did he think he was?

David Lloyd was duly appointed.

Those who thought the Illingworth situation had gone beyond a joke hadn't see anything yet. For there was still the little matter of who was going to sit on the new selection committee.

Once again Illingworth activated his stooges, Brian Bolus and Fred Titmus, and persuaded them to stand for election. Bolus was not convinced at first. He had had his fingers burned before when he was sacked as a member of Illingworth's selection committee at the end of England's Ashes trip in the winter of 1994-95 to be replaced by Graveney. He told Illingworth he was prepared to stand but only if Illingworth would guarantee that he would do everything he could to get him elected.

Now it boiled down to a straight fight between Illingworth's supporters and the rest. And the rest gave themselves every chance of making sure Illingworth did not railroad Bolus and Titmus back into his cosy coterie by flooding the field with alternative candidates in order to split the vote.

By the closing date for nominations for the two vacancies on the selection committee alongside Illingworth, Lloyd and Atherton, there were no fewer than nine runners at the post.

While those counties who stuck with Illingworth through thick and thin nominated Titmus, Brian Bolus and another one of Illingworth's ex-England colleagues John Edrich (Illingworth's appointment as England's batting coach), those who wanted change proposed myself, Kim Barnett, the Derbyshire captain, Graham Gooch, the ex-Derbyshire and England all rounder Geoff Miller, and ex-England captain (albeit for one Test only) Chris Cowdrey. I was flattered to be nominated by Northamptonshire and Derbyshire but I was fully aware that I had very little chance of being elected. My prime concern was to register my protest over the way Illingworth had been running the show for the last couple of years and to give people enough voting options to ensure that Bolus, Titmus and/or Edrich would not be there to prop up Illingworth's ailing regime.

It worked. Graveney and Gooch were nominated to join Illingworth as chairman, Atherton as captain and David Lloyd as coach.

What I could have done without but should really have expected bearing in mind the attitude towards me of those who still walked the corridors of power, was a concerted campaign against my candidature from within the TCCB offices.

Immediately after I announced I was happy to accept the nomination of Northants and Derbyshire to stand for election, A C Smith, the Board's chief executive wrote to all eighteen counties, pointing out the media commitments of 'at least one candidate'. There are no prizes for guessing who he was talking about. It was quite obvious to me that the Board officials were scared stiff that I might actually be elected and absolutely petrified of what might happen to the selection process if I and Illingworth were put together face to face. I had made no secret of my attitude towards Illingworth, his judgement over players, his bullying of Atherton and others and my belief that he was just too old in his thinking and out of touch with the modern game to be able to do the job properly.

I had also made it clear that I believed he should have stood down or been sacked after the disaster of the 1996 World Cup campaign. Had I been elected, the Board knew that there would have been fireworks and I'm certain it was this element rather than any procedure concerning selectors with media connections that was behind their decision to try and sway the outcome of the vote.

To justify the Board's position, AC dragged up some history about Bob Willis's nomination having been withdrawn by Surrey the previous year for the same reason.

He wrote: 'At least one of the nominations to date is, we believe, very heavily involved with a media responsibility. In the circumstances we believe you should be advised of the position taken up by the executive committee at roughly the same time last year.'

The letter revealed details of an executive committee meeting minute which stated: 'The committee noted that a nomination had been received as a selector for Bob Willis. After a brief discussion it was agreed, as a matter of principle, that someone who was employed full-time in the media could not be a selector.'

That may have been the case in 1995, but why should it have affected proceedings a year later? And what power did the executive committee have to influence the wishes of the counties in the first place?

Illingworth, who had made it clear he wanted Fred Titmus and Brian Bolus alongside him again also attempted to influence the voting by claiming that current players should not be considered. Both Graham Gooch and Kim Barnett fell into this category. At least the counties saw enough sense not to be suckered into giving Illingworth his way this time when Gooch was duly appointed.

At last Illingworth's power base had been removed. It is no coincidence that, apart from the controversy over his book, we hardly heard another peep out of him all summer.

THIRTEEN
MURDER
IN BULAWAYO

*'He [Illingworth] couldn't stand the fact that players would come
to me for help and advice rather than him ... he was damned sure
he was not going to let me into the England set-up...'*

THE 1996-97 winter tour of Zimbabwe and New Zealand was the
first occasion on which I was involved with the coaching and
preparation of the England team on an official, or semi-official basis.
For some time I had been operating privately as an advisor to several
England players: Dominic Cork, Darren Gough and Robin Smith were
among those who had been coming to me from time to time for help on
specific technical problems.

David Lloyd had wanted to get me involved almost as soon as he was
appointed coach in April 1996, and approached me to see if I would be
interested. I told him I was and looking forward to being involved that
summer. Unfortunately, Raymond Illingworth got wind of Lloyd's
proposal and put the block on it. Publicly, Illingworth's reason for
overruling Lloyd was that the coach should find his own feet first before
recruiting assistance. But his comments in the *Daily Express* where he had
described my approach to motivation as 'to squirt a water pistol, then go
off and get pissed', withdrawn while I was contemplating legal action, had
revealed his true feelings.

Illingworth had made his remarks in an interview with James Lawton of
the *Daily Express*, to publicise *One-Man Committee*, his book about his
time as Chairman of Selectors. Referring to my unsuccessful bid to become
a selector in the spring, Illingworth said: 'Everyone knows Botham was a
great player, but he wouldn't do for me as a Chairman of Selectors.

'I think it significant that none of the three counties he played for,
Somerset, Worcestershire and Durham, voted for him. For me that tells a

story. Botham never watched cricket even when he was a player. His idea of team spirit and motivation was to squirt a water-pistol at someone and then go off and get pissed. There's a bit more to it than that.'

As you might imagine I replied in kind. In my column in the *Daily Mirror* I said: 'If only Illy devoted as much time and energy getting the England team right as he does to slagging me off, we might not be in this mess.'

I wasn't going to sit around and let Illingworth walk all over me especially as he had got his facts badly wrong. He claimed that none of the three counties I played for had voted for me. In fact, as he would have found out had he bothered to engage his brain before opening his mouth, Somerset had voted for me, and I knew of a few people at the other two counties who had wanted to as well.

As for his assertion that my entire approach to motivation was a mixture of water-pistols and booze, this really was beneath contempt. Finally, after instructing my solicitor to instigate legal proceedings, I received the following apology from Illingworth, parts of which appeared in the pages of the *Daily Express*: 'The remarks I made were tongue-in-cheek. I'm sure the ones he has made about me are the same.

'We have had, and still have, our differences on cricket matters. But I totally accept that he is sincere in his wish to be involved in English cricket and its selection process.

'I know that he watches a lot of county and international cricket and always did as a player. He is a good and serious motivator of players which was reflected by the fact that one of his counties, Somerset, did vote for him as a selector. I am sure that before long he will give a further positive contribution to the England team.'

Spot the difference.

With one amazing somersault, that affair was brought to a close, but Illingworth still made sure my chances of being used by Lloyd to help motivate the players were sunk.

By now Illingworth was fully aware that the England players had lost what little respect they might once have had for him. He couldn't stand the fact that players would come to me for help and advice rather than him and I believe he felt my very presence within the camp would have undermined his authority even further. Certainly, he was damned sure he was not going to let me into the England set-up through the front door.

It was sad that Illingworth, for whatever reason, got in the way of something the captain, the coach and the players all wanted, but I am afraid that it is a measure of the man that he put his own sense of self-importance ahead of something almost everyone inside the England camp believed would be of positive benefit.

Fortunately throughout the summer of 1996 Illingworth had enough on his plate with the disciplinary case over comments in his book about Devon Malcolm to bother too much about the England team. As time went by he became more and more of a peripheral figure.

Atherton said all the right things about wanting to give Illingworth a good send-off by winning his last Test as chairman, against Pakistan at The Oval, but in reality most of the players were glad to see the back of him.

It irritates and frustrates me to think that Illingworth's intransigence cost me the chance to spend another six months helping develop the England team, but when he was finally out of the way, in fact almost the moment his reign as Chairman of Selectors came to an end, Lloyd approached me again. He knew I would be travelling to Zimbabwe and New Zealand to cover the tours for Sky television and he asked me if I was prepared to come to the nets from time to time to lend a hand on a purely informal basis.

Where on earth the term 'technical adviser' came from, I'll never know. I certainly never used it myself, and neither, to my knowledge did Lloyd. But the result of having the title bestowed on me by some headline-writer was to give the impression that I was going to be far more directly involved than either Lloyd or I had wanted. What it also meant was that my detractors were given an easy target if things went wrong, which, of course, at first they did.

I was more than happy to oblige but I never saw my role as anything other than to be of assistance when asked. It was never envisaged, for instance, that I would attend team meetings or even be present at all the net sessions, nor would I have any voice other than merely to suggest, in the business of picking the side. Even if I had wanted to, I would not have been able to be present at all times due to my Sky commitments.

I saw myself basically as a sounding board, to pass on a touch of experience, or a little piece of advice here and there. What is more there was never any question of a fee involved, unlike in the case of a certain Geoffrey Boycott.

In the event my position as a commentator actually helped rather than hindered. Having access to Sky's super-slow-motion pictures meant that on more than one occasion I was able to spot things that would be invisible to the naked eye and then go and discuss them with the player concerned almost on the spot during the next interval. By the end of the tour I was getting quite adept at timing my runs from the Sky box to the dressing room and back again just in time to pick up the microphone and start commentating again.

One thing I was determined not to do was to attempt wholesale changes to a bowler's action. Unlike those charged with getting the best out of Devon Malcolm in South Africa twelve months previously, my attitude is that fine tuning is normally all that is required to help a bowler rediscover the form on which he was picked in the first place. The middle of a tour is not the time to start suggesting that the action with which a bowler has taken wickets all through his career has to be changed fundamentally.

The kind of things I was looking out for were quite straightforward. Sometimes when a bowler starts to feel the effects of a long tour, for instance, you might notice that his run-up has lost a little bit of aggression and that, consequently he is not 'hitting' the crease as he should. At that point you might step in and have a word with him and the coach and advise a break to recharge the batteries. Or there might be occasions where a particular bowler wants you to help him with something new. For example I was happy to assist Chris Silverwood, the Yorkshire seamer on his first senior tour, almost as soon as I met up with the party a week before the first Test in Bulawayo.

Chris told me that he had been struggling and failing to perfect a slower ball. After a few suggestions from me and an awful lot of work from him he finally managed to master the trick. And I was absolutely delighted when Silverwood had almost instant success, taking his third Test wicket with the delivery in question.

The case of Ronnie Irani was quite different. I felt he had major problems with his action. Following a severe back injury he had been advised to try and develop a chest-on delivery technique. All well and good if your name is Malcolm Marshall, but with Ronnie it just meant that when he got to the crease he wasn't able to generate any pace. When he landed both his big toes were pointing straight down the track. He had become, for want of a better expression, a pie-thrower and any batsman worth his salt at the highest level would have been only too happy to tuck in.

Ronnie was keen to work and I think we actually managed to make some progress. Some you win, some you lose.

The most obvious problems during that tour concerned Dominic Cork.

Cork is a complicated lad who was hit hard by personal problems during the summer of 1996. Having arrived in a blaze of glory the previous season, taking seven for 43 against West Indies on his debut to help win the Lord's Test then doing the hat-trick against them in the fourth Test at Old Trafford, he maintained his rate of progress with excellent form on the winter trip to South Africa. By the time he took his 50th Test wicket in only his eleventh match, the first Test against India at Edgbaston, he had become the first name on the selectors' list and the man around whom the England attack was going to be constructed.

Cue the demons.

First he was roundly criticised for 'sending-off' India's Anil Kumble at Edgbaston, then, as he stretched himself to live up to the absurdly high level of expectation he had unwittingly created for himself, his action started to suffer. Trying to take a wicket with every ball is no bad policy as long as you understand it simply isn't going to happen. But the more he strained the worse matters became. There was also, clearly, something on his mind. Late in the summer and out of the blue came the announcement that his marriage had broken down.

By the end of the 1996 season I believe Dominic was perilously close to physical and psychological burn out and I really don't believe he was in any sort of shape or mood to undertake the three-month tour to Zimbabwe and New Zealand. It was no surprise to me when he pulled out of the African leg. In hindsight I'm convinced it would have been better for him to have taken the whole winter off.

I find it sadly predictable that some of our so-called experts seem to have taken such a perverse delight in Dominic's misfortune.

There is no doubt that he is the kind of bowler who gets right up the noses of other players; in fact he deliberately sets out to do so and there is nothing new or intrinsically wrong with that. Frankly, I couldn't care less what he gets up to on the field as long as he is taking wickets. He'll discover soon enough that if you get it wrong too many times you're the one who ends up looking like a pork pie.

But the occasions where he might have overstepped the mark are, I believe, evidence not of a big-head out of control, but of a simple guy trying desperately to do the very best he can.

Many of Cork's critics will tell you chapter and verse about how people like him should behave, how they should be able to handle being in the public eye. And how if they can't do so they should just be bombed out and forgotten about. They'll tell you all you need to know about how overrated are the so-called pressures heaped on young sportsmen by the media and they will talk with all the authority of someone who has been through the grinder themselves.

Well, I have been through it and I can tell them this: if you haven't experienced how it works and the effect it can have on you, your family and friends, you simply cannot conceive of what it is actually like.

Geoff Boycott has been through the process, which is why I was disgusted but not surprised when he went on BBC television in June to announce to the world that Cork was, in his words 'a show-pony' and a 'prima donna' and claimed that certain England players wanted to send him home from the New Zealand leg of the 1996-97 winter tour.

Boycott went on: 'Cork may have talent but he has an attitude problem. If you think I was bad, my God he's three times worse and I think I could play better than him. He flew out to New Zealand and they were ready to send him home. They'd had enough of him. He's just difficult.'

Although, sadly there may have been a grain of truth in what Boycott said about Cork's reception from some members of the England side in New Zealand, I'm sure Dominic was delighted to hear those constructive comments from a man who was, without doubt, one of the most selfish and disruptive influences inside an England dressing room it has been my misfortune to suffer. Funny how Boycott, who had nothing but praise for Cork when things were going right, had nothing but contempt for him when the reverse applied.

It sounds simplistic but the basic fact that should never ever be forgotten is that everyone is different. Some are better equipped to deal with the pressure than others. That is not to say those who have problems, like Cork, for example, are any less brave, determined or committed than anyone else. You do not achieve what Cork did at the highest level in such a short space of time without possessing those qualities in abundance. But some people simply need more help than others to deal with the inevitable consequences of success, the most obvious being the fact that from the moment of your arrival in the spotlight you become public property, to be analysed and scrutinised in minute detail.

I know from talking to Dominic at length that there came a point when he just felt the whole world was against him. One moment he had been the great hero for whom everyone had been searching for so long and it seemed he could do no wrong. When he was running in, bowling well and taking wickets, everybody loved him and the occasional excesses of his appealing were put down to exuberance. When the wickets dried up, his form deserted him and he started trying too hard to get it back; maybe he went over the top with his on-field aggression. And when the criticisms came, suddenly he felt he was merely a target.

Dominic was never going to be a starter for the 1997 Ashes series, and it was a cause of relief for him that a specific condition known as Gilmore's Groin (after the physician who first diagnosed the problem) was identified and operated on in June. But, once he gets himself going again what he must do from a technical point of view, is get back to the basics that enabled him to succeed in the first place.

When he made such an impressive start people quickly got it into their heads that he was a strike bowler. But Dominic's strength is not speed. It never was and it never will be. His main asset is the ability to bowl late away swing at lively pace with plenty of aggression, and if he is to enjoy a long career at the top, as he is perfectly capable of doing, he must settle for that. He should remember that very often it is the maiden over leading up to the wicket-taking delivery that is every bit as important as the ball itself.

Apart from his physical problems, from a psychological perspective, personally I think Dominic's biggest problem is fear of failure. I know that he became absolutely paranoid about dropping short of his own and other people's expectations. Nineteen ninety-six was a pretty tough year for him. First there was the disappointment of England's poor World Cup performance, then a steady but sure loss of form, and finally the break-up of his marriage and the associated trauma involving his young son Gregory. And the harder he tried to make sense of things by taking wickets for England the worse his situation became. Quite apart from his personal problems, I don't believe he was ever really 100 per cent fit all year.

Certainly, the last thing he needed was to fly out to New Zealand and walk straight into the pressure the England team found themselves under to perform out there.

He could also have done without walking into implied criticism from within the camp. Just prior to his arrival in Auckland, the England management let it be known that they were less than pleased that Dominic had failed to turn up for two fitness assessments, the second with the full-time trainer Dean Riddle, and that he had failed to let anyone at Lord's know why. They may well have been miffed and he certainly should have contacted them to let them know, but I cannot find any good reason why the management wanted this information made public, other than to protect themselves from criticism in case Dominic arrived short of fitness.

I also know that certain voices within the camp began a muttering campaign suggesting that no matter what personal problems he was having to deal with there was no excuse for him absenting himself from the Zimbabwe leg of the tour. This kind of negative talk was symptomatic of the frame of mind the England players had talked themselves into. Once they had started to turn in on themselves it was only a matter of time before some of them turned against each other.

This was also true when it came to the problems Mike Atherton was going through. While none of the players doubted that he would eventually pull himself out of his wretched run of form, the question of his captaincy was another subject that got quite an airing from the malcontents. None of them would ever say it to his face, but one or two were not backward in giving their opinion that maybe the time had come for a change at the helm.

Mind you, you could hardly blame them when Atherton himself on more than one occasion gave interviews indicating that if England failed in Zimbabwe and New Zealand he would give up the job. I admire Michael greatly as a batsman and as a character, yet surely he should have kept such negative thoughts to himself, or at least away from the players he had the job of trying to motivate.

One lesson I hope he learned was that if a leader starts to doubt himself, it is only a matter of time before the feeling spreads to those he is leading. I'm sure that the atmosphere of introspection that clouded the whole of the Zimbabwe leg of the tour came from Athers. He was unfit at the start of the tour and out of form throughout. And his mood rubbed off on everyone else.

England's other major error was in failing to replace Cork once it was known he was pulling out. To me that smacked of complacency, and I know the Zimbabweans thought the same. The message sent out was that England didn't require a full-strength squad to beat Zimbabwe and it made David Houghton & company even more determined to prove them wrong.

Of course everyone involved in the England set-up not to mention the press and public expected England to win. But I think too many of the players felt they only needed to turn up to do so.

Perhaps their attitude to the newest entry to international cricket was too close in spirit to an article I read in the *Googly*, the satirical magazine which, under the heading 'Cricket round the World: Zimbabwe' published the following article: 'Zimbabwe's most momentous season to date may be over, but there is plenty of work to be done by the administrators, who are currently engrossed in forming an internal first-class competition, the Mickey Mouse league, which will start next season.

'The two teams to take part next season will be Matabeleland and Matabeleland B. Matches will last three days if all players can get the necessary time off work. Umpires will be provided by the batting team and teas are the responsibility of the wives of the home side.

'There is also a one-day competition, the Matabeleland Cup. It will be a straight knockout tournament of one game between the two Matabeleland teams. The winner takes the Cup. Zimbabwe's skipper, David Houghton, highlighted the problems of making the step up to full ICC status: "Persuading the players to carry the team bag is very difficult now. They say that Mike Atherton and Richie Richardson don't have to, so why should they. We've had to implement stringent punishments, like collecting match fees or filling in the scorebook after the game."

'But Houghton is confident that the Zimbabweans can soon be a major force in Test cricket: "We've got some tremendous players at the moment and some promising youngsters. When we've got a sightscreen, we'll be ready for anyone."

For practical reasons as well the decision not to replace Cork was a poor one. It meant there was even less competition for places in the squad of only fourteen players which included just six specialist batsmen. Once the decision had been made that Russell was not going to keep wicket and Stewart was, in a dual role of wicket-keeper/batsman, all six of those batters, Atherton, Stewart, Knight, Thorpe, Crawley and Hussain were guaranteed to play no matter what their form. This lack of competition was evident. Not only do you need it to gee everyone up and make sure they perform to the best of their ability at all times, but it left England dangerously short should there have been an injury.

On more than one occasion England were down to the bare bones to send out a side for the warm-up matches and that is an unsatisfactory situation. But it smacked of the complacency with which England undertook the whole expedition to Zimbabwe and they got their comeuppance in the 3-0 thrashing in the one-day international series.

I was a privileged observer in Zimbabwe and New Zealand, and although I would walk through a brick wall to help any of the players, I have to say that a lot of what I saw distressed me. To my mind the players got Zimbabwe all wrong. They decided early on that they didn't like the place or the people and from then on they made little or no effort to understand it or them. If you go to a country like Zimbabwe you've got to get out there and experience the place. Most of the players confined themselves to the cricket grounds and their hotel rooms. It was completely the wrong way to go about touring anywhere, but in Zimbabwe it was a disaster. Some of the players seemed more concerned that the room service was not up to scratch or with the standard of television programmes available, than they were with getting to know the people and the country. Only Jack Russell took it upon himself to get out and about to do his painting and of course he had an awful lot of spare time to do it in because right from the start it was clear he did not figure in England's team plans. In fact he knew from about the first game that he was hardly going to play any cricket at all.

What the players failed to grasp, and for this I blame the management as well, is that you only get out of an experience what you are prepared to put in. The people of Zimbabwe were ready to bend over backwards to accommodate their guests. This was, after all, the first time a full England side had ever undertaken a Test tour of their country and in that respect the captain and his players had the perfect opportunity to win friends and influence people. How they wasted it.

Instead of taking the time and the trouble to have a beer after the early matches, to relax and unwind with their hosts, it was 'Where's the bus? Let's get back to the hotel.'

As the tour progressed they were criticised, rightly in my opinion, for their insular attitude And I believe Barclay, Lloyd and Atherton should have done more to try and open the eyes of the players to what was on offer in that wonderful country.

Furthermore the mood within the party was certainly not helped when, after early results went badly the siege mentality the players adopted extended to the touring pressmen. My attitude towards the press, as most people know, has been reasonably ambivalent. They are paid to do a job and they criticise you if you do badly and praise you to the skies if you do well. When England lost their first game of the tour, to Mashonaland, the press piled in and the players got the hump. Driving down to London on the first morning of England's match against Mashonaland I turned to

Radio 5 Live to hear the latest news: 'And now the sport,' read the announcer. 'We were not going to lead this bulletin with news from England's cricketers in Zimbabwe, but you are not going to believe this. England began their first match of the tour about half an hour ago and they are currently 10 for three.' Cue gales of laughter all round the Radio 5 Live office. English cricket as a music hall joke, again.

But what did the players expect? They were bound to get it in the neck, and they did. Very soon, however, it was a case of 'us and them' not only between the players and the press but, it seemed between the players and everyone else. This negative outlook should never have been allowed to develop. But it was, and the results were clear for all too see.

By the time I got out there I found attitudes were fairly well entrenched. Atherton and Lloyd were upset by the criticism of the team after the defeat against Mashonaland, particularly in the broadsheet papers like the *Sunday Telegraph* and the *Sunday Times*. But they were naive not to see it coming.

They must have known the effect that kind of result was going to have and they should have ridden the criticism instead of reacting to it. When, during the Test match in Bulawayo, I got wind of the trouble that was brewing between the players and the press I considered the whole thing to be an unnecessary distraction. And when I heard that the players had decided to boycott the traditional press Christmas panto I realised the situation had got out of hand. This Christmas function is never meant to be taken seriously. The touring press guys put on a bit of a show and invite the players to attend and watch them take the mickey out of themselves as much as the players or anyone else. It's also a chance for the players and press to unwind and have a drink together and exchange views and bury the hatchet if necessary. Preferably not in each other's heads. There is no three-line whip on these occasions but generally in my experience the players have been happy to go along and share a drink with the press at Christmas. What happened this time was that the matter was put to a vote, and as soon as it was it became a big issue among the players. It was all totally unnecessary but the end result was more bad publicity for the England team. And that's what they didn't need when they failed to win the first Test against Zimbabwe in Bulawayo. They made a great effort and Nick Knight's hundred on that last day was a memorable performance. So, sadly, was that of David Lloyd after the match.

Wound up by a Zimbabwe Cricket Union official over England's failure to win the match, Lloyd, a passionate man who lives on his nerves, exploded – in full view of several other ZCU officials and their families, not to mention a cluster of touring England supporters.

Lloyd took the man in question to task and let himself down by his behaviour (and that's putting it mildly). In some ways I can fully understand his reaction. In order to try and prevent England succeeding in their desperate final-day run-chase the Zimbabweans adopted the questionable tactics of bowling wide down the legside at the England batsmen, but not actually wide enough to be penalised according to the strictest interpretation of the laws. I don't blame them for trying whatever tactics they could to hold on for the draw, but I have to say that in my opinion the umpiring let them get away with far too many borderline decisions. Many of the England guys were involved in the fourth Test against South Africa at Port Elizabeth on the previous winter tour when Cork was called by the umpire Cyril Mitchley for bowling out of the batsman's reach in a period when England were trying to restrict South Africa's lead. Yet here the rules appeared to be different. Time after time Heath Streak sent the ball way down the legside or offside and not once did the umpires intervene. Streak admitted afterwards that he and the other bowlers had got away with murder. To my mind he was right, the umpiring was atrocious and England were consequently robbed of a Test victory that would instantly have relieved the pressure on them for the rest of the tour.

Instead all the frustration that had built up inside the passionate and patriotic Lloyd, what with the criticism he felt they had taken unfairly for their slow start to the tour, meant that he was a bomb waiting to go off. When he did, in the immediate aftermath of the match, the message relayed to me was straightforward and urgent: 'You'd better get down to the dressing room quick. "Bumble" has blown a fuse.'

Quite what tour manager John Barclay was doing at this time, I don't know. Perhaps in the chaos of the last ball tie he was too busy trying to arrange press conferences and the like to notice the state his coach was in. But when I got down to the pool area behind the stands it was clear that Lloyd was out of his mind with rage. I put my arm around him, pulled him into the dressing room and told him: 'Look, Bumble. This is not the time or the place.' I shut the dressing room door behind him and in time he cooled down.

It was all over quite quickly but word was out and the fuss rumbled on all tour. I know he himself thought he was badly done over in the press, but this kind of thing is just not on. When reports got back to MacLaurin, the ECB chairman and Tim Lamb, the chief executive, they were not best pleased. The last thing English cricket needed at this time was to make enemies.

When MacLaurin was appointed the chairman of the new board, he made it his business to insist that England's public image would be improved. That didn't just mean shaving or looking smart on official occasions, it also meant doing the right thing in the right place at the right time. Lloyd's exhibition was emphatically not. And he got a flea in his ear from the chairman and chief executive as a result. Most of the complaints that MacLaurin and Tim Lamb took notice of were not those that appeared in the national papers. I know for a fact that a couple of travelling England supporters were so upset and angry about what had happened that they took it upon themselves to seek out Lamb and MacLaurin when they arrived in Harare for the second Test and give them chapter and verse of what exactly happened.

Although he'd calmed down a bit by the time he met the press in the post-match conference, it didn't take much to get Lloyd going again. Those who watched the whole match could sympathise with the thoughts behind his words, 'We murdered them, we hammered them. We know it and they know it,' because England had been in the ascendancy and were one ball away from winning the Test match. But the tenor of his comments was right out of order.

Apart from just sounding daft, Lloyd could not have done more to stiffen the resolve of the opposition. It was pointed out to Lloyd that the next time he talked about killing the opposition he'd better make sure they had actually stopped breathing. By the time the team assembled in Harare for the second Test the pressure was really on.

Having blotted his copybook so publicly, by the time England travelled to Harare for the second Test and the last two one-day internationals Lloyd was under scrutiny, particularly from MacLaurin and Lamb, and Atherton was struggling with his form and confidence.

What made matters worse for both of them was what happened on the first day of that second Test, when England collapsed in a heap of undisciplined batting. They managed to drag themselves back into contention but the match ended in a disappointing draw because of the weather. Again the comments offered by Atherton after rain washed out the final day could have been more diplomatic. He said: 'We would have won both games given five days of good weather.' This may have been a true reflection of Atherton's thoughts but someone should have told him that, after what Lloyd had come out with in Bulawayo this was not the time for plain speaking.

The Zimbabwean captain Alistair Campbell had his own thoughts. 'For them to say they outplayed us is truly astonishing. Why can't they just admit that there have been two very good games of cricket between two evenly-matches sides? In the 22 Tests I've been involved in this has been the easiest series of all. We've spent most of our time playing in the sub-continent where even the likes of Australia and South Africa get beaten. What happened to England the last time they were in India and Sri Lanka? Four-nil, wasn't it? It's about time they got rid of their superiority complex. This "we murdered you and you know it" business is frankly monotonous. They're clutching at thin air as far as I'm concerned, and conning themselves into thinking they've played well. There's not much between ourselves, England and New Zealand among the minnows.'

Some might say Campbell was merely stirring things up. I say he was just giving as good as he got. And how his words were borne out in the following week, the lowest point of the tour, some might say the lowest point of any England tour in recent memory.

England's performances in the last two of the three one-day internationals were abject and underlined that there was now a real crisis of confidence inside the camp. Even Lloyd admitted as much. He said, 'Everyone will tell you and the statistics tend to support the theory that our top six are good Test match players. But we are not consistently batting well enough as a unit. On the first day of the second Test and in all three one-day internationals our batting was unacceptable, abysmal. There are no excuses and no hiding places. In the second one-day international we had the game won but just petered out. Not one of the batsmen had it in them to grab the moment and say "I will win this match". It was as if they were all hoping somebody else would take the responsibility. That is not good enough. The performance in the third and final match spoke for itself.'

Indeed, it did. England lost by 131 runs.

So England travelled to New Zealand knowing that nothing but victory would be enough. This applied particularly to Atherton for this was, without doubt, his darkest hour as captain of England so far.

Although he insisted he had no intention of pulling up the drawbridge everyone understood that his future was on the line. Whereas in the past he had been able to count on himself as a batsman to try and get his side out of trouble, his batting form meant that even his most trusted ally had deserted him. When he failed again in the last warm-up match before the first Test in Auckland, against Northern Districts in Hamilton, his prospects looked bleak. I honestly couldn't see where he was going to get another run.

The transformation from virtual liability to England's man of the New Zealand series was quite remarkable. And it all started when he took on the bowling machine behind the England dressing room in Hamilton. He'd clearly had enough of batting against human beings. After discussing his problems with Alec Stewart, the Surrey man told him how he had dealt with his own loss of form in South Africa the previous winter. Then, on return from the World Cup Alec had dragged his father Micky and his long-time mentor Geoff Arnold off to an indoor net and practised playing shots against a bowling machine for hour after hour until his footwork and timing just returned of their own accord. His magnificent run over the next twelve months told the story of the success of the move.

Athers took Stewart's advice and when the team moved on to Auckland for the first Test the results were immediate. In the nets at Eden Park prior to the match he was already looking more confident and, once at the crease in earnest he looked the picture of confidence and aggression, making a stylish 83 in what was, by streets, his best innings of the tour.

Once again, however, England failed to press home their advantage, having to settle once more for a draw. After victory in Wellington, achieved thanks to the brilliance of Darren Gough and Andrew Caddick in helpful conditions, the whole winter's efforts and Atherton's future as captain would still be judged on events in the final Test in Christchurch. And it was here that Atherton played one of the matches of his life.

England allowed New Zealand to make 346 after putting them in at Lancaster Park. This was about par for the course, but it soon assumed match-winning proportions when England batted abysmally in reply. Without Atherton's unbeaten 94 they would have been severely embarrassed, but conceding a deficit of 118 on first innings they were still on course for the defeat that would have given New Zealand a share of the series and, by the criteria for success he himself had laid down, might well have cost Atherton the captaincy.

What happened next constituted an extraordinary turnaround. First

Phil Tufnell and Robert Croft got among the Kiwis on a turning pitch, as hurried along by Gough they capitulated for 186. Then, faced with the task of making more than 300 in the fourth innings to win a Test match for only the second time in England's history, Atherton took control with one of the most crucial innings of his career, making the 118 with which he dragged his reluctant heroes to the brink of glory. In the end it was left to Cork and John Crawley to keep their heads and finish the job. Only Atherton knows what was going through his mind as the match reached its climax. England 2 New Zealand 0 looks a hell of a lot better on your CV than 1-1.

Ten years of hurt may have come to an end in a reasonably optimistic fashion for England. Their two Test wins in New Zealand gave them that series 2-0 and to a certain degree dispelled the doom and gloom that had surrounded their efforts in Zimbabwe.

And perhaps in the selection for those last two Tests there lie clues as to what had been going wrong for so long. For the last Test in Christchurch England selected the same eleven that had taken the field to win the second Test match of the series in Wellington. This, almost unbelievably, was the first time they had done so in more than thirty Tests. It is no coincidence that the last time they had enjoyed such luxury over selection was in the two Tests immediately prior to Ray Illingworth's appointment as Chairman of Selectors in the spring of 1994. England's victory over West Indies in Barbados in the fourth Test of the 1993-94 winter tour was a fantastic achievement and, quite rightly, they nominated the same team to take the field for the final Test in Antigua. By achieving a creditable draw England had given themselves a platform on which to build for the future. Atherton was convinced that the early traumas had been dispelled and that the courage and commitment they displayed thereafter had given him the nucleus of a young side to build on.

Back home, however, the appointment of Illingworth meant that all that was about to change. In the next three years the common thread in the selection of England teams was inconsistency. Not only did Ray Illingworth rip up the plan to select a young side and let it develop, his shotgun selection meant that no one was ever sure of a place, and I believe that contributed to England's poor performance during that period. England's cricketers do not want to be mollycoddled but they want to know they are going to get a reasonable chance. That doesn't mean one or two Tests, but a minimum of three.

During that period there were some crazy selections and I've covered them in detail. But one in particular caused me to believe that Illingworth had totally lost the plot, the award of one single Test cap to Alan Wells, the Sussex batsman, at the end of the 1995 summer Test series against West Indies at The Oval. Wells had been one of the most successful batsmen in county cricket over a number of years. He might have been given his chance at any time during the previous seven or eight. When he was finally picked he made nought in the first innings, three not out in the second innings, and never played again. I have looked at his selection upside down and inside out but it still makes absolutely no sense to me. If Wells was worth a place in the side he was surely worth a place in the side for more than one match. Yet he was always extremely unlikely to be on the plane for South Africa for that winter tour in 1995-96. In the end Wells did the selector's job for them by failing in the match but what if he had succeeded? Was he, at the age of 33, really going to replace one of John Crawley, Alec Stewart, Mike Atherton, Graham Thorpe, Graeme Hick, Robin Smith or Mark Ramprakash in that tour's squad?

More generally, under Illingworth England's selection had become a lottery. In out, in out, shake it all about; this was the Illy hokey-cokey. No wonder England had been spinning round and round in circles.

1997 ASHES TO ASHES

FOURTEEN
THE NEW ORDER

'It was clear to me that he [Ben Hollioake] had talent, but what struck me even more forcibly was his temperament … he looked made for the big stage.'

WHILE county clubs returned from their overseas tours to gear up for the start of the 1997 summer programme, and cricketers all over the county began to fine-tune their techniques in pre-season nets, an elite group of the best of them were doing something completely different.

Towards the end of England's winter tour in New Zealand, the coach David Lloyd informed the squad that they would be meeting again to begin preparation for the forthcoming Ashes challenge rather sooner than any of them might have imagined.

Normally the first time England's players re-introduced themselves following an overseas tour would be during the couple of days prior to the Texaco Trophy one-day internationals at the end of May. They would barely have enough time to shake hands and swap stories of what they did on their holidays before being pressed into battle against the touring sides in front of capacity crowds and mass television audiences.

This time things were going to be different.

At the Cornhill Player of the Year lunch at the Landmark Hotel, Marylebone, on 14 April the new Chairman of the England and Wales Cricket Board, Lord MacLaurin spelled out how things were going to change.

To an audience of invited guests that included the England captain Mike Atherton, Chairman of Selectors David Graveney, coach David Lloyd and players, plus representatives of the media, MacLaurin announced the arrival of a breath of fresh air.

He said: 'We took a lot of flak in Zimbabwe and quite rightly so. But we pitched the side into 36 degrees centigrade temperatures and asked them to play their first game after just three days of practice. Before the tour we went to Portugal where there were no facilities for cricket practice.

'We said to them that they wouldn't be seeing their wives, girlfriends or families for three and a half months, which won't be happening again, and asked them to share hotel rooms which was unacceptable.

'From now on our Test players will be a top priority. Their preparation to that end is our responsibility. They are under the spotlight for 24 hours a day and we need to help them cope with the pressures and strains. From now on nothing but the best is good enough for our players. But I want a big return on our investment. When I say I want them to die for England I am not joking.'

Put simply, the deal was this: MacLaurin and the Board would support the players all the way and in every way. But they had to have something to show for their commitment. They had to have results.

The first part of the plan to give the team the best chance of success was to take place immediately.

Straight from the function, all the players who toured Zimbabwe and New Zealand, except for Alan Mullally, unavoidably absent in Australia, plus Mark Butcher, Mark Ealham, Adam Hollioake from the A team and Graeme Hick set off for their assignment at Heythrop Park, NatWest's residential training centre, in Oxfordshire, for a three-day team-building seminar course run by Will Carling's company Insights. Erroneously described in the press at the time as a charm school, the course had very little to do with the correct method of holding a tea-cup, the right order for knives and forks at the dinner table or balancing books on top of the head, as the players soon found out.

Instead, they were spilt into groups and given various problem-solving tasks to carry out as a team, including paddling across streams and driving with their eyes closed. The world gone mad? Far from it. According to Atherton, 'It was to do with teamwork, team ethics and team dynamics.'

Two of the exercises in particular illustrate the point. The first involved each group being driven by one of the number through a forest in a jeep. Nothing too tricky in that, except that each driver was wearing a blindfold and was directed through and past obstacles by his colleagues barking instructions and directions.

While that Test was intended to encourage trust among the group, the next was all about ingenuity. Each group would take on an orienteering course during which they had to build a raft on which to paddle across a river. The element of difficulty here was that each group would be given the tools to fashion such a craft, minus the vital part required to finish the job.

All teams and individuals were monitored throughout and at the end of each series of Tests had the opportunity to talk though and review what they had achieved or failed to do. All in all everyone connected with the squad agreed that the exercise had been worthwhile, even those who got wet. Apart from anything else it enabled the players to learn more about themselves and each other in an atmosphere of mutual reliance. Atherton and Lloyd said afterwards that part of the thinking behind the course was to discover what their players were capable of achieving as a team.

The best parallel I can draw is with one of those Army Recruitment advertisements on television. A group of soldiers carrying a wounded colleague on a stretcher reach their intended crossing point over a deep ravine to find that the bridge has been destroyed. The question flashes up on screen: 'What are you thinking?' Then it provides the following answer: 'If it's "How am I going to get across?" we're not interested. If it's "How are *we* going to get across?" ring this number.'

The bottom lines were individual resourcefulness and collective responsibility.

All this was far cry from the haphazard approach to the start of an international season that had been the norm and, of course, the employment of such sciences should have been commonplace for years.

What the exercise did underline was the fact that Lord MacLaurin was prepared to put the Board's money where his mouth was. And he had other ideas too, even at this early stage, months before his strategy for cricket was released to an eager cricketing public.

The next innovation involving the players was to do with image. MacLaurin may have been criticised in some quarters for going slightly over the top in one area. It was his decision to pay Lowe Bell Associates, the company founded by Maggie Thatcher's image adviser Sir Tim Bell, a considerable amount of money for a thorough review of the Board's public image and advice as to how to proceed from then on. That fee caused some to raise an eyebrow or two, especially as the announcement coincided with the appearances in the media of some rather unfortunate information regarding Bell himself. In an unauthorised biography of Bell, entitled *The Ultimate Spin Doctor – The life and fast times of Tim Bell* the author Mark

Hollingsworth revealed Bell's 1977 conviction for indecent exposure and detailed his use of cocaine from then to the early 1980s. Those past problems apart, however, Bell was regarded as the most effective political 'fixer' of the Thatcher years and the engagement of his company's expertise proved the level of seriousness with which MacLaurin was taking on the job of rejuvenating English cricket.

In any case MacLaurin had the perfect answer to those who might have accused him of profligacy with the Board's money, for it was he, as a non-executive director of the mobile phone company Vodafone who was instrumental in attracting them as England team sponsors to replace Tetley, for the not inconsiderable sum of £13 million.

In terms of his public image, Atherton himself had been on the end of some strong words from MacLaurin in New Zealand. On the chairman's return from Zimbabwe, his chief executive Tim Lamb had spelled out their views, saying: 'We were not happy with the way the England team presented themselves. We understand their demeanour was fairly negative and not particularly attractive. Things improved in New Zealand but there is still a long way to go.'

Indeed as Lord MacLaurin later revealed, his early impressions of the England captain were less than favourable. He said: 'During the tour of Zimbabwe and before I arrived in Harare, I suppose I had perceived Michael as the press had portrayed him, as being quite a dull sort of chap, maybe a bit grumpy occasionally and not really the sort of person that I thought should be the England captain.'

But during their meetings in Harare MacLaurin was won over. As he underlined: 'When I got to know Michael my opinion changed right on its head.' And from that moment both men found much common ground. Atherton said: 'I've had two or three meetings with him and he's an interesting guy to talk to because he comes from a different background and has a different perspective on things and obviously has a very successful business record, so you have an immediate respect for the things he says. And it also struck me that he wants to be a bit of a doer...'

His first instructions to Atherton had an instant effect. On his return from pre-season fishing holidays in France and Scotland, Atherton came out with some quotes that could have been scripted for him by the man at the top, insisting: 'The image and projection of the England team is very important. I have no difficulty with understanding this approach because it is essential to our future if we are going to be successful in encouraging youngsters to come into the game who want to be England cricketers ... I have made an agreement that I will be clean-shaven and that will carry on being the case as long as I am England captain. Shaving is not a big issue with me, or the rest of the England team, but I can promise that the England side will look immaculate this summer.'

As for his 'Captain Grumpy' image Atherton explained: 'Concentration is sometimes mistaken for grumpiness. If you go out of your way to be loved, or if you are so concerned about your image that it's all-consuming at the expense of your form, then you have a problem. I hope people will understand that I love my cricket. I love captaining England.' Those who knew Atherton well never had any doubt that this was the case, of course. But the message from MacLaurin had obviously got through. It never hurts to tell the people what they want to hear, especially if one of them is your boss!

Just to make sure they were under no illusions about what would be expected of them as their part of MacLaurin's new deal, the players were issued with *The England Players' Handbook*, a 26-page document spelling out exactly what was required of them.

If England played poorly and lost, at least they were going to look good doing it. According to the document: 'You have been invited to represent England and as a consequence you will be expected to conduct yourself and dress in a manner befitting an international sportsman.' The following dress code would be adhered to at all times:

ARRIVAL AT ASSEMBLY POINT: Smart casual.
HOTEL TO GROUND ON NON-MATCH DAYS: Smart casual.
HOTEL TO GROUND ON MATCH DAYS: England blazer, white shirt, England tie and grey or beige colour trousers.
AT GROUND ON PRACTICE DAYS: Blue tracksuit trousers (white tracksuit trousers at Lord's), ECB or Tetley headgear, training shirt, or blue sweat shirt.
AT GROUND ON MATCH DAYS: Only the current ECB issue clothing will be worn outside the dressing room. Training shorts and T-shirts will *not* be worn away from the dressing room area. Tracksuits are acceptable. No bare torsos or branded T-shirts or clothing unrelated to the England team on public view at anytime.
DINING ROOM AT GROUNDS: (a) On the field cricket clothing. (b) Tracksuit. (c) Training shirt. (d) Blue shorts and collared shirts, no headgear, no cycle/beach shorts.

AT GROUND MATCH DAY PRESENTATIONS: Blue tracksuit trousers (white tracksuit trousers at Lord's), cricket shirt or training shirt (not T-shirt), cricket sweaters.

IN HOTEL AND ALL PUBLIC ROOMS: (a) England blazer, shirt, tie and grey or beige colour trousers. (b) Tracksuits and collared shirt. (c) Smart casual (smart jeans permitted). (d) Lounge suit.

NO HEADGEAR PERMITTED.

No chance of catching Athers in his normal post-match gear of tie-dye shirt, loons and open-toed sandals, then.

Increased payments, pension arrangements and emphasis on media-friendliness ('in the interest of promoting cricket in a positive manner it is essential that every appropriate opportunity is taken'), as well as the dress code, made it perfectly clear to the players that playing for England was now a seriously 'professional' business, and that from now on the absolute priority in the English game was the preparation and performance of the national side.

All in all these measures added up to an impressively proactive start for the new regime, but, inevitably some cynics wondered what all this was leading. To prove this was not all beside the point, MacLaurin needed something tangible to show for his efforts.

The next indication that a greater degree of imagination would be at work to support the England effort came at the same time as they set off for Heythrop Park.

At the start of the season, David Graveney had finally ascended to the position of Chairman of Selectors the majority of counties had wanted him to have twelve months earlier, and his first act after officially replacing Ray Illingworth was to give his captain Mike Atherton the kind of real support he had never enjoyed under Graveney's predecessor.

Clearly uninterested in playing the power game that Illingworth had indulged in from the moment he took office in the spring of 1994, Graveney made it clear that there would be no question over Atherton's position as captain of the England side. At the press conference which followed the announcement of the Cornhill Player of the Year award to Alec Stewart (a man incidentally written off as a Test player by Illingworth at the end of England's 1995-96 tour to South Africa) Graveney not only announced that Atherton had been re-appointed as captain, but that the job was his for the entire summer.

This was a huge break from normal protocol and, of course, carried a risk. 'What if Atherton fell into the kind of slump that dogged him in Zimbabwe?' asked the doubters. Graveney would not entertain any such thoughts. Indeed he could not have sent out a more positive indicator of the level of confidence the selectors placed in Atherton. And this came right from the top.

Atherton was thus given the kind of backing no other England captain had ever enjoyed before. And this was not the only innovation in store. At the same press conference Graveney confirmed the rumour that had been circulating in advance, that although he and the coach Lloyd would have a strong input into the selection process, Atherton had asked not to have a vote.

Atherton's decision was based on two factors. First, and most importantly, unlike the position when Illingworth was in charge, it demonstrated how confident the captain was in the ability of the new selection panel – Graveney, Graham Gooch and the most recent recruit, the former Middlesex and England captain Mike Gatting – to think along the same lines that he did and his trust in their judgement over players. For longer than he cared to recall Atherton had been banging on about the need for younger selectors more in touch with the modern game. Now he had them, in the form of two current players and a recently retired one, he was happy to let them use their experience and expertise. With that there could be no argument.

The second factor in his decision provoked more controversy, inside and outside the selection panel. Atherton had made it clear that one of the areas of captaincy he had always found difficult was telling players that they had been dropped. He had had to do so on a number of occasions. It had never been easy for him, for instance to let down his great friend Angus Fraser whenever the axe had to fall on the Middlesex paceman's neck. And he recalls the famous incident prior to the final Test against Australia at The Oval in 1993, his second in command as England captain, when he came to the painful conclusion that Robin Smith had to be omitted after a run of 45 consecutive Tests. Atherton happened to be playing for Lancashire against Hampshire at Southampton during the week before The Oval Test and had been happy to accept the invitation of his friend Smith to stay with him during the match. On the Sunday morning, the day when the squad was due to be announced, Athers peered at his mate through the packets of cornflakes on the breakfast table and greeted him with some rather unwelcome news; namely, 'You're dropped.'

The example he quoted now happened during the final Test against Pakistan at The Oval at the end of the 1996 series. The squad for the Texaco Trophy series was due to be named on the Sunday morning, so, prior to leading them out onto the field for the fourth day's play in the final Test, he had to inform Nasser Hussain, John Crawley, Chris Lewis, Dominic Cork and Ian Salisbury that they would not be required for England duty the following week. 'I found that very hard,' he admitted.

In the new scheme of things, without having the vote over who should or shouldn't play Atherton freed himself of the danger that his personal feelings might be compromised or that they might indeed be perceived to be coming into the reckoning. The experience he had had with Illingworth over the years, telling all and sundry in his articles in the *Sun* and elsewhere that Phil Tufnell and Phil DeFreitas to name but two could not get a game for England because the captain either didn't trust them or didn't like them, had encouraged Atherton to believe he was better off not being so directly involved in the final choice. It was, however, made plain that as well as having substantial input, the final decisions on who to leave out of the squad on the morning of a Test match and what tactics should be pursued would be down to him.

Reaction to this news was mixed. For instance, one of the selectors, Gatting, was surprised that Atherton had adopted this position. Gatting's approach to the business of captaincy had always been hands-on. At Middlesex, as far as selection was concerned, he had always been left more or less to his own devices and if a player had to be told he was dropped, he reasoned that news was best coming from the man who dropped him. He was also of the opinion that a vote in selection was one of the privileges of the job rather than one of the burdens and, as such was not to be given away lightly.

The fact was, however, that Atherton had weighed all these factors in the balance and was quite prepared to take the consequences. I believe he was right. Apart from anything else, he was such a vital member of the side for his batting alone, that the fewer potential distractions he had on his plate the better.

The next clear evidence of the new impetus within the England set-up came in the selection of the squad for the Texaco Trophy series to be played at Headingley, The Oval and Lord's.

Graveney had said right from the start that age and experience would not necessarily be a barrier to selection and he and his co-selectors were as good as their word. Adam Hollioake, whose all-round abilities had been obvious during his England debut in the one-day internationals against Pakistan at the end of the previous summer and who had received rave reviews from Graveney and Gatting, the A team manager and coach in Australia, was a certainty to play, but at the start of the season who would have given his younger brother Ben, the slightest chance of making the squad? Apparently, Ben had made his first real impression on the selectors during the match between England A and The Rest at Edgbaston, even bowling out his brother Adam. I had my first extended view of him when Sky television covered the Benson & Hedges Cup match between Gloucestershire and Surrey at Bristol on 30 April and I liked what I saw.

As an upright strokeplayer he hit hard and straight and when bowling he sent the ball down at a lively pace, playing his full part in Surrey's win, en route to their Benson & Hedges Final appearance against Kent in July, a match he was later to dominate in emphatic style with the Gold Award winning innings of 98.

It was clear to me that he had talent, but what struck me even more forcibly was his temperament. At 19, and with only a handful of first-team appearances under his belt he looked made for the big stage.

Ben had to wait his turn, as the selectors decided to stick with Phil DeFreitas for the first two one-day internationals but the impression he made in the third at Lord's will not be forgotten in a hurry. Five years the junior of his brother Adam and the youngest England cricketer for 48 years at the age of 19, he took the full house at headquarters and a debut appearance against some of the most talented players in world cricket in his stride.

No one who saw the off-drive for four against Glenn McGrath from the third ball of his innings will ever forget the sheer command of the shot. McGrath didn't, deciding that this young upstart needed teaching a lesson. He knew his bouncer would be called no-ball, according the one-day regulations but he reckoned it was worth it just to put one up young Ben's nose. It was a snorter too, jagging back and rearing up at high pace. Ben simply didn't give it the time of day, swaying out of the line at the last moment with imperious ease. When he swept Shane Warne into the Tavern Stand for six, the noise reached a deafening crescendo.

Ben had not even been to Lord's until the day he made his England debut, Sunday 25 May, but his fabulous innings of 63 from 48 balls, including 11 fours and a six justified at a stroke the policy of the selectors in giving outstanding young talent its head.

The second part of Atherton's moan over selection strategy under Illingworth was that too often the chairman had opted for 'experience' ahead of youth. Under Illingworth Gooch, Gatting and John Emburey had all returned to the England side at a time when they should never have been in contention. Ben Hollioake's success showed what England might have been missing as a result of Illingworth's over-enthusiasm for looking back rather than forward.

Indeed the key element in England's 3-0 Texaco whitewash of Australia lay in the youthful exuberance and dedicated team spirit that Heythrop had been all about. Taking his lead from the work done there, Lloyd and his fitness coach Dean Riddle got into the minds and hearts of the young squad from the start with some mind-boggling fielding practices, maintaining their focus and high level of optimism and, because the exercises were competitive (between groups of players), generating the kind of team spirit that can swing tight matches.

The result was obvious for all to see. Whereas only a year before in the 1996 World Cup England had displayed all the vibrancy and enthusiasm of slugs on valium, here they were on fire. Run-outs, catches and lightning ground fielding made the Australians blink and think twice.

Perhaps the best all-round fielding performance came in the second match at The Oval, when England produced no fewer than four run-outs. Batting first on a belter of a pitch Australia would have expected their vastly experienced line-up including a top five of Mark Waugh, Mark Taylor, Steve Waugh, Michael Bevan and Michael Slater to amass a crushing score. In the event their total of 249 for six was perhaps thirty runs short of par and the single most crucial factor was that every time England fielders lined up direct throws at the stumps, they hit. Taylor was the first to go after a custard-pie throwing routine with Mark Waugh. But there was nothing humorous in the dismissal of Waugh himself, three balls later, caught out by Robert Croft's throw at one-and-a-half stumps from just behind square on the legside. Nor did either Slater or Ian Healy see the funny side of stunning efforts from DeFreitas and Graham Lloyd and all of these successes lifted the England team and sent the crowd into a frenzy.

Apart from their lethal liveliness in the field, the most compelling evidence of the real backbone that ran through the side had been offered in the first match at Headingley. England had done well to limit Australia to a low total of 170 for eight. But the crunch came when England slumped to 40 for four in reply. Had they failed to recover, all the optimism that had been engendered in advance might well have disappeared. The Headingley crowd clearly recognised that fact and they were eerily silent when Adam Hollioake came to the crease.

He struggled at first, particularly against Shane Warne and the atmosphere in the dressing room would have been decidedly nervous. But with the help of Graham Thorpe he battled his way though and as the Surrey colleagues built their match-winning partnership you could sense the confidence returning to the side and to the terraces. Adam's winning hit was the shot of a man who expects to win and when he finished off the next two matches in similarly emphatic style, the announcement that England were going to offer their opponents the fight of their lives in the months ahead could not have come through more loud and clear.

Among them, Mark Waugh especially was forced to change his opinion. Prior to arriving in England Waugh had given a long interview in which he more or less wrote off England's chances in the Ashes series. He identified that lack of team unity that had rendered England such a disorganised pushover during the previous three Ashes encounters he had taken part in, saying: 'England's players are not mentally tough enough or hungry enough. You got the impression that they were playing as individuals, not as a team.'

He could have no doubts now just what the current crop were made of.

From what I saw this group of players was already a team. How gratifying that was for Atherton, who even in his darkest moments in Zimbabwe clung onto the hope that if he could only get through the winter tour with his game in one piece, he could yet confound his critics by developing a side to take on Mark Taylor's men.

Even while England were struggling, Atherton kept a close watch on the progress of events in Australia. He noticed how much flak had been aimed at Taylor during Australia's poor run in one-day cricket, at one stage losing ten out of twelve in that form of the game and failing to reach the final of the World Series competition for the first time. Although Atherton respected their record and the fact that they held on to defeat West Indies in the Test series prior to winning in South Africa, I know he just had a sneaking feeling that his lot might just have half a chance, given careful preparation and planning.

And how sweet the Texaco Trophy victory must have tasted to

Atherton, following the all-too-predictable comments of Ray Illingworth in the week before the series began.

Both Illingworth and his former Yorkshire and England team-mate Geoff 'Speedy' Boycott insisted that Atherton shouldn't even play in the Texaco series. Boycott, of all people branded Athers a 'slowcoach', this from the man I was given instructions to run out on purpose during the second Test of the 1977-78 Test series against New Zealand in Christchurch because not only was he boring the pants off everyone but also because his refusal to get on with it was reducing our chances of winning the match.

As for Illingworth, I do believe that by now the cricketing public who had heard so much from him over the past three years, were simply sick of the sound of him. Why couldn't he simply have gone quietly and let those involved get on with the job? He cannot have believed that in harping on about Atherton's supposed unsuitability to play in the one-day XI let alone captain it, just days before the guy was trying to focus on beating Australia, his comments would be of any positive benefit to Atherton or the team. Why couldn't he just give it a bloody rest?

Maybe the words of Boycott and Illingworth did help in as much as they encouraged Athers to shove them back down the throats of those who spoke them.

In a brilliant unbeaten century at The Oval Atherton did that and more. Just five months after the poor performance in Zimbabwe had led him to threaten resignation should the tour of New Zealand bring no improvement, Atherton led England to their first series victory over Australia in any form of cricket for ten long years, and he did so from the front.

Afterwards he admitted: 'It's a good motivator when people write you off and it's nice to prove a few people wrong.'

So far so good.

FIFTEEN
ATHERTON'S DREAM

*'Never in their wildest dreams could England have imagined
their pre-match planning and preparation would have had
such a devastating initial result.'*

ENGLAND'S Texaco Trophy victory over Australia, coming as it did
in such unpredictable and emphatic style, instantly altered the mood
of the cricketing public.

Whereas they had feared that the good intentions expressed by those at
the top of the game might come to nothing against the strongest side in
world cricket, the 3-0 result in the one-day international series proved
there was more to this new era than mere talk.

And the new optimism and enthusiasm on the field was mirrored by the
behaviour of those who for too long had had to sit and suffer England
coming a distant second to the oldest enemy.

Now, buoyed by the achievement of England's footballers at Le Tournoi
in France and reminded of events during Euro 96 the previous year, the
supporters of Mike Atherton's team had begun to chant their own version
of the anthem that had accompanied the exploits of Alan Shearer & co
during those summer days at Wembley.

Whoever came up with the words: *'It's coming home, it's coming home
… Ashes coming home'* would not have won any school prizes for
grammar, but the message was clear enough. Such had been England's
superiority in the early skirmishes that there was real confidence that the
major battles ahead could also be won.

What is more, the England management team felt it as well.

Some of the ingredients missing for so long had been in glorious
evidence in the Texaco matches. The vitality and vibrancy of a young and
athletic fielding side, for instance, and the resilience that had enabled them

to bounce back from the parlous position of 40 for four at Headingley. Underpinning all their efforts had been the keyword 'intensity', something Atherton and the former Aussie coach Bob Simpson discussed at length over dinner in Wellington during the winter tour.

What England needed now was a solid and achievable game plan for the battles ahead, and using the combined brains of Graham Gooch, Mike Gatting and Atherton, who knew full well from experience just what they were up against, as well as the input of David Graveney and David Lloyd, they devised a strategy for dealing with Australia's biggest threat.

Four years previously, during the 1993 series with Australia, by preparing in the main dry, grassless wickets which, thanks to a roaring hot summer merely got drier and more bare as the series went on, the Test match groundsmen had more or less handed the Ashes to Shane Warne on a plate. Granted, at first they had had no real knowledge of what was about to hit England, but even after the Aussie leg-spinner showed what he could do in the first Test on an Old Trafford pitch that because of initially wet conditions turned into a big turning track from day one, no concerted effort was made to deal with his massive threat.

This time Graveney and his co-selectors were determined to give themselves as near to a level playing field as possible on which to take on Warne, and also Michael Bevan, the left-arm chinamen bowler who had done severe damage to West Indies during their winter series and who they regarded as something of a secret weapon.

The selectors had noted what impact Bevan had made. Carl Hooper, the West Indies middle-order batsman had admitted that many of his team-mates had had acute difficulties in 'picking' Bevan, as he proved when taking ten wickets for 113 in the fourth Test at the Adelaide Oval, helping Australia to win by an innings and 183 runs and clinch the series.

Specifically what England wanted were pitches that had enough grass on them to encourage movement off the seam for their own bowlers, while dampening down the amount of turn Warne and Bevan could be expected to produce.

While such manoeuvres were clearly not in keeping with tradition and some Australian supporters might have grumbled that this approach was akin to pitch-doctoring, there is no doubt in my mind that the move was entirely justified. It seems to me that alone among Test playing nations, we have bent over backwards to give touring sides every assistance against us. Imagine groundsmen in the West Indies for instance, ever preparing slow seamers for their fearsome pace batteries, or those in India preparing flat non-turners for their spinners.

As Atherton explained: 'At Lord's last year against Pakistan we might as well have been playing at Peshawar, it was so slow, low dry and arid, perfect for the Pakistani swing bowlers and leg-spinner.

'Until now when people said that someone like Matthew Elliott was inexperienced in English conditions, that was no problem for him, because conditions here are much the same as in Australia or anywhere else.'

Furthermore, for too long England's requirements had been secondary to the desire of those county clubs who stage the Tests to make sure that the matches lasted long enough for them not to have to hand back money for unused tickets and who feared too much grass for the seamers to exploit might produce shortened contests.

The most obvious exception to the rule had been the rogue pitch at Edgbaston for the third Test against the West Indies in 1995, which had not exactly been a five-day featherbed. Yet that was more down to a combination of a lack of attention to detail from Chairman of Selectors Ray Illingworth and soil conditions out of the control of Steve Rouse, the Warwickshire groundsman. But the pitches for the final two Tests of that series were just too good for batting for a positive result to be achieved, making it inevitable that Brian Lara would cash in, which he did making 152 at Nottingham and 179 at the Oval. With the series poised at 2-2 when the teams arrived at Trent Bridge, a little help from sympathetic groundsmen might have given England a real chance of beating the Windies at home for the first time anywhere since 1969.

This time England didn't care if the games lasted three days, or three hours, as long as they were given the best opportunity to win.

Planning was everything. With Dominic Cork absent through injury, England needed to choose their bowlers with care. Darren Gough was a certain starter, while Andy Caddick's improvement in New Zealand meant he was well worth persevering with. The most testing conundrum was the question of who should spearhead the attack.

From very early in the season, having seen him back in form and fully fit, my vote went to Devon Malcolm. Throughout the 1996 season it was clear to me that the only real obstacle to the big man regaining his place in the team was nothing whatsoever to do with ability. Devon's much-publicised moan about his treatment by Raymond Illingworth at the end of the 1995-96 tour to South Africa had left the chairman fuming. But

Malcolm believed he was only exercising his right to defend himself from Illingworth's disgraceful treatment of him throughout the tour. Then in responding to Malcolm's words in his book *One-Man Committee* Illingworth incurred the displeasure not only of Malcolm's club Derbyshire, but also more damagingly perhaps, Mike Atherton's club Lancashire. Although Illingworth survived a concerted effort to remove him as chairman, only because of the pressure put on his rival David Graveney not to stand, those counties pressed for action over Illingworth's comments and won the day when the chairman was found guilty of bringing the game into disrepute and fined £1,000.

Illingworth later won his appeal, but the public row meant that Malcolm had two chances of being called up by him all summer; one of them was slim and the other non-existent. Malcolm knew what the form was, but that didn't stop him putting in a huge performance in the championship for Derby, racking up 73 championship wickets for his county and finishing the leading England-qualified first-class wicket-taker in the country, second only to Courtney Walsh overall. Not surprisingly, that still wasn't enough to get him in the frame for the tours to Zimbabwe and New Zealand, the final selection being in the hands of you-know-who.

It wasn't coincidence that as soon as Illingworth was out of the picture, Malcolm came right back into it, and he duly raced ahead of the pack to lead the first-class wicket-taker's table with 34 strikes at an average of 19 prior to the first meeting of the new selection committee before the first Test. In my book he had to be worth a go against Australia, if nothing else for his shock value alone.

The story of the controversial circumstances behind his eventual selection gives a good indication of the kind of flexible thinking now operating within the Illingworth-free selection panel. It was also one in which I was closely involved.

It so happened that Australia's final match before the first Test at Edgbaston was against Derbyshire at the Racecourse Ground, to be televised by Sky. Devon had contacted me in advance and asked if Sky could put together a team to play in his Benefit golf day at Breadsall Priory the day before. Also in attendance were Mark Taylor, Geoff Marsh and Ricky Ponting, with whom Devon made up a foursome.

When I met Devon at Breadsall Priory before the start of the competition, I could sense that something was troubling him. The fact was that he was in two minds over whether to play against the Australians the next day or not. He had heard and read all the speculation indicating that he was going to be in the Test squad. The game against Taylor's men would give him the opportunity to show what he could do, but he was unsure whether to play on several counts. First he had the sneaking fear that all bowlers have on these potentially make-or-break occasions that, while a good performance would only confirm his place, with a poor one he could effectively bowl himself out of the reckoning.

Secondly, whereas he was encouraged by the fact that to date during the season he had managed to get his outswing going, he was reluctant to reveal that fact to the Australian batsmen. Finally, as Kim Barnett, his vastly experienced county colleague and former captain confirmed, Devon had bowled a vast number of overs already and could have done with a break.

There were two other complications. At this stage, Graveney, the Chairman of Selectors, had got the impression that Devon was suffering from 'Benefititis', a common complaint among those handed the collecting buckets by their county clubs, which can blur the attention and focus of the player in question. Indeed it was not until Graveney contacted Barnett that he realised Devon had already bowled more than 200 overs by the beginning of June.

The final element was that the Derbyshire skipper Dean Jones, who as a former Australian Test star could not have cared less about England's interests in the matter, was desperate for Malcolm to play in order to give his side the best chance of a morale-boosting victory over the tourists, not to mention landing the £12,000 up for grabs from sponsors Tetley to those counties who achieved such a result.

Malcolm didn't know what to do. He didn't want to speak to Graveney direct because he felt that any sign that he was reluctant to play might be misconstrued. After discussing all the pros and cons with Devon, I realised I had better take the bull by the horns. I rang Graveney on his mobile phone and left a message telling him the story and suggesting that he should tell Devon he was in the squad come what may and not to play against the Aussies. This merely seemed common sense to me as I could see how wound up Malcolm was becoming.

I finally made contact with Graveney in person just minutes before Devon and I went into the post-golf tournament dinner function … when I rang him on Devon's mobile phone! Graveney explained that he had got my message and had left a message of his own with Devon's wife Jennifer at their home. I reiterated my feelings and handed the phone to Devon, who was duly told by Graveney that he was in the squad. Graveney later contacted Jones and the Derbyshire chairman Mike Horton to formally request Malcolm's withdrawal. The chairman was sympathetic, the captain, most decidedly was not.

The next morning at the ground, Jones did an interview on Sky announcing that Graveney had asked Jones to withdraw Malcolm from his team, making it quite clear he was far from pleased with the situation. Graveney moved quickly to try and pour oil on troubled waters, saying: 'I take full responsibility for the decision to rest Malcolm and I regret how this has turned out. I know Dean Jones is not happy; our phone call was short and not very pleasant. I hope the Derbyshire members have not been burning effigies of me outside the ground.

'These club versus country situations must be handled sensitively and I accept that I haven't covered myself in glory. But in this instance I feel that the interests of the national side must come first. I should have made the decision earlier in the week but at that stage I had not realised how much Devon has bowled this season, 50 overs more than any other bowler. I understand how upset Dean is but I would just ask him whether in similar circumstances, Shane Warne would be expected to play for Victoria against an England touring side the week before an Ashes Test.'

Graveney was dead right and the whole affair highlighted the nonsense that at this stage England selectors still had to go cap in hand to counties and beg for co-operation.

To my mind Graveney's actions were fully justified and demonstrated that he was willing to make difficult decisions and also take responsibility for them if the muck hit the fan as a result. Furthermore, not only was he open to outside opinion on the matter, namely mine and that of Barnett, more crucially he was prepared to listen to the player concerned. Perhaps, as he says, he should have made the decision earlier in the week, thereby saving the Derby supporters the disappointment of Malcolm's late withdrawal, but that's showbiz. At least when he realised he needed to act, he did so positively and quickly.

Having decided on the right pitch and the right players to exploit it the next part of the plan was to devise specific strategies for doing so – that meant, primarily, a plan to make life as uncomfortable as possible for the most consistent batting side in world cricket.

For help with this, coach David Lloyd turned to the former England batsman Bob Woolmer, now the highly successful coach of South Africa. Woolmer had watched his side lose to the Aussies in their recent series and was only too happy to be of assistance. Woolmer confirmed to Lloyd that the task ahead would be extremely difficult, but eminently achievable. Woolmer said: 'With careful planning, skillful bowling and gutsy batting it is not impossible to beat them. The key for England is to raise the confidence level of their own players. A really positive mind set and a stubborn attitude will be required.'

As for his player-by-player analysis of Australia's leading batsmen, Woolmer was convinced there were possible weaknesses to target. Lloyd and Woolmer spent hours on the phone discussing ways and means.

The prime target was the captain Taylor. Brilliantly successful as his leadership of the side had been, genuine doubts had been expressed from within the Australian camp and their media over whether Taylor was worth his place in the side as a batsman. Taylor himself had admitted the validity of those doubts just prior to leaving for England, when he said: 'Whatever one might feel about individuals, the priority is to do whatever is necessary for the sake of the team. If that means me dropping out, if it comes to the crunch I will stand down.' Prior to the first Test, pressure was coming at him from all sides. Particularly damaging were the words of the former Australian captain Greg Chappell, a man revered in his native country as one of the best batsmen they have ever produced. Just five days before the first Test was due to begin at Edgbaston, Chappell claimed, 'Taylor is in no fit state to be captain of the Australian cricket team. If he was mentally fit, I know he would have stood down long ago. He may not admit it, but people who know about cricket realise that Australia are being hurt by what is going on. Mark is in a classic state of denial. He is not capable of admitting he has a problem. He is in a mental whirlpool and can only keep going down.'

Just for good measure, Simpson added his name to the list of Taylor's critics when he weighed in with his opinion that Taylor should not play.

Taylor's frame of mind would not have been eased by a sordid publicity stunt attempted by one of the tabloid newspapers, when they tried to present him with a 3ft wide bat at the county ground in Bristol during Australia's match with Gloucestershire. They claimed this was only a bit of fun. Hilarious, I'm sure.

As far as Woolmer was concerned, not only was Taylor under mental stress, he had developed a major technical defect. He told Lloyd: 'Taylor's feet are just not moving and he leans back as he drives, restricting his options as far as placement goes. He looks as though he is playing straight but in fact the bat is chasing the ball, making him vulnerable to anything slanted across him.'

For Mark Waugh, Woolmer passed on the following advice. 'We tried bouncing him – he wasn't all that confident against the short-pitched stuff – and we tried to hit his off stump through the gate. He looked a little vulnerable against the nip-backer.'

Greg Blewett, Woolmer suggested, might be undone by 'the ball angled into his off stump from wide of the crease.'

Of Steve Waugh, Woolmer believed: 'If he has a weakness it is to the outswinger, which can square him up. He got nicks to the keeper a couple of times against us.'

And he gave Lloyd this clue as to how to dislodge Michael Bevan. 'He has a problematic temperament, which can lead to dismissal when he gets himself wound up or worried, and he has a weakness against the short-pitched ball against the genuine quickies.'

Lloyd took all this on board, while during Australia's game against Derbyshire he saw something in Matthew Elliott's technique that opened his eyes. Early on in the Aussie opener's first innings knock of 67 Lloyd noticed how often he played around his front pad. After one delivery from Phil DeFreitas which swung into his pads late and would have had him stone-cold lbw had he not got the faintest of inside edges, Lloyd exclaimed: 'Did you see that? Lovely.' That incident and Woolmer's comments were duly recorded and stored away for future use.

The day before the Test Lloyd simply instructed his players: 'You know what to do. Now go and do it.'

How they did. Taylor won the toss and decided to bat on a dampish pitch. By lunchtime his side were, astonishingly, 54 for eight and England, put in by the bookies at 3-1 against to win the game beforehand, were 1-4 on. And what made their success so extraordinary was that every single Australian top order batsmen was dismissed according to plan.

Elliott was bowled by a ball from Darren Gough which swing into him and in between bat and front pad. 11 for one. Taylor, driving at a ball slanted across him by Malcolm, nicked a catch to Mark Butcher at second slip. 15 for two. Mark Waugh was bowled by a wonderful ball from Gough which swung away then nipped back on pitching. 26 for three. Then Gough, in an inspired spell, struck again at 28, angling the ball in at Blewett from wide of the crease and having him caught by Nasser Hussain at slip. 28 for four. Steve Waugh, the number one rated batsman in world cricket, edged Andy Caddick's outswinger to wicket-keeper Alec Stewart. 48 for five. And finally, after Ian Healy had become Caddick's second victim in similar fashion from the very next delivery, in the next over and with no addition to the score Bevan was hurried up by a quick delivery from Malcolm aimed at his chest and sent a simple catch looping to Mark Ealham in the gully.

The cream of the best batting side in world cricket was blown away at 48 for seven. Caddick then made it a barely believable 54 for eight.

Some spirited hitting by Shane Warne ensured Australia avoided the embarrassment of failing to reach three figures, but only just, as they were finally bowled out for just 118 in the sixth over after lunch.

The dismissal that gave me the greatest satisfaction was that of Blewett, for it proved to me just how much Darren Gough had progressed as a cricketer. The star attraction of England's last Ashes contest, on the 1994-95 tour, before being struck down with injury, Gough had suffered further injury setbacks on the road to recovery. But he had also attracted to my mind unfair criticism from those who believed he was too much of a showman. I know that Athers needed some persuading that Darren was rather more than merely a self-promoting cabaret act and that this was behind the decision to ignore his claims throughout the 1996 home season. Now in the *two* balls with which he dismissed Blewett he proved beyond question that he had become a mature talent. The first was a wonderful late outswinger which bowled Blewett all ends up. It was Gough's reaction to what happened next that was so impressive. Gough had heard the call of umpire Peter Willey signifying he had overstepped the mark. But instead of making a fuss over his bad luck, Goughie stopped and smiled at Blewett, turned sharply, went straight back to his mark and concentrated on the next ball. Clearing his mind of his disappointment he stuck to the plan, went slightly wider on the crease and produced a jaffa which Blewett edged to slip. Great bowling.

When England batted, in their first innings, the confidence that came from successfully completing the first part of the plan was clear to see. Suddenly the players believed they could do what they had only hoped they might, while their efforts were aided by the fact that the slow seaming pitch they had asked for and got, had effectively disarmed the threat of Warne. Although wobbling somewhat when Atherton and his opening partner Butcher were removed at 16 for two and Alec Stewart followed them at 50 for three, Nasser Hussain and Graham Thorpe came together in a fourth wicket stand which by the close had produced 150 and given England a first day advantage of 82 with seven wickets remaining.

Never in their wildest dreams could England have imagined their pre-match planning and preparation would have had such a devastating initial result. That night as Lloyd supped a welcome pint or several in the Prince of Wales pub he could barely contain his delight. 'People will say simply that we had a good day and Australia a bad one. They just have no idea how hard we worked out there and how hard we planned.'

By the time the partnership between Hussain and Thorpe was ended they had put on 288 at a run a minute. Hussain's double-century of 207 was the innings of his career so far, and probably of his life, Thorpe's 138 no less valuable.

Australia spent all of the third day clawing back a deficit of 360 and how well Taylor responded under the greatest pressure he can ever have experienced. The way the Australian media and a posse of former Test players were calling for his head, had he failed then there is little doubt that this would have been his last Test as captain, possibly even his last Test. But on a more friendly pitch and under cloudless skies, in a five-hour effort of will Taylor battled his way to his first century in 25 innings, amassing 194 for the second wicket with Blewett and making sure England had to bat again to win.

At one stage it seemed Australia might be on course to do even more than that. Whether imagination or desperation lay behind Atherton's decision to throw the ball to Ealham on a slow pitch, the result was stunning.

Ealham's first over went for 10 runs. His next was the beginning of the end. Ian Healy, cutting a wide delivery straight at Atherton in the gully, Michael Kasprowicz, two balls later, edging to Butcher and Warne, giving the bowler a dolly catch meant Ealham had figures of three for none in ten balls. In between, Jason Gillespie was run out as Australia lost their last four wickets for 12 runs.

When England batted, even the normally unemotional Atherton got into the spirit of the crowd's euphoria, and couldn't stop playing shots. After Stewart slapped the winning runs it was smiles and champagne shampoos all-round. For Atherton. Zimbabwe must have seemed a different and distant planet. Warne's figures read one for 137.

Hussain summed up the emotion of the moment and the effect the result had nationwide. 'There's a buzz around the whole team and we feel we can't let anyone down. All round the country in the offices, everywhere, they want to know the score and it's so important for us to do well for them. These are the best four days I've had in cricket. The crowd made a big contribution towards us winning. They were phenomenal, roaring us on and inspiring the bowlers. If that doesn't lift you, nothing will.'

So far even better.

SIXTEEN

STILL DREAMING

'[Fred] Titmus's declaration that he had been anti-Atherton ...
was an astonishing admission which finally nailed all those lies
that had been peddled by Lord's about the harmony between
the captain and his selectors.'

A FTER the Lord Mayor's show, the Lord's Test provided Mike Atherton's team with its stiffest Test of the summer so far. While England's efforts until that point had been underpinned by a collective confidence in their ability to put a well considered plan into operation, it was obvious that Australia had been performing well below the standards they had set themselves.

Their record in recent years had established them as the most successful Test team in world cricket. No side attains that status by accident. What Atherton and his men had to do was make sure that when the revival came they were prepared and ready to deal with it.

The build-up to the second Test at Lord's was dominated by Atherton himself and (guess what?) overshadowed by more criticism of him from the Illingworth camp.

By leading England in the second Test at Lord's Atherton would establish a new captaincy record. This was to be his 42nd Test in charge of England since he took over from Graham Gooch in 1993, surpassing the previous record held by Peter May. Atherton's own opinion of his achievement was typical. He sets little store by records for their own sake and he made it clear that the pride he felt in setting this one came from his satisfaction that, despite everything, the controversy over the dirt in the pocket, conflict with Illingworth, his chronic back condition not to mention poor results, he had survived. Ted Dexter, the man who appointed him four years previously commented: 'Since Athers came in as captain, it's interesting to note he has survived two Chairmen of Selectors, Ray Illingworth and myself, plus a team manager, Keith Fletcher. Is this a coincidence or down to the strength of Atherton's own personality?'

I personally was astonished by the determination he had shown to outlast Illingworth. To my mind, following the disappointment of losing to South Africa on the winter tour of 1995-96 and the subsequent disaster in the World Cup, one of the main reasons why Atherton was prepared to carry on as captain at the start of the summer of 1996 was that he knew that, come what may, Illingworth was going to be out of the equation at the end of it. The worst aspect of his relationship with Illingworth was that it caused so many unnecessary distractions for him. As well as getting on with the job of being England captain, which is hard enough as it is, he was constantly having to deal with Illingworth spouting off about him and his players in the media. And of course the closest he did come to losing the job was when Illingworth and his crony on the 1995 selection committee, Fred Titmus, closed in on him for the comments he made during the 1994-95 winter tour to Australia in response to Illingworth's own criticisms back home, his job only being saved by the intervention of the new selector David Graveney.

When Atherton himself made these points in the biography *Athers* whose publication was timed to coincide with the Lord's Test, Illy & co climbed in again.

Firstly, Illy denied that he had wanted to get rid of Athers back in 1995, but then Titmus, who had been a selector from 1994 to 1996 revealed the true depth of his own feelings on the matter. He said: 'I wanted Atherton out in 1995. I admit that. I was anti-Atherton throughout my time as a selector because I don't think he is a very good captain. Atherton is a fine player, yes, but I think he's one of the worst captains we've had since the War. For him to get Peter May's record is a travesty.'

Bearing in mind the tenor and substance of these comments, I find it very difficult to believe that had Brian Bolus, who Illingworth admitted was 'livid' over Atherton's comments about the age of selectors and them being out of touch, not been replaced by Graveney, the terrible trio of Illingworth, Titmus and Bolus would have found it in them to spare Atherton.

Titmus's declaration that he had been anti-Atherton 'throughout my time as a selector' was an astonishing admission which finally nailed all those lies that had been peddled by Lord's about the harmony between the captain and his selectors. Surely it also called into question Titmus's place on the selection committee. If he was so against the captain for so long, how could he, in all conscience, have carried on as a selector for as long as he did? If he had no confidence in Atherton as captain why didn't he prove it by resigning from the committee ? How could he have sat there through all those selection meetings discussing players and tactics with a man who he never wanted as captain in the first place? Surely the expenses weren't that good!

And what a time to come out with all this tosh. The mood of the cricketing public was at its most buoyant for years. What the England team and its captain needed was support, not more carping.

At least it was getting support from those who mattered. The rain which dominated the entire Lord's match may have washed out the first day's play but it failed to dampen the enthusiasm of Lord MacLaurin. Perhaps persuaded that the comments of Illingworth and Titmus demanded a positive response, he delivered it.

He told reporters he was 'thrilled' with the improvement in performances since the 'shambles in Harare', explaining, 'The England team were told in Harare that we were all in this together. We told them we'll do anything you need for us to help you. Harare was a pretty miserable time, but 80 per cent of those players remain the same. What we have seen is, I believe, proof that our cricketers are as good as any in the world. What they needed was a bit of leadership and understanding. They've responded magnificently, first in New Zealand and then with the way they have started this summer. They've delivered and they should be lauded from the rooftops. At Edgbaston our guys never shirked anything. They bowled like demons and fielded like dervishes. After being on top for two days, the team spirit shone through with the way they handled the Australians' comeback and after sticking at it, the champagne batting on the fourth day finished it off. Our guys never shirked anything. They broke Aussie hearts.'

MacLaurin also revealed that after the win, he made sure every player received a bottle of bubbly from the Board. The difference between that approach and the words of Illingworth and Titmus could not have been more acute. Indeed although MacLaurin declined to play their petty game, he did emphasize what Athers had been talking about all along, the importance of having younger men in charge of selection, in the form of Graveney, Gooch and Gatting. According to MacLaurin: 'The players identify with them. They admire them.'

Typically, of course, events on the field once the rain relented made all this stirring stuff sound a tad premature. Bowled out for 77 thanks to the brilliance of Glenn McGrath on a helpful pitch, England's batting performance could hardly be described as the stuff of which world beaters are made. And when England began their efforts to drag themselves back in the game, the outlook went from bad to worse.

England's fielding, the most obvious indicator of all-round improvement in confidence throughout the season thus far, simply went to pieces. Dropping five catches and missing two clear run-out chances suddenly resurrected memories of the bad old days England supporters believed were dead and buried, and when Matthew Elliott (dropped three times) completed his century to lead Australia to 213 for seven declared, a lead of 136 with one full day's play remaining, it seemed all the good words might end up sounding like so much hot air.

That a morale-damaging defeat was avoided said a lot about the new spirit at large within the team.

There is no doubt in my mind that had the England team of 1994-95, 1993 or 1989 for that matter been faced with the same final-day circumstances that this XI had to confront, the result would have been victory for Australia. Not only would the Aussies have expected to achieve it, but, crucially, deep down the England players involved would have anticipated it as well. With Warne and McGrath ready to pounce, the slightest encouragement to the Aussie attack would have been gobbled up and the all-too familiar pattern of head-scratching collapse would inevitably have set in.

Indeed, as connoisseurs of the great England collapses pointed out, that scenario is exactly what was played out during England's last Test match at headquarters, the first of the three-match series with Pakistan, in July 1996. Atherton had batted through the final morning and the draw seemed secure. Then the Pakistan leg-spinner changed his angle to bowl around the wicket. Atherton edged a slip catch. England lost their last seven wickets for 18 runs, the match, their confidence and optimism and finally the series.

The parallels with Lord's in 1997 were obvious. Having enjoyed a huge slice of good fortune when Mark Butcher, for whom after three consecutive failures, this innings was make or break, was grassed by Mark Taylor at slip off Michael Kasprowicz having made only two, Butcher battled through and with Atherton in commanding form at the other end, he played his full part in an opening stand of 162.

In theory the game should have been safe. But you couldn't escape the sneaking feeling that once Atherton was out, the pack of cards might just come crashing down. This time round, however, although they wobbled, they refused to fall and that said so much about the resilience this new team, backed by the new order now possessed.

How fitting it was that Atherton should once again be the central figure in England's rearguard action. Had he not stepped on his stumps to end that first wicket partnership he would surely have scored his first century at Lord's and maybe that would have been enough to stop the carping for good. In any case, as events turned out, he ensured that England held onto a lead many had believed they would never come near in the first place.

The manner of England's salvation was particularly pleasing for coach David Lloyd. Ridiculed for his over-the-top comments at the end of England's drawn first Test against Zimbabwe in Bulawayo, the draw at Lord's meant he had presided over an unbeaten Test run stretching back seven matches. He was satisfied that, whatever else his team would achieve they were at last clearly playing for each other.

All the trials and tribulations they had gone through during the winter tour, all the lessons they had learned after their poor attitude in Zimbabwe had been exposed and all the preparation they had put in had brought them together. And now they were producing the results to prove it.

Lloyd told me: 'When I took over as coach I identified various areas where we had to improve. In my eyes the players needed to toughen up, to harden themselves mentally and be prepared to take more responsibility.

'From a coaching perspective my job was to give them the back-up they needed, whether videos, specific technical work or whatever and create an environment of enjoyment and intensity. Lord MacLaurin gave us all the lead when he said that the England team was the priority and that he would make sure they had the best chance of realising their potential. There is still an awful long way to go and the chairman has said that he has only just started to get to work on the problem areas in the game he wants to address. But we all get the feeling that, from top to bottom, we are pulling in the same direction.'

He didn't say it, so I will. About bloody time.

SEVENTEEN

'GOOD MORNING, MICHAEL'

'My main criticism of the [England] team is that they didn't seem to be tough or nasty enough when it really mattered.'

AND then we woke up. England's collapse to 77 all out in the first innings at Lord's should have been a grave warning. But no one could have been prepared for the sheer strength of the Australian backlash that began in the third Test at Old Trafford and culminated in the surrender of the Ashes in the fifth Test at Trent Bridge.

Things had started to go wrong for England even while they were battling to save the match at headquarters. Heavy rain in Manchester in the fortnight preceding the Test match had hampered the preparations of Lancashire groundsman Peter Marron and when the Test pitch was finally revealed to the England hierarchy, it was clear that this was not what the doctor had ordered. There was grass on the wicket, but it was obvious that the ends were bare. As a result Shane Warne was given the first opportunity of the summer to prove that he still had the class and skill to be a match-winning force.

Even though Mark Taylor won the toss for the third time of asking, then decided to bat, early in the piece the signs had looked reasonably optimistic. Dean Headley, who made such an impression on England's A tour down under in the winter, quickly settled into his new environment on full international debut. In his first over he hit Taylor on the helmet and in his third he had him caught at slip with the kind of outswinger to the left-hander with which he accounted for all three of them in both Australian innings.

With support from Darren Gough and Mark Ealham, Headley reduced Australia to 113 for five. Then Steve Waugh broke out. He later described the first of his two centuries in the match as the best innings of his career.

In the context of trying to stop England in their tracks it was a tremendous innings. Without it Australia would have done well to reach 150; as it was they made a respectable 235, but nothing to concern Mike Atherton's men unduly, it seemed, provided they batted well.

Enter the old double-act of Shane Warne and Ian Healy. England were cruising at 74 for one when Warne struck a decisive blow, having Alec Stewart caught by Taylor at slip. It was the first of seven England wickets to go down for 49 runs as Warne (and England) turned back the clock. With each wicket the mood darkened. Memories of *that* ball, with which Warne took his first English Test wicket on the same ground four years previously grew and grew. Nasser Hussain, Graham Thorpe and John Crawley had no answer to Warne's magic. England were skittled out for 162.

Steve Waugh's second century was every bit as vital as the first and twice as brave. This time he came in when his side was in the mire again, at 39 for three and with a lead of just 112 but this time he had the added problem of batting with a jarred and bruised hand which forced him to let go of the bat in agony on a number of occasions. But this remarkable batsman showed why he is rated no.1 in world cricket, and gave a magnificent demonstration of what can be achieved with guts and will allied to skill and technique.

First, in a stand of 98 with twin brother Mark he eased the game out of England's reach. Then, the following morning, now pain-free he cashed in, leading his side to 395 and a lead of 468.

As if Warne's return to form was not enough for England to contend with, they were now shown just why paceman Jason Gillespie is so highly rated in his homeland. After Atherton hooked him for six, England lost their top four batsmen for the addition of eleven runs, three of them to Gillespie in 19 deliveries. Warne ended the match by having Andy Caddick caught at mid-on then flew home to visit his wife and new-born daughter.

The reaction of the England selectors, though well-intentioned, was misguided.

The next Test at Headingley was not due to begin for a fortnight because of the place in the fixture list of the Benson and Hedges Final between Kent and Surrey at Lord's the following Saturday. David Graveney and his co-selectors were keen to demonstrate that the days of shotgun selection policies were over and to give their backing to those players who had started the summer in such positive style. With such an abnormally long gap before the resumption of hostilities they were also intent on stamping on any speculation over selection before it could get started. But to name an unchanged side for the next Test so soon after suffering defeat by 268 runs was dangerously close to being the kind of 'bright idea' that overtakes common sense.

England's batsmen had made a stack of hundreds in the previous year – fourteen to be precise – but they had been bowled out for 200, 162 and 77 in three of their last four innings. Was that the kind of form that warranted such a pat on the back? By picking the same men without a second thought the selectors were expressing satisfaction with the men in possession. When you are up against the best team in world cricket the last thing England needed to be was satisfied with anything.

The next part of their plan I endorsed wholeheartedly, even though they laid themselves open to criticism in the act of it. On the Saturday before the Test was due to start David Graveney and Harry Brind, the Board's inspector of pitches, met at Headingley to view the Test track. It didn't take long for news to leak out that as a result of their visit, the Yorkshire groundsman Andy Fogarty was instructed to switch pitches to the one next door. Although Brind claimed that this unusual step was taken because the new strip had a more even covering of grass than the first-choice pitch, it didn't take an Einstein to work out that the move might have had something to do with the England management's desire to negate the threat of Warne.

Brind was wheeled in front of the television cameras to insist that nothing underhand had taken place, but the Australians took full advantage of the opportunity to kick up a stink. Their tour manager Alan Crompton, a solicitor by trade, perked up and piped up for the first time in the summer with the following observation, which sounded what it was, an official complaint and an accusation of skulduggery: 'We have no problem with the decision to change pitches and no evidence that the reason was other than to produce a better Test match. But it is totally inappropriate that the decision should be made by the chairman of selectors.'

Graveney protested his innocence, and after meeting with him and Tim Lamb, the chief executive of the Board, he issued another statement. The tone was a little more conciliatory:

'They both assured me that David had not been involved in the decision and I have accepted Tim's assurance', though I notice he didn't say 'David and Tim's assurance.' A Freudian slip?

Lamb insisted: 'David is a bit concerned with the implication of sharp practice. The decision was made by the ground authority in conjunction with Harry Brind, the ECB's pitch consultant. It was two weeks ago when the groundsman Andy Fogarty first told Chris Hassell, the Yorkshire chief executive, that he felt the pitch might not be good enough for a Test match.'

Oh, so now it was Fogarty's decision?

What a load of tosh. To my mind the truth was obvious. England wanted a grassy pitch, as they had wanted all summer long, and they tried to make sure they got one. And why on earth not? It seemed to me that the England management was only doing what has been accepted as common practice in other countries for decades.

In Shane Warne we are talking about one of the best spin bowlers in the world. If you give him an inch he will take a mile so why give him help that he doesn't need? When the West Indies were at their peak with four of the most lethal fast bowlers alive, I don't recall batting on slow, low turners. When Jeff Thomson and Dennis Lillee were having opposing batsmen carted off to casualty every five minutes I don't remember Australian curators producing many slow seamers. And when India played England at home in 1993 with three twirlymen I don't remember much encouragement for our seam-based attack.

But we in England only just seem to have woken up to the possibility of actually creating conditions that suit our bowlers. Then the moment we have a go ourselves, first we deny we are doing it then we apologise and blame the groundsman. That's crap.

In the meantime we had already confused ourselves out of picking the best attack for the match. Graveney signalled his intentions when drafting in Mike Smith, the Gloucestershire left-arm swing bowler to join the squad and although it is easy to say so in hindsight to me the decision to play him ahead of Caddick was a mistake. Okay, Smith had taken stacks of wickets as he helped his county to briefly head the championship but throwing him in at the deep end against Australia seemed to me to be asking for trouble. Caddick had taken 11 wickets in the first three Tests, he was regarded as England's biggest danger by the Aussies themselves and though not consistent was the only England bowler with the ability to get extra bounce from a length.

Once the match started, Jason Gillespie showed how important that was when he cleaned up England's first innings, taking seven for 37, the best figures by an Australian at Headingley as the top-order once again failed, skittled out for 172. As things turned out Smith should have had a crucial first wicket when, with Australia struggling on 50 for three, Matthew Elliott edged a straightforward chance to Graham Thorpe at first slip. And as Elliott went on to make 199 (albeit dropped twice more) you might say this was rather an unfortunate miss. But the fact is that try as he might, after that Smith simply couldn't get the ball to swing. Without that movement he looked merely ordinary. Thanks to Elliott, Australia rattled up 501 for nine declared. England managed 268 in their second dig, the highlight being Nasser Hussain's second hundred of the summer, and Australia cruised into a 2-1 lead which was never going to be overtaken.

The preference of Smith over Caddick took me back to Atherton's choice at the start of the summer not to have a vote in selection. As I have said I thought this was the right move for him to take, as long as he could be assured that the final choice of the eleven players he took on the field from the squad of 13 or 14 would remain with him. This time it appeared that was not the case. As the Test progressed word reached me that Atherton had wanted to retain Caddick, but had found himself over-ruled by the other selectors. He was not happy about it at all, even before the start of the match. By the end he was probably fuming.

But that selection error apart the facts of the matter were by now clear. England had started the series well, had the full backing of the Lord on high and their preparation had been first-class. Their players had even enjoyed the luxury of a vote of confidence and another team-building exercise prior to the Headingley match, yet the bottom line was that they had been outclassed for the second Test in succession. Australia were looking ominously strong.

Atherton put his best stony face on the defeat but I think it was becoming clear to him deep down that things were slipping away. The selectors reacted by admitting the team needed an injection of new blood, and by the time they reached Trent Bridge for what turned out to be the decider they had administered it in the shape of the Hollioake brothers.

Encouragingly for the future of English cricket they looked at home and didn't let themselves down. Adam's six off Paul Reiffel was a statement of intent, although his dismissal to a full length delivery from the same bowler two balls later showed a touch of inexperience, while Ben looked totally unfazed. At 19, the youngest player to win a Test cap for England since Brian Close faced the New Zealanders in 1949, his first scoring shot, a sweetly timed push past mid-on for four was a stroke of real class.

Unsurprisingly, going flat out for the win they needed to keep their

Ashes hopes alive, to use a soccer term, England left themselves exposed at the back. When it came to defending the 451 they had been set thanks to Ian Healy's top quality late order batting, they were picked off like First World War soldiers charging over the top.

And so thoughts turned once again to Atherton's position as captain of a side that had started so brightly but ended up steamrollered by the Australian cricketing machine to become the fifth England side in the decade since 1986-87 to lose an Ashes series.

To me, his disappointing form with the bat apart, Atherton could not have done more in his attempts to alter the trend of recent Ashes history and it was no surprise to me or anyone who knows him that he reacted to calls for his head by insisting he would see the summer and the job through to the very end.

Even though the final Test at The Oval was still to be played, Atherton was the subject of huge speculation and not just in the media.

The first suggestions that he might be on the verge of quitting had emerged on day three of the Trent Bridge Test when the *Sun* ran a story claiming that, prior to the match, over dinner with Lord MacLaurin and Bob Bennett, the chairman of the England Management Committee and Atherton's county chairman at Lancashire, Athers had made the offer to resign.

The *Sun* were mistaken over some details of their story as an ECB statement made on the same day pointed out. According to Brian Murgatroyd, the Board's Press Officer: 'On Thursday night England captain Michael Atherton had dinner with Bob Bennett and Lord MacLaurin. Also present were David Lloyd, David Graveney, Graham Gooch, Wayne Morton and Medha Laud.

'This group represents the heart of England's management and organisation, and it was felt that following the loss of successive Tests it would be a good idea if they dined as a unit to discuss any issues which may have arisen during the course of those matches.

'At no time did Michael Atherton offer to resign as captain and the captaincy of the England team was not discussed.'

Atherton commented: 'I said at the post-match press conference at Headingley that, having been appointed as England captain for the whole of the summer, I intended to see that appointment through. That remains the case.

'I confirm that I have not offered my resignation as England captain, and the matter of the captaincy was not referred to during Thursday's dinner.'

Chairman of Selectors Graveney said: 'At the start of the season we appointed Michael as captain until the end of the summer. Nothing has happened to change that situation.'

The day England subsided to defeat both men spoke again.

Atherton was slightly less forceful. Asked if he would now resign, he said: 'We will have to wait and see. I have not played at my best this series. Statistics will confirm that. I have underperformed and that leaves me disappointed. I have always said that I'll know when the time comes for me to go. After the euphoria of Edgbaston I am now expecting a backlash. There seems to be no middle-ground. It's black and white and nothing in between.'

Graveney, on the other hand gave his captain an even stronger vote of confidence. He insisted that if the decision was left to him Atherton would keep the job. He said: 'I have spoken to Michael and he is well aware of my views. I want him to go on and I think it is in the best interests of the side for him to remain as captain this winter.'

Atherton himself decided that the best thing to do was to get away from all the speculation. He headed off to sort his head out and put his priorities and thoughts in order.

I had no quarrel with his decision either way. I was certainly not one of those clamouring for his head.

My main criticism of the team is that they didn't seem to be tough or nasty enough when it really mattered; on that final morning at Trent Bridge for instance, having got rid of Steve Waugh they should have piled into Ian Healy with everything they had. Instead they seemed to ease off and allow the opposition to dominate. That passage of play alone speaks volumes about the lack of intensity to which all English players become accustomed in the county game.

As far as Atherton himself is concerned I don't subscribe to the view that all England captains have a set life-cycle. To me you go on for as long as you believe you are the best man for the job.

In that respect I understood Graveney's efforts to make him stay, for none of the contenders – Alec Stewart, Nasser Hussain or Adam Hollioake – exactly jumped out of the page and demanded to be appointed.

The important thing was that the decision was left in Atherton's hands. He is the only man who could tell whether the time was right to go. He is the only man who could weigh up all the factors and decide whether the pluses to him and the team of him being captain still outweighed the effect on him of the burden of having to lead a losing team.

HOW NOT TO RUN ENGLISH CRICKET

EIGHTEEN

MARKING TIME: THE NICHOLAS AFFAIR

'The story of how he [Nicholas] failed in his bid [to become chief executive of the TCCB] provides a typically depressing insight into the confusion and self-interest that have prevailed at the top of our game for so long.'

I N the autumn of 1996 Tim Lamb, the cricket secretary of the Test and County Cricket Board, was appointed to succeed A C Smith as chief executive of the TCCB, soon to become the new England and Wales Cricket Board.

Lamb's success was a partial victory for those county clubs who had feared a more radical approach to the change required in the domestic game, put forward by Lamb's main rival for the job, Tony Cross, the vice-chairman of Warwickshire, on behalf of the group he represented, the Test Match Grounds Working Party.

The Test Match Grounds Working Party comprised Lancashire, Surrey, Nottinghamshire, Warwickshire and Yorkshire and sought greater powers for those clubs who staged the major international games and therefore earned the Board most revenue. Noises emanating from within this powerful group on more than one occasion hinted at the possibility of forming a breakaway league of counties, along the lines of the FA Premiership, free to negotiate their own deals with sponsors and television companies.

An accountant by profession, now running his own venture-capitalist business, Cross and those he represented were seen as dangerously subversive by the rest of the counties, radicals who believed that revolution not evolution was the only way forward for English cricket.

As early as the summer of 1995, the Test Match Grounds Working Party under Cross's chairmanship demonstrated that they were not interested in half-measures. Their working party report not only supported the principle of a two-division county championship but extended the idea to incorporate a much larger structure inclusive of the minor county clubs in a new nationwide cricket pyramid.

Although the more reactionary counties reacted in predictably negative fashion to the concept that this should eventually involve promotion and relegation from top to bottom, the idea of an all-encompassing domestic cricket framework did come to pass in the shape of the new ECB, comprising 38 members, the 36 English counties, Wales and MCC.

But other ideas for wholesale change devised by the Test Match Grounds Working Party were anathema to those counties whose conviction that if they stuck their heads in the sand long enough everything would turn out nice in the end has been and still is the greatest threat to the progress and development of the national summer game.

Had the decision been left entirely in the hands of the interviewing panel, Cross would almost certainly have got the job. But powerful men hell-bent on preserving the status quo finally held sway within the corridors of power. When he met the panel, Lamb said all the things those backers wanted to hear, namely that there was far more right with the game than wrong with it and that as far as possible the sport should be kept free of what they perceived as the mucky hand of business.

In the final reckoning, however, the decision smacked of compromise. The Test Match Grounds Working Party were placated and encouraged by the appointment of Sir Ian, now Lord MacLaurin as chairman of the board, and by the installation of Bob Bennett, the Lancashire chairman, at the head of the England Management Advisory Committee, along with MacLaurin and Lamb, David Acfield, John Barclay, Brian Bolus, David Graveney and Doug Insole. But it remains to be seen whether, when push comes to shove, the ostriches will allow MacLaurin to put his own vision of the future of English cricket into place. MacLaurin revealed his strategy for cricket to the world on 5 August 1997, but the crunch will come when the counties are asked to rubber-stamp his most innovative measures. Throughout the summer of 1997, worryingly conservative noises were emanating from the most died-in-the-wool counties, notably Essex, over the prospect of restructuring the county championship into two divisions. MacLaurin has made his position clear. If, finally, the counties resist his moves for change, he will walk away. But if they feel that the opportunity for real change within the present structure has been lost, possibly for good, I anticipate the Test Match Grounds Working Party will once again crank itself into action, this time their implied threat to break away from the rest carrying real substance.

What seems certain is that the man whom many considered more suitable than either Cross or Lamb for the vital role of chief executive will now never have the chance to occupy it.

Mark Nicholas, the former captain of Hampshire and more than one England A touring team has clear and well-considered ideas regarding the direction in which English cricket should be heading. The story of how he failed in his bid to be given the opportunity to put them into practice provides a typically depressing insight into the confusion and self-interest that have prevailed at the top of our game for so long.

Nicholas initially had his interest stirred by two conversations during England's 1994-95 winter tour to South Africa. The first was with John Barclay, the England tour manager. Barclay raised the subject of the new chief executive position and urged Nicholas to stand. According to Barclay, what was required was someone young and fresh and full of enthusiasm who believed in English cricket but also believed it needed a new emphasis. He felt Nicholas filled the bill.

The next chat Nicholas had on the subject was with Mike Atherton, the England captain. Over supper in Johannesburg Atherton bemoaned the fact that so many former players who might be useful to English cricket were slipping away from the centre of the game and into careers in the media – a nice lifestyle for them, thought Atherton, but unhelpful to English cricket as their media commitments precluded them from taking a full part in the direction and running of the game. Nicholas told Atherton of the conversation he had had with Barclay and Atherton supported the suggestion that Nicholas should put himself forward.

Nicholas was encouraged in his thinking by the fact that two men so close to the modern game believed he had something tangible to offer. And that made him start to consider seriously the possibility of applying for the position.

Dennis Silk, the Chairman of the TCCB was the next to raise the idea with Nicholas. In Ahmedabad, the venue of England's first game in the 1996 World Cup against New Zealand, Silk asked him if he had thought about standing. They had a brief discussion regarding what the job might entail and Nicholas asked him how he should proceed. Silk told him to write a short note as an application. No CV was necessary, according to Silk. 'Everybody knows your CV,' Silk told him. Nicholas recalls: 'I got the impression from Silk that if I applied I would be quite likely to make the final two or three and that I would have his full support and backing.'

Silk was a Nicholas fan. He had had dealings with Nicholas before, principally when he tried to get him involved in his eventually abortive attempts to get a national cricket academy off the ground. During the previous winter tour to Australia Nicholas had written a piece in the *Daily Telegraph* extolling the virtues of the Australian academy and pressing strongly for the foundation of a similar facility in England. Silk, who had firm ideas of his own on the subject and had been working hard behind the scenes to get the ball rolling – as far back as November 1994 he had asked the former Australian leg spinner and team coach Peter Philpott to present papers on the possibility of an English Cricket Academy – had read the article and, while in Australia Nicholas introduced him to Rod Marsh, who ran the Australian academy.

Plans were well-advanced by the time Silk next contacted Nicholas. Philpott had been formally offered the job of principal coach in June 1995 and soon afterwards, at their August Board meeting the counties confirmed the plans should go ahead, voting 16 to 2 in favour of their adoption. In October, just before the England squad departed for the long winter schedule of a full South African tour followed by the 1996 World Cup, Silk and Nicholas drove to Shenley in Hertfordshire to the proposed site of the Academy. En route, to Nicholas's surprise, Silk asked him to become the head of the Academy. He told him that he wanted Philpott and Mike Gatting to be the coaches and that a secretary was in place, but that he wanted a chairman to be the central figurehead. It was to be a non-paid job, but would carry a high profile. Nicholas was flattered and interested.

Eventually however, progress came to an abrupt halt.

Shortly after Silk's trip with Nicholas to Shenley, the Board's executive committee performed an amazing about-turn, overturning the plan adopted by an overwhelming majority of the counties, entirely off its own bat.

On 23 November Philpott received a fax from A C Smith stating that the Academy was on hold, indefinitely. Having refused a coaching offer from South Africa and another in England as well as teaching positions in England and Australia, Philpott was understandably miffed.

He asked: 'How can an executive committee responsible to a board overthrow the board's 16-2 decision? Surely, of all countries England needs a concerted plan to develop its cricket standards. An academy is not everything but it should be an integral part of any developmental decision. What was planned was an improvement on the Australian academy. Geographically, England has great advantages but the egocentricity of county cricket is destructive to the game. Who does rule? Is there an overall plan? Or simply a selfish in-fight?'

He could ask that again. Officially the reason given for the u-turn was that the executive committee felt that Silk had overstepped the bounds of his authority. Yet if he had been given a 16-2 mandate by the counties how could that be true? Unofficially, certain observers suggested that the real problem lay with self-interest. For some time Yorkshire had been running their own version of the academy at Bradford, and producing some talented young players to boot. At one stage the Yorkshire club might have believed that the national academy might even have been situated on their complex in Bradford. Was it merely coincidence that once it became clear that Shenley and not Bradford was the chosen site, Sir Laurence Byford, the Yorkshire chairman and member of the executive committee, withdrew his support for the idea?

Presumably this was the moment Silk first realised quite how solid was the wall of conservatism he was up against, but although he had been humiliatingly rebuffed over his master plan, he did not give up all hope that he could make a contribution to future progress in other areas.

He knew Nicholas was enthusiastic about the idea for an academy among other measures and continued to back his candidature for chief executive. Silk took Nicholas's hand-written application back to England with him at the end of the World Cup campaign and in April contacted him to tell him that interviews were about to take place.

Silk told Nicholas that he would probably be interviewed by Silk himself, Lynn Wilson, the chairman of Northamptonshire and Sir Ian MacLaurin, at this stage nothing more in the set-up than an MCC committee man and, as chairman of Tesco, a commercial advisor to the TCCB.

Nicholas knew little about the two men due to examine his credentials so set about doing his homework on them. In preparation, he also put his ideas on paper in the form of a document called 'Implementing a Strategy for Cricket', to show them he meant business.

At this stage Nicholas was confident that Silk's support would be influential. On the basis of their previous discussions he had been given the impression that whoever he talked with would be ready to listen. The first hint that his passage was not running as smoothly as anticipated came in a phone call from Silk two days before the interview was due to take place in MacLaurin's London office.

Silk told him that, regrettably, MacLaurin would not be able to attend, but that a man named Alan Dowling, an Australian schoolmaster who had been a colleague of Silk's at Radley College, had lived in England for years and had been involved with MCC would be present instead. Nicholas was a bit taken aback but not as much as he was when on the eve of the interview Silk rang him again to tell him that Wilson wouldn't be there either, but that another schoolmaster, a Rodney Exton, formerly headmaster of Epsom college, would replace him.

Nicholas was surprised that he was to make a presentation on the future of a £60 million business to three retired teachers. Moreover he was told that after making the presentation to them he would go into another room to be interviewed by M J K Smith, the chairman of Warwickshire and Mike Murray, the former chairman of Middlesex who was the chairman of the finance committee of the TCCB.

'Implementing a Strategy for Cricket' comprised three distinct sections, entitled:

1. A vision to take English cricket into the next century.
2. The best democratic process to convince people to buy into the vision.
3. Getting it done!

And the proposals it contained were radical.

The first section, Nicholas's 'Vision' of English cricket concentrated on two main areas: the playing structure of domestic cricket and the formation of an academy which would become the finishing school for all cricket education in the country.

He proposed two divisions for county cricket, with nine teams in each section playing each other home and away. He envisaged promotion and relegation for the bottom and top three teams, prize money for the top six in the premier division and the top three in the first division and suggested investigating the possibility of semi-final and final play-offs.

As for one-day cricket, he proposed two limited-over competitions only. His preferred option was to leave the 60-over competition as it stood as a

Right: David Graveney was a much more modern-thinking chairman of selectors than his predecessors. After all, at the time he succeeded Ray Illingworth he still had to pay full fare on the buses. But strategic errors were still made.

Left: Lord MacLaurin of Knebworth. The former chairman of Tesco whose blueprint for cricket, entitled *Raising the Standard,* disappointed those seeking radical change. Unencumbered by having to please county chairman he would have gone further.

Right: England coach David Lloyd trying desperately to get the message across to his players.

Above: Angus Fraser, a great trier for Middlesex and England whose Test career was hampered by burn-out.

Above: Darren Gough will never stop trying. But he needs handling with care. For years the English game has destroyed talent like his with remarkable efficiency.

Below: Dominic Cork burst onto the Test scene in 1995 with his dramatic exploits against West Indies, but within a year his career had left the rails. A prime candidate for special treatment under a Board contract.

Above: One of the great rearguard actions in England's Test history has ended in triumph. Mike Atherton embraces Jack Russell after saving the second Test of the 1995–96 winter series against South Africa at The Wanderers' Ground, Johannesburg – the high point of a tour that turned sour for Atherton, Ray Illingworth and Devon Malcolm.

Below: Mike Atherton sticks his head over the parapet during England's dismal 3–0 one-day thrashing by Zimbabwe at the end of the 1996 winter tour. There were plenty ready to take aim and fire, not least Atherton's former chairman of selectors Ray Illingworth.

Above: My first 'official' involvement with the England team in a coaching capacity came during the 1996–97 winter tours to Zimbabwe and New Zealand. Plenty went wrong, but it could have been worse.

Below: A happy end to the 1996–97 tour as England players celebrate their 2–0 series win over New Zealand, a result that guaranteed Mike Atherton the captaincy for at least another series.

Left: Not exactly the darlings of the establishment – me and my fellow Sky TV commentators tell it as we see it. Clockwise: Allan Lamb, Paul Allott, Mark Nicholas, Bob Willis and me.

Right: Robert Croft was the success of the 1996–97 winter tour to New Zealand, but struggled against Australia.

Left: Darren Gough and Mike Atherton decide that there is always time for a quick sprint under the new fitness regime inspired by coach David Lloyd.

Right: Mike Atherton and Mark Taylor have a high regard for each other. I wonder what Athers might have achieved given the players at Taylor's disposal.

Left: The false dawn of victory at Edgbaston in early June 1997 preceded weeks of Ashes disappointment. At least, thanks to their magnificent record stand, Nasser Hussain and Graham Thorpe delayed the inquests by one Test.

Below: England's joy on the dressing room balcony at Edgbaston after their first Test win was unconfined. But just look at the expressions on the faces of the Australians. Their mental toughness and their greater skill enabled them to have the last laugh.

Left: Nasser Hussain was the only England batsman to enhance his reputation during the 1997 Ashes series, so much so that by the end he was a leading contender to take over from Mike Atherton as captain.

Right: Graham Thorpe is a magnificent striker of the ball, easily our best left-hander since David Gower. But he seemed to lose his way against Mark Taylor's Aussies in 1997.

Below: The latest great hopes of English cricket, Adam and Ben Hollioake quickened pulses with their performances in the Texaco Trophy series with Australia at the start of the 1997 season. But they had to wait until the Ashes were all but lost before they were given their chance at Test level.

Ray Illingworth, former Chairman of Selectors and the man who couldn't stand the fact that players would come to me for help and advice rather than him. The expression says it all…

sort of FA Cup of English cricket, but to play a 50-over league under the same regulations as applied to all international one-day cricket.

His second option was to have one 50-over competition and one 25-over mid-summer evening league playing with substitutes and specialists.

He proposed strict pitch control carried out (on an ad hoc basis) by roving inspectors in the 48 hours preceding the start of each championship match.

And he proposed sweeping changes to the programme for overseas touring teams. He suggested the creation of five regional teams, plus England A and Young England to play four-day matches against the tourists; one-day matches against the tourists to be played by non-Test match hosting countries, major Test playing countries to tour England every five years to create a space for 'newer' ICC members and a mid-season triangular one-day tournament between England, the visiting major nation and a second visiting nation.

As for the Academy he proposed the following objectives:

'To be a world leader in the creation of a cricketing centre of excellence and
   education.
'To provide elite technical coaching and advice in science and medicine.
'To provide state of the art practice and teaching methods and facilities.
'To use the academy as a development ground for young cricketers and to
   provide accommodation and further education.
'To provide a permanent institute for coaches.
'To provide a media training centre for all potentially "high profile"
   cricketers.'

In the second section, 'The best democratic process to convince people to buy into the vision', he stated his objective as to encourage, persuade and reassure existing parties, with a road show of ideas sent around the counties, confidential discussions with county committees and a review of the findings and recommendations thereafter.

The third section, entitled 'Getting it done' concerned the England team and the administrative structure of the game.

For the England team he proposed a full-time management team to comprise a team manager, to administer the day-to-day business of the team, a coach, a media liaison manager, to act as go-between and improve relations between players and press and a physiotherapist.

This would be backed up by a chairman and two other selectors to join the captain in the selection of the team, and a trainer, nutritionist and medical advisor.

He also stressed the need 'to immediately implement the employment of all England cricketers by the Board.'

In his plan the administrative structure governing the domestic game would be put in place as follows:

1. A managing director to work with the chairman and his democratically elected board and to be given absolute power in the running of the business that is English cricket, in the way that they would have absolute power in a public limited company.
2. To report annually to the shareholders, i.e. the counties, the minor counties and the MCC, in the way suggested in the proposals for the new English Cricket Board.
3. To appoint a small advisory council (similar to non-executive directors), from outside the day to day running of the game, who would be paid a retainer in order to ensure access to their experience and specialist skills. Examples: To financially appraise projects and business plans. To put a value on television rights and sponsorships. To advise on public relations in the launch of the new constitution.
4. To streamline all existing sub-committees, abandoning some and simplifying others.
5. To streamline county playing staffs.
6. To begin a process by which all club and school cricket is managed by the county in which it takes place.
7. To encourage senior league club cricket to assume a greater importance and to be played over a longer period.
8. To work with government and local education authorities in bringing cricket back into schools.
9. To dramatically improve the levels of communication between the headquarters of the game, its subsidiaries, the media and, most importantly of all, the counties themselves.

Nicholas ended the presentation with this conclusion:

'The key is to get the product right so that the English team thrives at the top of a pyramid whose foundations are built around a strong and committed domestic structure.

'This will come through the provision and implementation of a clear national development plan and a clear national business plan, whose aim is to take English cricket to the forefront of the world game within the next decade.'

Nicholas felt he had delivered his presentation well. According to him: 'It was clear that they were interviewing more than one person and so had decided to split the sessions. To be fair the schoolmasters asked extremely pertinent questions, like 'What makes you think you can change the long established views of the county clubs who run the whole show anyway?', most of them more relevant than questions he was to be asked later by the cricket administrators.

'When I went through the presentation for a second time, to M J K Smith and Murray, I sensed they were less responsive from the start. I got the feeling that Murray might have been in favour of two divisions, but doubted my capacity to convince anyone else. M J K Smith was clearly so much against changing the Sunday League format that he couldn't see the wood from the trees.'

Eventually Nicholas was seen out by Silk who asked him to keep free some dates in his diary in order to go to the next stage of the process. He said that they would be narrowing down the choice to two or three people and that they would all make presentations to the Board's executive committee.

Nicholas waited for confirmation, but was encouraged to receive a supportive phone call from Silk who told him: 'Your presentation was really good. I'd been staunchly against the idea of two divisions but you've completely convinced me that it would work. I'm backing you to the hilt.'

Nicholas's next communication with Silk surprised him. Silk rang Nicholas to tell him that there had been a re-think and that a decision had been made to employ a management consultancy to interview the remaining candidates.

'We want an expert in recruitment to take a view,' Silk told him.

Nicholas asked what would be required. 'Just make your presentation to him exactly as you did to us,' came the reply.

Nicholas recalls: 'I went to the West End offices of a company called Whitehead-Mann and gave my presentation to a man named Ian Butcher, a director. He asked me a couple of questions about certain aspects of administration, what I thought of the staff at Lord's etc. Then, just before I left I asked him for clarification of my position. I told him that the people at Sky Television were waiting for me to sign a contract, that they had been very understanding and told me that they wouldn't hold me to any promises if a job at the centre of cricket came up. I explained that I didn't really want to leave them hanging on the end of a leash.

'I said to Butcher: "I really don't mind you telling me straight that you don't think I'm the man the board is looking for. If I'm not, please tell me so that I can let Sky know." Butcher said that he couldn't say anything definite then, but that I should ring him in a few days. I did so and he said something like "If there were an election tomorrow I think you would get the vote. At this stage you are probably leading the contest." I understood he was dropping a broad 'off the record' hint that I was going to get the job.'

Nicholas was encouraged but, by this stage, another puzzling element had entered the story. At the same time as Nicholas had first discussed the role of chief executive with Barclay and Atherton in South Africa, he had also had a conversation with Bob Bennett, the chairman of Lancashire, one of the counties on the Test Match Grounds Working Party pushing Warwickshire's Tony Cross for the job. As tour manager and captain on the A team tour to Zimbabwe in 1990, Bennett and Nicholas had always enjoyed a close working relationship.

Back in South Africa, Nicholas had sought Bennett's views over the position. Bennett had told him that he thought it would be in essence an administrative role, that however strong the chief executive was the counties would always really retain control and hinder rather than help any move for change, and that the role was unlikely to allow the free rein enjoyed by Ali Bacher in South Africa – a man much admired by Nicholas for his ability to get things done and envied for the freedom he has do to do.

The next time Nicholas had any contact with Bennett was in May 1996 … well after Nicholas had entered the running for the job. Nicholas recalls: 'Sky were covering a match between Derbyshire versus Lancashire at Chesterfield. It was cold and rainy and play was delayed. I had gone out to the middle to do a piece to camera when who should sidle up to me but Bob, wearing a big sheepskin overcoat with the collar turned skywards and looking as dodgy as Don Corleone.

"Hi, Bob. How are you, mate?" I greeted him.

'He mumbled back, somewhat to my surprise: "You don't want it, you know. You don't want it."

'I was slightly taken aback and after a few moments asked: "What are you talking about?"

'He said: "You know. What we talked about in South Africa. You don't want it. It's not for you. It's all paperwork."

'By this time, the penny had dropped. I told him it wasn't for him to decide whether the job was for me or not. He said again: "It's not for you. No power. You want to be an Ali Bacher."

'I said that was exactly right and that was exactly what anybody worth his salt should be if they were going to make English cricket big again.

'Bob replied: "I'm warning you off. Keep away. You're doing far too well in the media."

'With that, he walked off. So I walked after him and said, "Bob, what is going on? Why are you sidling up to me then sidling away now like this, treating me like a leper. What is going on?"

'He said: "I can't say anymore. It's not for you. Trust me."

'It was an absolutely staggering performance.'

Although bemused by Bennett's behaviour, Nicholas heard no more from him and let the matter pass. He spoke to Silk regarding dates for making his presentation to the executive committee and mentioned that if he was successful his 'dream ticket' would include a strong chairman with business acumen and serious credibility. He proposed the name of Sir Ian MacLaurin. Silk told him this was a 'fantastic' idea and that he would set about trying to contact the chairman of Tesco to see if it appealed.

Nicholas felt things were moving. But a week after this conversation with Silk about MacLaurin, he got a call from Ian Butcher which threw the issue into confusion. Butcher told him that the Board had decided that the interviews had not gone as they would have liked and that a new 'search committee' had been formed. Butcher spoke to Nicholas on the Tuesday of that week, informing him that he would have to make his presentation again, this time to the search committee, at his offices at the end of that week.

This stopped Nicholas dead. Prior engagements, including exchanging contracts on a new house at midday on the Friday meant that it was more or less impossible for him to attend a meeting at such short notice. He was also keen to rewrite some of the proposals in his presentation and was concerned that he would not know anyone on the new search committee with whom he might have a rapport. 'But you do know them,' Butcher told him. and read out the list of names: M J K Smith, Mike Murray, Dennis Silk, Doug Insole, David Acfield, Ian MacLaurin and Butcher himself.

Nicholas rang Silk to find out exactly what was going on. Silk told him that a new man had come into the race, Tony Cross, and that he was being pushed heavily by the Test Match Grounds Working Party. 'I'll be honest with you,' Silk confided, 'A head-to-head has been set up between you and Tony Cross. You simply have to be there.'

Nicholas's problems began the day before the final presentation. He received a phone call to tell him he had been gazzumped on his house. He set off for Hereford to fulfil a speaking engagement as a favour to the *Guardian* journalist Frank Keating. He left Hereford at one o'clock in the morning to drive back to London and finally got to bed at his sister's house at 4.30 am. After getting up at 7.30 am he tried to see the man whose house he was trying to buy, but when he got there the man had gone. He went back to his sister's house to collect his papers, made a few quick changes to the presentation, took it to the printers, got the printers to do the alterations, got on the phone to the estate agents, had a row with them, then had another row with the vendor because he hadn't been there when he went to see him earlier as arranged and because he now wanted another £6,000 for his house. As he was walking up the steps to the room where the presentation was to take place he was still talking to the vendor on his mobile phone.

'In I walk,' remembers Nicholas, 'and there they are sitting around the table. I'm tired and I'm not focused and I'm upset. I'm worrying about the house and whether I can find six grand and my mind is just not all there. What is more I am about to give this presentation for the fourth time to many of the same people who had heard it all before. In the event I gave a pretty poor performance.

'Then the questions started. Perfectly reasonably, MacLaurin says: "Mark, you've clearly got the ideal credentials cricket-wise, but if there was a question mark it would be over your business experience. What plans do you have business-wise?"

'And I suddenly realised that I'd made a balls-up. All along I had been asked by Silk to present a cricket plan. I had been convinced that the plan I had devised allied to the enthusiasm and beliefs and diplomatic skills I had were exactly what was needed on the cricketing front. But the fact was that I didn't have a business plan.

'I could easily have come up with one but it hadn't occurred to me. My idea had been to get MacLaurin involved as chairman and address the business criteria with him. I had left it at that. I was exposed.

'I was cross with myself and I gave some weak answers.

'Then Acfield chipped in and I could feel the whole thing slipping away from me. "But Mark," he said, "You've no administrative skills for running an office." I said: "Well, that's an astounding observation and I commend you for making it. The fact is that I've been playing cricket for the last 18 years, as you knew full well before you invited me into this room."

"Well," he said, "You can't expect to run a £60 million business and all the employees and staff and so forth without any experience." And I thought 'here we go, coming at it from the negative again … the glass is half empty not half full … etc… Now I was starting to boil a bit. I told him, "It just makes me cross that you've said that David. We've known each other a long time and always got on well and to my mind you've made a totally irrelevant point. At Hampshire I ran a county club for 12 years and it was a happy and contented place."

'Then M J K Smith started to lay into me about wanting to get rid of the 40-over competition on Sunday. He said that I had no right to tamper with the one thing that kept the counties afloat financially and then, I'm afraid, it happened.

'Doug Insole, the silent power behind so much of what the Test and County Cricket Board had stood for so long whose basic principle was that success in cricket was and is cyclical, started to have a go at me over the idea of two divisions. And I'm afraid I blew.

'He said that two divisions would ruin English cricket and that clubs would go to the wall. He trotted out all the old arguments. I told him I disagreed and I got more and more frustrated. Without actually having a stand-up row we had a loud and heated argument which culminated when I looked at him straight and said, "Doug, the problem with English cricket is you." You could have heard a pin drop.

'I went on: "I don't necessarily mean you individually, Doug, but what you represent, because what you and your kind do is that you always refer back to how things used to be. You know too much and you've been involved for too long and any new idea that is put before you receives an examination to discover what is wrong with it rather than what might be right. Just because something didn't work in 1958 doesn't mean a revised version is not going to work in 1998. To be on the fringe, advising and consulting younger people, that's fine, but while you hang on to positions of great power and influence and in your case effectively run cricket from behind the scenes, I don't think anything will ever change. You'll tell me that its all cyclical and I simply don't believe that. Things are only cyclical if during the down part of the cycle work is done to ensure that there will be an up part of the cycle."

'The only thing I didn't do was trot out Will Carling's line about 57 old farts, but I may as well have done. By now my finger was stuck on the self-destruct button and I couldn't have removed it even if I had wanted to … which I didn't.

'I thought: "You've let yourself down," but maybe I had let my hair down as well and maybe, I realised, in the circumstances this job was just not for me, what with the constraints that I would be under.'

Nicholas was followed downstairs by Silk who looked shocked. He tried to reassure Nicholas that the interview had not gone as badly as Nicholas knew it had but Nicholas apologised for letting him down. He told Silk: "I think you've worked really hard for me and I think you worked really hard for the academy and if it really is me that you believe in I'm sorry because I know they won't go for me now and after that I don't blame them."

Nicholas rang Silk later that day to offer to pull out. He was going to say that even if he did get the job there were so many things that he would like to do that would meet with insurmountable resistance that maybe the time was just not right. Before he could utter a word, Silk confirmed what both men already knew. 'I'm afraid you are not the chosen one,' Silk told him.

In fact Nicholas believed Cross was bound to get the job. The word was that Cross had performed well at interview and that was that as far as Nicholas was concerned. All the while Silk had told Nicholas that Cross would get it over his dead body, that he felt Cross would merely be a mouthpiece for the Test Match Grounds Working Party who wanted to take over the game and that Silk felt that was not the right way to go.

Certainly Cross had had influential backers as Nicholas was later to discover, when, out in Christchurch during the New Zealand leg of the 1996-97 England tour, Bennett approached him on an entirely different matter.

Bennett explained that one of the reasons he was there was to find out if Nicholas was interested in becoming the new chairman of England selectors. He told Nicholas that of the shortlist of candidates, he was the only person they had had any correspondence about from the counties. Nicholas had a bit of a sinking feeling about all this but told him that of course he would be interested. Bennett asked if they could have further talks.

Nicholas agreed but on one condition. 'I told him,' Nicholas recalls, 'That I wasn't going to talk to him about anything until Bennett told me the truth of what was behind his extraordinary performance at Derby the previous May when he had warned me off the job of chief executive.

'He said he couldn't tell me. I said: "Well, then. I'm not going to talk to you. Thank you for coming and I'll talk to Sir Ian MacLaurin (who by now had been installed as the chairman of the ECB) when I get back to England."

That evening Bennett changed his tune. He said that he had to find out from Nicholas whether he wanted to be considered for the job of Chairman of Selectors and agreed to explain the 'Don Corleone' business at Derby.

The following morning Nicholas went to Bennett's hotel room. What he heard left Nicholas stunned.

Bennett said: 'The reason I warned you off was that Dennis Silk was pushing Tony Cross for the job and that you were being used to take the trail off him.'

Bennett told Nicholas that every time Silk spoke to Cross he had told him that he was his man and that he needn't worry because the other candidates were just being interviewed for show.

When he got his breath back, Nicholas thanked Bennett for the information but told him he didn't believe a word of it. The interview over the job of Chairman of Selectors duly took place. Nicholas said that he was prepared to drop all his media work except for television presenting which was a new and interesting career for him. He was not remotely surprised that he never heard another word.

The story reached its conclusion at the start of the summer of 1997, several weeks after David Graveney's appointment as Ray Illingworth's successor. At a dinner to celebrate the 90th birthday of the veteran *Daily Telegraph* cricket writer Jim Swanton, Nicholas bumped into Silk, told him he had to get something off his chest and reported to him his conversation with Bennett.

Nicholas describes the look on Silk's face as one of shock. Silk assured him that what Bennett had said was untrue. 'I was not in favour of Cross getting the job. I was absolutely behind you.'

When Nicholas heard Silk's denial, his immediate response was anger at Bennett. In the interests of fairness, however, he decided to ask Cross for his recollection of events.

Cross told Nicholas that what Bennett had said was accurate; namely that Silk had approached Cross and asked him to stand for the post of chief executive and that at every step along the way he had told Cross he was right behind him, just as he had also said to Nicholas. Perhaps Silk had been pushed into bringing Cross into the race by the members of the Test Match Grounds Working Party, Nicholas reasoned, and then felt obliged to back each man with equal enthusiasm. Whatever, Nicholas still feels that although Silk had set his heart on improving English cricket, the politicians in the corridors of power quite cleverly manipulated him and made his ambitions impossible to achieve.

Nicholas was relieved that Bennett had not lied to him, but was disappointed that he hadn't told him the truth of the matter when they first spoke. Most relevantly, Nicholas believes that this charade and the whole shambles was a typical demonstration of the way English cricket is administered – slap-dash, old-fashioned and self-interested.

He believes Lord MacLaurin remains the only hope for the future and reckons that he must spend his early days as chairman uncovering inadequate management by some pretty ordinary people. 'Tesco to TCCB,' says Nicholas, 'Some culture shock. What a job he's got. I pray the counties support him. He's an exceptional man and tough enough to brush aside the self-interest which is the biggest problem in our game. That, and the fact that the counties and their members control cricket. It is a ridiculous state of affairs and hopeless for the future of our game. If only the members could understand what really goes on.

'It's sad,' Nicholas says, 'that the administration of our game does not do justice to the amazing and continued enthusiasm for it throughout the country.

'Cricket is our national summer game, but it is run selfishly as if it is a private recreation. It's such a shame.'

NINETEEN
TROUBLE WITH PATRICK

'The England cricket team have certainly paid dearly for the Board's refusal to embrace the Whittingdale Cricket Plan wholeheartedly.'

I CANNOT help but feel one of the greatest cricketing tragedies of recent years has been the way Patrick Whittingdale and his Cricket Plan were treated by Lord's. I suppose that Ian Botham may appear a rather strange champion of organised coaching and planning, but here was a genuine cricket-lover whose main motivation was to help make England's Test team more competitive in whatever way he could. Despite those good intentions, as well as the millions of pounds invested by his company, this cricketing benefactor was treated very shabbily by those empowered with running the game at Lord's.

The greatest irony is that the current England set-up is now employing many of the ideas that were part of the original Whittingdale Cricket Plan. It seems incredible to me that the Board managed to bite off the hand that would have fed them the resources required to provide top-class coaching and expertise for our Test team.

Few sponsors have been as well-liked or well-respected as Patrick. A players' man, first and last, he felt their well-being was a prime concern. I should have realised that such an attitude would not go down well with cricket's bosses. Such was his concern, that when he announced his sponsorship was to end, he went public over Ray Illingworth's treatment of Mike Atherton at the start of the 1995 summer and attacked the England boss's lack of man management as one of the reasons behind his decision.

'Criticism of the players through the media is bad man management and simply does not get the best out of the players. Mike Atherton had a rotten

job taking over the captaincy from Graham Gooch and was treated like a child by long-range criticism during the winter. The treatment of Angus Fraser who works for me when he is not playing cricket, has not been acceptable either. I cannot continue to work with anybody who is going to deal with players in this way. While the management persist like this, there is no way they will be getting my money. Ray Illingworth said when he became manager that his job was to instill confidence and "make the most of the limited talent at my disposal." I don't subscribe to the view that talent is limited, but we are not going to get the best out of the talent.'

Strong words with plenty of emotion. His efforts had been thrown back in his face for the entire length of the sponsorship which began in 1991. This was nearly four years down the line. Illingworth's elevation to an all-powerful role of Chairman of Selectors and Manager in the spring of 1995 was the last chance for Lord's to redeem itself in his eyes. It vanished when Whittingdale travelled to Edgbaston during the England A match a few weeks later, at the start of the summer of 1995 for a meeting with the new supremo. In the event they never did get together. This was the final straw for Whittingdale whose comments above created quite a reaction, not least from Illingworth who responded with:

'I don't want to get into a slanging match. All I'm prepared to say is that we've had a lot of good sponsors over the years who are still with us and don't try to run the game. Any sponsorship is welcome, but not any cost. What I feel is most irritating is all the criticism we're having and we're haven't started yet.'

Obviously, part of the sponsorship's appeal was to improve the profile of Whittingdale Fund Managers, a financial company in the city of London. Yet, I never got the impression that commercial considerations interfered with the cricket intentions of the Whittingdale Plan. Ultimately, it was only Patrick's love of the game and his relationships with the players that held him back from taking the Board to court over the way his sponsorship contract appeared to have been breached, ignored and abused.

I first got to know the man, his hopes and his many problems with the Board during my Leukaemia Walk along the South Coast at the end of 1992. Patrick kindly sponsored me on one of the days and joined me as we trekked halfway round the Isle of Wight. It soon became clear that he was unhappy and frustrated. He felt his attempts to provide the best for the England team – in terms of coaching, preparation and back-up – were being undermined by a long-running dispute with the TCCB. His comments were tinged more with sadness and regret than anger.

Patrick had got involved with cricket along a familiar route, the beneficiaries. Those early efforts brought him into contact with the likes of Graham Gooch, Clive Radley and John Lever. Cricket is always on the lookout for rich and successful benefactors. Many are happy to hand their money over and sit back. That is not Whittingdale's way. As well as at Essex, he became a familiar figure at Lord's and The Oval, where he took a box. Several schemes were discussed with the likes of Ted Dexter, who had just taken over from Peter May as chairman of selectors and had become chairman of the England Committee. Whittingdale found Dexter receptive to the idea of helping the players, but Dexter, who ran his own PR company at the time, was trying to find a sponsor for what later became the Whyte & Mackay Rankings. Whittingdale felt there was a slight conflict of interest in Dexter's dual role, a feeling confirmed when Dexter wrote that he would support his sponsorship plans; the same letter explored the possibilities of Dexter's company handling the sponsorship.

The businessman's long-term objective was the Whittingdale Cricket Plan, a blueprint for England's Test team. He also wanted to help the most promising of England's youngsters. To that end, his first direct involvement, named The Young Cricketers' Scheme, was announced at Trent Bridge towards the end of the disastrous 1989 summer. Two cricketers, a batsman and bowler, would be nominated, with the company paying the equivalent of their summer wages in the winter. The basic idea was to free youngsters of serious financial worries to allow them to pursue the best methods of improving their cricket.

The initial Young Cricketers' Award launch at Lord's had all the hallmarks of the Board's lack of professionalism. The announcement of the choice of players was made right in the middle of David

Gower's sacking, Graham Gooch's elevation to the captaincy and the selecting of the squad to tour the West Indies. The sponsors Whittingdale, new to such matters, went along with the Board's arrangements and waited in the Indoor School at Lord's for the journalists to arrive and salute this brave new initiative. In the event, very few attended for the simple reason that the TCCB had earlier held their own press conference that day to present Gooch as the new England captain. The media rushed to the press box to write heaps on the new man in charge, the man who had suffered at the hands of Terry Alderman all summer. The naming of the first two Whittingdale Young Cricketers became little more than a side-show.

The Board would have done everyone a great service by holding back the announcement. The fact that the sponsorship was buried beneath other cricket news was damaging enough, but a delay would also have prevented an avoidable error being made in one of the choices. The Whittingdale panel, chaired by Tom Graveney – Patrick Whittingdale's boyhood hero and whose name was given to the Oval Box used by the company – also included John Lever, David Hughes and Clive Radley. As one of the main objectives was to ease the financial worries of young players, there seemed little point in choosing someone going on the senior England tour that winter. The Whittingdale panel had a slight logistic problem in that they had to meet before the England selectors made their winter choices. No real problem here. The old pal's act and a discreet phone call would do the trick to ensure they chose a player not bound for the senior tour to the West Indies. Indeed the Whittingdale panel was informed that their first-choice batsman, Michael Atherton, who had appeared in the final two Ashes Tests, would be jetting out with Gooch's team to the Caribbean. So they switched the award to Nasser Hussain, who had not been far behind Atherton in their deliberations. Therefore, the first two Whittingdale Young Cricketers were Hussain and the Surrey paceman, Martin Bicknell. The following morning there was little publicity for his scheme. Later that day it was announced that Hussain would be travelling to the West Indies after all and that Atherton had been named vice-captain of the England A party, which was visiting Zimbabwe. Word of the cock-up soon leaked out. Hussain celebrated the double jackpot, while it was a double blow for Atherton. Unfortunately, that first sponsorship venture with

Lord's set the trend for his future involvement, although the lacklustre launch of the Young Cricketers Scheme was nothing to the problems that were to plague the Whittingdale Cricket Plan.

This time the sponsor was not prepared to stand back and see his money squandered and his ideas abandoned. I've never seen anyone so emotionally involved with a cricket sponsorship. Perhaps the Whittingdale Cricket Plan was too dear to his heart. Perhaps, he had too clear an idea of how it should be constructed, organised and developed. Patrick Whittingdale hates compromise and mediocrity. The TCCB was not used to sponsors having anything to say for themselves about cricket. Most sponsors were happy to hand over the money and let the board's marketing department get on with it. Most of them invest in an event – not the future. Their money is spent on something that already exists and is well-established in the public's mind. But Whittingdale's involvement was about a dream, a long-cherished ambition and a desire to help England catch up with the rest of the cricket world.

The Whittingdale Cricket Plan was a long-term strategy to assist the development of the England cricket team. It was to make available to the England team manager a wide-range of facilities, ideas and techniques to monitor and enhance performance, for use as and when he considered appropriate. Although most of the publicity centred on England's pre-tour coaching, the Plan covered a wide variety of areas. One concerned England fringe players. The best young players were to be identified, monitored and assisted, and receive specialist coaching. As far as Whittingdale was concerned, Specialist Coaching and Masterclasses meant the best. But the Board refused to entertain the likes of Sunil Gavaskar and Dennis Lillee being called upon. The Board's view was that England's players were as good as anyone else's and the governing body and the counties did not want to be seen to be looking abroad to find the best. The Plan proposed that the team manager should be provided with the resources to study coaching techniques, home and abroad, and in other sports. Whittingdale felt that modern developments in American sports, such as baseball, could be of benefit; the set-ups, the techniques of hitting and throwing etc. Before the 1992-93 Indian tour, the sponsorship paid for team manager Keith Fletcher to travel to watch India in South Africa. The Plan also allowed for the coach to take Specialist Coaches and Players on tour. On the Indian tour, Ian Salisbury travelled in that capacity and was eventually added to the official party. The Whittingdale Plan also provided for net bowlers.

The Plan also allowed for personal videos for each member of the squad, as well as Player Care, with individual reviews of progress and development plans. This was backed up by Fitness Monitoring/ Rehabilitation Programmes, plus post-tour debriefings. For the coaches, there would be an annual seminar. These measures were wide-reaching and, for the TCCB, quite a radical departure. Yet, it was the way forward. Events in other countries have proved that conclusively in the last few years.

I am sorry to say that the England cricket team have certainly paid dearly for the TCCB's refusal to embrace the Whittingdale Cricket Plan wholeheartedly.

The Plan did have one great supporter, Graham Gooch. The arrival of Gooch as captain signified a more professional approach to preparing for tours. 'If you fail to prepare, you prepare to fail' became a familiar catch-phrase at the time. No one has worked harder than Gooch to get the best out of his cricket talent.

Whittingdale flew to Perth at the end of the ill-fated Australian tour in 1990-91. The team hotel, the Hyatt, was holding an exhibition, a photographic look at the series called the 'Ashes Flashes' which had been sponsored by Whittingdale. It allowed Patrick to get the views of Gooch and several senior figures, like David Gower, Richie Benaud and Tony Greig.

By now the company was certain the way forward was to become the first coaching sponsor of the England team and the summer of 1991 was spent negotiating the contract. It was aware that the TCCB was looking for a shirt sponsor and, although the company felt such a deal might be out of financial reach, it did request a copy of that sponsorship document. The reply from Lord's was that it had yet to be finalised. To this day, despite repeated assurances by Lord's to the contrary, Patrick has never laid eyes on what was on offer in the 1991 shirt/team deal.

The launch of the Whittingdale Cricket Plan, though there was no 'blueprint' actually published for a further year, was another botched job. The announcement was planned for the Saturday of the final Test of the summer of 1991, against Sri Lanka at Lord's. As Whittingdale's geared themselves for the biggest marketing day of the company's life, the plug was pulled at the last minute. Cornhill, sponsors of England's home Test series since 1978, were not happy that another financial institution was going to steal its thunder in the middle of the match. That, anyway, was the message relayed to the company, although subsequent conversations with Cornhill revealed that the TCCB's marketing department had not even asked Cornhill about the matter. The other basic problem was that Whittingdale was told that they could not call themselves 'official coaching sponsors to the England Test team.'

Another difficulty, although it was not apparent at the time, involved the several late changes made to the contract by the Board's marketing director, Terry Blake. He explained there was nothing sinister in these changes. It was just a question of tidying the contract up as normally happens at the end of negotiations. Whittingdale, of course, was keen to get the deal signed.

A few weeks later just prior to the 1991-92 winter tour to New Zealand and the 1992 World Cup, Tetley were appointed as England team sponsors. Interestingly, the phrase 'England team' had not been available to Whittingdale on 9 September, but now, on 7 November, Tetley *could* use the word 'team'. Whittingdale had been assured by Lord's that it would be contracted immediately if the team/squad situation in the Cornhill contract ever changed. No such notification had been received.

Seeking assurances, Whittingdale was informed that Whittingdale and Tetley could work in harmony and that none of Whittingdale's rights had been lost or given away to the other side. As a way of countering the Tetley deal, Whittingdale, who had been using England cricketers in his financial advertisements (Graham Gooch/ Whittingdale – top-class performers) came up with a picture of Robin Smith, without his shirt, coming out of nets all padded up. The message was 'England cricketers are putting their shirts on Whittingdale this winter', a reference to the pre-tour sessions at Lilleshall and The Oval. It seemed pretty clever to me. But, as it turned out, there were objections from the Board.

There was also a problem with the counties. The sponsorship was paying for the best specialist coaching for their leading players and making them better, as well as employing some of their coaches. It was a 'pay-as-you-spend' sponsorship basically footing the bill for giving these counties better performers. Yet the company was told that there would be a price for of the deal and for the counties' approval. Whittingdale hoped that once the pre-tour sessions began, these early problems would sort themselves out and both sides could work together for the sake of the England team.

The Lilleshall and Lord's launches went well, the sight of the recovering Angus Fraser on crunches with Dexter offering good photo opportunities at the Indoor School. The company had been told that to back-up a sponsorship, you need to spend the same amount in support to get full value from any involvement. It did not skimp and quickly realised that this support was necessary. Getting decisions and actions from Lord's, however, was not easy, especially when other TCCB sponsors appeared to be coming a poor second to Tetley.

That was confirmed in the first week of the New Zealand tour. The England tourists were wearing Tetley's gear, not Whittingdale, during the first few days of practice. The response from the TCCB was hardly designed to erase the coaching sponsor's worries. As far as they were concerned, the contract did not give Whittingdale any rights abroad. That turned the skirmishing into something more serious.

A document that expanded the various grievances with the Board was prepared at the request of the TCCB's solicitors, Slaughter & May, to set out Whittingdale's position. It was fifteen pages long and it is not known whether members of the Executive ever looked at it. Their lawyers urged caution, afraid that the Board might have to take action should the Whittingdale complaints prove justified. The breaches of contract included exclusive rights and TCCB under-taking not to grant rights to another person as well as maximum public recognition of the sponsorship, the possible bad faith on the granting of rights to Tetley, the postponed launch, and Specialist Coaching. Much as I would love to reveal the exact details of that Whittingdale document, Patrick feels that would be inappropriate, even now when his sponsorship is over. It is believed that the document handed to the Executive was also critical of the TCCB marketing director, Terry Blake and his relationship with Tetley's.

Blake, who had been head boy at Radley when Dennis Silk, the Chairman of the TCCB, was headmaster there, was a long-time friend of Marcus Robertson, one of the directors of Craigie Taylor, the company appointed to look after the Tetley sponsorship. The TCCB's other sponsors felt Tetley was receiving preferential treatment, and in certain quarters the TCCB's marketing director was referred to as 'Tetley' Blake. Other companies, including those involved in the England Players' Pool, found themselves excluded from official team gatherings, although the Tetley contract specifically allowed them access. When Blake was on site that access was refused.

When Gooch appeared on a live 'Sportsnight' link-up wearing a Whittingdale sweatshirt during the Indian trip, tour manager Bob Bennett was woken up in the early hours by Blake, who had been given a hard time by one of the Tetley's hierarchy. But there was no official dress code outside practices and official functions. That came in later. Blake actually sent Bennett a fax, which the Lancashire chairman has kept to this day. A dress code was soon imposed and touring players were actually told at Lilleshall that Whittingdale kit should not be worn outside practises, even as leisure wear. Before an earlier A tour the players were told not to take any Whittingdale gear with them.

One of the reasons the Whittingdale gear was worn was that it was quality stuff. The company used Russell Athletic for Sweatshirts and Beefy-T for Shirts. Cricketers, like all sportsmen, like good gear and Whittingdale certainly had the edge over Tetley in that department. Even here, the Board found a way to penalise Whittingdale. The Whittingdale gear would never be worn during official televised matches, so there was no restriction on the size or number of logos. That was compensation for having no television coverage. The company used a large 'W' logo with a cricket ball on the front of T-shirts and sweatshirts. It was big, but not vulgar and looked quite striking. Yet, when the 1993 season began, the company was told that its gear had to conform to the television restrictions. The Board cited the complaints about the players' dress in India, especially at the post-Bombay Test ceremony. Yet all the gear on show that day was Tetley's and had to been approved by the Board. It was pretty clear that the relationship was reaching the point of no return.

One area where the sponsor felt badly let down was over publicity for the scheme. The delay of the launch was an obvious example, but another was the incident that occurred during the Edgbaston Test against Pakistan in 1992. While the general announcements of the sponsorship received reasonable coverage, it was specific examples of sponsorship in action that would capture maximum exposure. Specialist coaching and Masterclasses were opportunities that would do that. While the early stages of the match were disrupted by rain, the press corps asked to see the England team manager, Micky Stewart, to find out what plans there were for the rest of the season. Deadline time was approaching and the journalists had very little to write about. They struck a minor seam of gold when it was revealed that Devon Malcolm, who was not playing in the Test, was to receive Whittingdale-supported specialist coaching from Geoff Arnold. It was just the sort of high profile publicity that the sponsor had been hoping for, but there was just one slight problem. Throughout Stewart's half-hour discussion with the journalists in the Edgbaston press-box, the name Whittingdale was not mentioned once and the sponsorship was never referred to.

Patrick himself was aware that such sessions could be sensitive and often would be held in private, so photo opportunities would be extremely limited. The sponsor was happy to put the player's consideration first. But the minimum requirement was that due credit be given to the sponsorship and the participants should wear Whittingdale gear, for which Lord's had a special supply. Neither happened on this occasion. Malcolm returned to the England side for the first time in a year, took four for 70 in the first innings at Lord's and Whittingdale's part in the entire exercise was not given any acknowledgement in the masses of publicity that greeted Malcolm's return. There were other instances of Lord's failing to inform the sponsor of specialists being brought in, but this was the most serious because it was only likely to happen to someone of Malcolm's high profile a few times during the sponsorship and those occasions had to be maximised.

Another problem was Geoff Boycott. Now that England had official coaching sponsors, obviously there could not be unofficial ones. Boycott was used to wandering around in the nets and advising players. Early attempts to make him part of the scheme proved fruitless. Boycott, who had always claimed that he was keen to help, wanted more money than any of the other coaches and even contacted Whittingdale to see if he could strike a deal with the company directly. As with Lillee and Gavaskar, Whittingdale had no problem with the idea of paying Boycott more if he was the best, but the TCCB insisted that all coaches had to be paid the same rate. They would not accommodate Boycott. Once that had happened, the TCCB should have taken all reasonable steps to keep him out of the nets. Unfortunately, the Board were never too keen to address the situation and he continued to wander in and out as he had done in the past. Several years later, Ray Illingworth tried to involve Boycott as England's batting coach, but, again, the price was too high to pay.

Money was another problem. This was a pay-as-spend sponsorship, the sponsor wanting the bulk of the money to go to supporting and improving the senior England team, yet any contractual moves to guarantee this were seen by the TCCB as efforts by the sponsor to interfere in the running of the game. It took the Whittingdale office several weeks to put the invoices in order. The effort was worth it. When the original sponsorship launch was delayed, Whittingdale had been left with the cost of national newspaper advertisements which had been bought to coincide with the announcement. After some discussion, the TCCB agreed to compensate Whittingdale.

Despite all these problems, the company spent over a year and a six-figure-plus sum to its lawyers to try and resolve the matter and produce a new contract. But, as word of the difficulties spread through the cricket world, it was announced that the company had a hidden agenda for the dispute. Whittingdale Fund Managers were in financial trouble, it was suggested, and this disagreement was a way for the company to get out of the contract with the TCCB. The facts did not bear this out. If that had in fact been the case, why spend all that extra money on lawyers? If the sponsor wanted out, it seems there were enough breaches to justify walking away and seeking compensation.

The 1993 summer did remind Patrick Whittingdale of the real reason for this sponsorship. Allan Border's Australians, the tourists, were the proud possessors of the Ashes and back in England. In the sponsor's eyes at least, the Plan had been devised and designed to help get them back. The problems with the Board had not been resolved, yet the sponsor came up with a new initiative that it hoped would help the players focus on the contest ahead. The proposal was that the Whittingdale Cricket Plan would include an incentive scheme for the players. Every Test win and series victory would see the players rewarded with units in one of the Whittingdale investments. No-one would be able to retire on the proceeds, the amounts proposed would be in the hundreds, but it was hoped that successful players could build up a small fund during the course of the sponsorship. The intention was to reward success and link the players with one of the Board's official sponsors. In addition, each player would be offered a luxury weekend for two on Concorde/The Orient Express if the Ashes were regained, to be used on an individual basis over the next year.

In order not to upset the delicate re-negotiations over the sponsorship contract, Whittingdale's incentive scheme would not come out of the current sponsorship, but be an extra cost to the company. Despite the problems with the Board, the company was not prepared for the negative attitude of the TCCB, basically because the new contract that was being formulated at the time included the principle of such an incentive scheme. But this scheme, known as the Whittingdale Cricket Challenge, was turned down by the England committee, who felt it would cut across event sponsors like Texaco and Cornhill. The committee found it difficult to understand why the question of the bonus scheme should be agreed before fundamental points in the new draft contracts had been resolved. The answer was the Aussies were about to arrive in England. In some ways the bonus scheme was unimportant. But its rejection gave Whittingdale the clearest indication that there was still very little 'goodwill' in the TCCB's attitude towards the sponsorship. A conciliatory gesture from Lord's at that stage would have gone a long way to showing there was a way forward with the sponsorship.

The matter was eventually resolved. There was no champagne popping. It was not just an end to the warring, but an end to the Whittingdale dream. A year later Ray Illingworth banged in the final nail.

For all the disappointments with the TCCB, Patrick maintains that he enjoyed his time in cricket and values the friendship he made with players, journalists and other sponsors. His Celebrity Lunch with Viv Richards at The Oval in 1991, his trip to India with Gooch's mum and dad, Alf and Rose, his Leukaemia Walk and many afternoons in his Oval Box with the likes of Gavin Hastings, Will Carling and Gary Lineker are just some of his favourite memories. But it was sad to see someone beaten by the English cricket establishment through no fault of his own.

I have no doubt that the England Test team is still paying the price for the failure of the Whittingdale sponsorship. The loss of the Ashes at Trent Bridge in August, for a fifth consecutive time, was a disappointing reminder of what might have been.

TWENTY
LIAM'S CHOICE

'Regarding Liam's decision, and looking back over my career ...
I have to say that, given the same choice now that I had to make then
I would not hesitate in choosing a career in football.'

T HE first significant cricket of the 1997 season in England was the four-day match at Edgbaston between England A and The Rest starting on Friday 18 April. Not that you would have known it by being there.

The young talent on show should have made this a showpiece occasion. Plenty had been written and read about the performances of the young stars of the England A team tour to Australia during the winter of 1996-97; Mark Butcher, the Surrey left-handed opening batsman many believed was next in line to replace Nick Knight of Warwickshire as Mike Atherton's opening partner in the senior side, his county colleague Adam Holioake, the all-rounder and A-team captain who had made his England debut in the Texaco Trophy series against Pakistan at the end of the 1996 summer season and had been mentioned as a possible replacement for Atherton had the latter not dragged his way out of the doldrums in New Zealand, and Dean Headley, the Kent paceman who had been knocking on the door for Test selection for some time. Son of Ron Headley and grandson of 'the black Bradman' George, who had both played Test cricket for the West Indies, Dean was in line to become the first third-generation Test cricketer in history.

Here was a chance for them to demonstrate how much real progress they had made down under to the new England selection panel of David Graveney, Mike Gatting and Graham Gooch, plus coach David Lloyd and captain Mike Atherton, and an opportunity for the cricket public to view at first hand the emerging stars of the English game.

Extra spice was added to the pot with the inclusion of Ben Hollioake, Adam's younger brother, who, according to sources at The Oval, possessed an even greater talent than his sibling. And those who have been longing for a new young pace star to fill one of the most obvious gaps in English cricket since the retirement of Bob Willis would have been eager for the chance to observe the 19-year-old Surrey quickie Alex Tudor in action.

The star attraction in The Rest XI was their captain Mark Ramprakash, the highly-gifted Middlesex batsman. Although thus far unsuccessful at Test level, Ramprakash, the one member of the 'bat-pack' of Graham Thorpe, Nasser Hussain and himself to have failed to take his chance at Test level, was desperate to prove a point after having been unceremoniously dumped from the England reckoning by Raymond Illingworth following the senior tour to South Africa in the winter of 1995-96.

Even though the sun refused to be fooled by the flannels into coming out to play, all in all the fare on offer should have been tempting enough to attract a reasonable crowd, particularly for the Saturday play.

In the event the paying spectators on all four days were heavily outnumbered by those players, officials, stewards, groundstaff and media who had been paid to be there. Official figures from the Warwickshire club reveal that the total paying attendance for the four-day match was around 1,000, the total gate receipts being £3,112.

Meanwhile, on the Saturday when three men and a dog turned up at Edgbaston to watch the brightest young cricketing talent in the country, the England Under-15 schoolboy soccer XI was taking on France Under-15 at Old Trafford, home of Manchester United. The attendance for that event? According to the English Schools Football Association, 35,000-plus, more than some county clubs attract for championship cricket during an entire season.

The example I have highlighted here is, of course, put in the shade when you consider that the average home gate attracted to the rebuilt Old Trafford football ground for one single Premiership match far outstrips the total season's championship attendance figures for almost all of the 19 first-class counties. Warwickshire, one of the more progressive counties, did throw open their gates on the Sunday, attracting some 3-4,000 for their annual Open Day, but the difference in those figures remains a clear indicator of the huge gap in popularity between soccer and cricket in this country.

As any state school teacher will tell you when the kids make for the playground it is to emulate Shearer, not Stewart, Anderton not Atherton. Ask a cross-section of sports-mad youngsters these days and they are far more likely to be able to identify the Liverpool back four (or Man Utd's, Arsenal's, Tottenham's, even Coventry's) than the England top six.

And soccer stadia aren't the only theatres of sporting dreams to be the focus of the hopes and aspirations of the next generation of British athletes. To them, rugby union, and in some areas rugby league, athletics, tennis and golf enjoy at least an equally high profile as cricket, while the emerging sports such as ice hockey and basketball are marketing themselves into the youth culture and consciousness at a rapid rate.

All of which means that the sad fact facing those who run English cricket in 1997 is that, given the choice of sports to take up as a profession, or even a hobby, the vast majority of eligible young talent will put cricket way down the list of preferred options.

I spoke to Malcolm Berry, chief executive of the English Schools Football Association, for his views. 'Cricket is simply not being played or taught in our state schools as it ought to be. There was a time, not all that long ago when cricket and football shared the attention of pupils. It was football in winter and cricket in summer, both in the school playground, on the playing field and later, back home in the parks afterwards.

'But for too long the majority of schools have not had the resources either in manpower, time or equipment to give their pupils the opportunity to discover what cricket actually is, let alone play it. All you need for a football match is a ball and kids who want to play.

'There was a feeling that the local clubs should take responsibility for teaching cricket to kids. They do their best, but there is a limit to what they can achieve on a national basis. The lack of cricket in schools means that not only are there fewer youngsters playing the game than ever before, fewer are finding out what the game is all about. Is it any wonder, then, that so few go to watch?'

Berry continues: 'When it comes to actively encouraging support among schoolchildren we make sure we give ourselves the best chance. Every season we stage an Under-15 schoolboy international at Wembley and one also at Old Trafford. Through our network of affiliated local schoolboy associations we ensure that the crowds for those two match regularly top 35,000. Not only does that make the schoolboys feel they are part of something worth striving for, on a more basic level it provides much needed revenue for the ESFA, which, apart from a small grant from the

Football Association, is almost entirely self-funding.' Such a thorough approach to grabbing the attention of youngsters in other sports as well as soccer is only one of the reasons why the most naturally gifted ball-players in this country are being lost to the game of cricket. First and foremost, of course, and as I know from first hand experience, the financial incentives on offer from cricket's rivals mean that more often than not there is really no choice to make.

But there is more to this than mere cash. My son Liam recently made the decision to turn his back on a career in cricket in favour of rugby union. Although I never put the slightest ounce of pressure on him either way, I have to say I believe his decision was without question the right one. In fact, I go so far as to say it was the *only* one.

Throughout his childhood Liam was cricket-mad, and highly talented to boot. What is more he achieved what he did in the game, at national representative level, despite being saddled with the burden of his father's name. I never told him in so many words but his performances and his progress thrilled me to bits. And what delighted me most of all was that he reached the top at his age level despite all the snide cynicism of those critics of mine who were all too eager to shoot him down simply because of his surname. In my book that demonstrated that not only did he have the talent to prosper at whatever sport he chose, he also had the determination, application and desire to do so whatever obstacles may be put in his way.

There was no doubt in my mind that Liam possessed the ability with bat and ball to go a long way in cricket and when he made his first-class debut for Hampshire towards the end of the 1996 season, he produced a performance to confound the doubters. Two days after his 19th birthday, on 28 August, after the Hampshire captain John Stephenson had been forced to withdraw through injury, Liam was pulled out of a second team match against Middlesex at Southampton and rushed to Portsmouth to take his place with the seniors.

The match had already started when he arrived to take the field, thus becoming, contrary to popular opinion, the first cricketer named Botham to turn up late for a county match. He had to bide his time before being given his cue, but when he did, he quickly moved straight to centre stage. Coming on to bowl as second change, he took a wicket with his seventh delivery, dismissing Mike Gatting, something I myself had never managed in sixteen years of trying.

Liam went on to finish with five for 67 in his debut first-class bowl and, when he telephoned me that evening to talk through the day's events I could hear the excitement and pride in his voice. I made sure the reverse did not apply!

Not that I needed any convincing, but his obvious delight at what he had achieved was clear evidence to me of what cricket meant to him. When, within only a couple of months of that match against Middlesex at Portsmouth he announced his decision to concentrate on rugby union by taking up the offer of a contract with West Hartlepool, I knew just how much he was giving up.

It was a tough choice and when we discussed the options it was clear to me that he had not taken it lightly. Now he sums up his position like this: 'It had never really entered my head until quite late in the day that I might have a career in rugby. All through my schooldays cricket was the number one sport for me.

'Obviously I knew all about what my old man had achieved but there was no way I was going to be put off. I was not the slightest bit intimidated by having to follow in dad's footsteps. I was good at cricket. I loved playing it and I was determined to make my own way in the game. The day Hampshire decided to offer me a playing contract was one of the proudest in my life.

'But, while I was still at Rossall school and progressing through England representative sides, it gradually dawned on me that there might be a choice to make.

'As time went on I was happy enough with how things were progressing with Hampshire, and my first-team debut was encouraging, but I had to look at the wider picture.

'West Hartlepool had been interested in offering me a contract to play full-time rugby for some months. Although there was much talk of what was on offer financially from rugby compared to cricket and that obviously came into my thinking, the decision was based as much on how the two games were perceived at national level. I asked myself one simple question: where do you see the two sports in ten years time?

'All through 1996 I had seen the high profile that the national rugby XV was enjoying and at the same time watched while England's cricketers were getting it in the neck from all and sundry. The avalanche of criticism aimed at English cricket after the World Cup in India and Pakistan meant that the whole future of the game in this country as a major international sport seemed to be precarious.

'It's impossible to look into a crystal ball, but I just had the feeling that of the two sports, rugby had the greater potential for development.

'People said that mum and dad were delighted at my decision because it meant I wouldn't have to carry dad's name on my shoulders, but I don't think that ever really came into my thinking. The prospect would certainly not have put me off cricket had all the other factors been in favour. Rugby just felt right. Cricket just felt wrong.'

During the period that Liam was making up his mind I chewed over the decision I had had to make twenty-odd years earlier. At the same time as I was making progress in cricket, a career in soccer was also a very real possibility.

Bert Head, the manager at Crystal Palace, had already offered me a contract with the club and a handful of others were also interested. Had one of them been Chelsea, the team I had supported since before the King's Road days of Peter Osgood, Alan Hudson, Charlie Cooke and Ian Hutchinson, my life might have taken an altogether different turn. In those days it really was as simple as deciding which was your 'favourite' sport. Although you could earn more money in football than cricket the difference was no so great as to rule out cricket on financial grounds. Indeed, until relatively recently it wasn't actually necessary to choose between football and cricket at all. Before the mid-1980s there were several instances of guys playing both sports professionally, perhaps the last of their kind being Phil Neale, my former Worcestershire colleague, Chris Balderstone, who played cricket for England and, briefly, football for Carlisle United, and Arnie Sidebottom of Yorkshire and England. Denis Compton was perhaps the most famous example of the post-Second World War generation of footballing cricketers. Apart from being one of the greatest batsmen of all time, he was a more-than-useful winger for Arsenal, with whom his career culminated with an FA Cup winners' medal in 1950.

In my case, the choice was more or less a straight one concerning which game I enjoyed more and which I felt I was better at. According to those criteria, cricket came first. I threw in my lot with Somerset and never regretted the decision for a single moment. But, looking back over my career and knowing what I was able to achieve in the game of cricket thanks to my god-given talent, I have to say that, given the same choice now that I had to make then I would not hesitate in choosing a career in football.

That may sound bizarre considering all the highlights I was lucky enough to experience at club and international level. Don't get me wrong. I had a wonderful life in cricket. The game took me to places I would never have seen and allowed me to meet people I would never have known. My experiences in the game have given me the kind of memories others only dream about. I'm grateful for everything the game enabled me to do and apart from a couple of rocky years in the mid 80s, I wouldn't have missed any of it for the world. But the plain fact is that, these days the picture is very different. Unless you have what used to be called a 'private income', professional sportsmen do what they do for a living and they owe it to themselves and their families to support them as best they can.

I am not, by nature, a greedy person, indeed some have said that over the years a tendency to be over-generous has worked against me.

Nor am I pleading poverty. The game has been good to me financially and although there is clearly no comparison between what I earned in an international career spanning two decades and the amounts of money being collected by the top stars in soccer, golf or tennis, for example, I have no complaints on a personal level.

It is merely that if you were to give any teenage sportsman the choice between a career in soccer and a career in cricket these days, the difference in what is on offer is now so vast that there is only going to be one winner.

Take the example of Phil Neville, the Manchester United and England defender. Both Phil and his brother Gary were excellent schoolboy cricketers. Their father, now the commercial manager at Bury FC was renowned as a big-hitter for Greenmount CC and held the record for the fastest century in the Bolton League. Phil's twin sister Tracy played netball for England. And those observers who watched Phil at close range during his formative years were convinced that he was a special talent, with the ability and temperament to go right to the top.

The story of Phil and Gary's first sporting experience was the classic tale of the sons of a cricketer playing on club outfields from the close of play until pitch darkness. Both were noted as good soccer players, but both were mad keen on cricket as well.

John Heaton, Headmaster of Hayward's School in Bolton and secretary of the Lancashire Youth Cricket Executive Committee, remembers both youngsters well. He recalls: 'Gary was an excellent cricketer in his own right but Phil was the one who stood out. He appeared to possess everything required to make the grade right from an early age.

'He first came into the Lancashire schools reckoning at primary level, at the age of eleven. In 1988 he scored 621 runs in 13 innings at an average of 62.1, including the first ever century at primary school level, 117 not out.

'In the next season, in the Under-13 section he made 262 runs, then in 1990 he made 841, making a grand total of 1103 in two years of Under-13 cricket, breaking the existing record held by John Crawley. At the English Schools Cricket Association Under-14 festival in Taunton that year, he broke another record set by Crawley, the highest ever score by a Lancashire schoolboy. John's record stood at 167. Aged thirteen, Phil made 193 not out against Nottinghamshire schools, in forty-four overs.

'It was at this point that the clash with soccer first became obvious. During the Under-14 year he played for England Schools at cricket and football, but next season he played very little cricket. On 30 June 1992 he played an innings for Lancashire schools against Yorkshire schools at Burnley that is still talked about by those who saw it. The wicket was damp and the opposition included Liam Botham and Alex Morris. Phil was captain and played a captain's innings. He fought his way through the early difficulties, then, as the pitch eased and the bowlers tired, he cashed in, making 125 out of 190-odd. It was his last innings in representative cricket. From then on football, and more specifically, Manchester United took over his life. Cricket simply couldn't compete.'

Heaton has no doubts: 'Phil had it all. He was playing first team cricket for Greenmount in the Bolton League at fourteen. That year the club professional was Mark Taylor, the Australian captain, and they won the League. There are no places in that League for passengers. Top Aussie players like Jamie Siddons and Matthew Hayden, as well as Taylor, are a common sight. But Phil had the whole range of shots, was equally good in defence or attack and always appeared to have loads of time.

'Did it frustrate me that he was lost to cricket because Manchester United had him under lock and key? Not really. When a lad is that talented you have to say good luck and on you go. He's made it to the very top in football and many people are convinced he would have done the same in cricket. But no matter how much Lancashire might say they want you, when Manchester United come knocking on your door, you don't turn them away.

'I don't find that frustrating. But I'd love to have been able to see just what Phil would have achieved had he chosen cricket. Looking back over the years at all the top cricketers who have come through the Lancashire schools system, I'd have to put him up there at the top, alongside Mike Atherton, John Crawley and Frank Hayes. Let's just say I would have been extremely surprised had Phil not gone on to make it at the highest level.'

Although Heaton is realistic about the prospects of cricket managing to hold onto the cream of the crop should football clubs target them seriously he does believe cricket could do more to help itself.

He explains: 'County cricket clubs are just not as proactive as football clubs. Clearly Manchester United have more money at their disposal than Lancashire, for instance, but young cricketers who need financial support and help are just not as well looked after by county clubs. In most cases young players are just left to fend for themselves.

'Quite apart from the price of kit, it costs a lot for parents to ferry their kids about from match to match, taking them all over the country for schools events and the like. Yet at that level there is almost no contact with the county club whatsoever. And there is very little structure for feeding talented kids into the county system. Quite often it's just a case of a county club hit by injuries or unavailability ringing up a lad or his school and saying, "Can you get here to play for the seconds this afternoon?"

'And sometimes counties will sign a player they have no real intention of trying to develop into a first-teamer just to avoid the embarrassment of him going off and making a name for himself with another county. Then those in the middle are just left to drift along.

'At United the approach is far more thorough. Phil Neville, for example would have been spotted playing football at primary level, United would have had the scouts out watching and at around the age of thirteen he would have been enrolled in the Manchester Schools development of excellence scheme. As such he would have been invited on regular weekly trips to Old Trafford and at around fifteen he would be assessed and a decision taken as to whether to offer him a contract. Once signed, the lad will have the best of everything available to him, in terms of diet, fitness training, facilities, sports science, the lot.

'As far as cricket is concerned, the system is far more haphazard. A talented young cricketer will come under intense pressure to play for all sorts of sides: his club, his Town schools side, the local League representative XI, the county schools XI. During the summer months a lad could play cricket every day of the week, sometimes twice in the same day. There is no overall strategy for the development of young players, no agency to say that a kid should play this much cricket and for whom. And then people wonder why any talent coming through is knackered by the age of twenty.'

In other words, whereas football clubs view their young players as priceless assets to be protected at all costs and do everything they can to make sure talent blossoms to its full potential, once a young player signs for a county club quite often he is left more or less to his own devices. I know from experience that the majority of cricket played at second XI level is a joke. The pitches are too often substandard, the level of coaching almost non-existent and the teams stuffed full of players who will never make the grade who have to turn out merely because they are employed to do so by their counties until their contracts expire. How appetising a prospect is that for young players thinking about a career in the game?

In football the players' well-being is paramount. Not only is the pay better, but the working conditions bear no resemblance. For years cricketers were contractually bound for instance as regards what work they could and couldn't do during the winter months.

Realistically, of course, cricket will never be able to compete with top football clubs on a purely financial basis. What the game must endeavour to do is make a career in cricket as attractive as it can possibly be. The old saying that 'if you pay peanuts, you get monkeys' may be harsh when applied to cricket, but when you look around at some of those earning a living in the county game with no ambition and no hope of further progress, perhaps it's not that harsh.

TWENTY ONE

PILLS AND ILLS: THE BURN OUT FACTOR

'I have witnessed at first hand the effects of burn out on a player around whom England would have hoped to build their side for years to come...'

WHEN Angus Fraser arrived at Edgbaston to report for England duty prior to the third Test of the 1995 summer series against West Indies, he made a bee-line for the physiotherapist's room. As he got there, he promptly collapsed on the treatment table in a heap.

'Which bit hurts?' enquired Dave Roberts, the England team physio.

'All of it,' confirmed Fraser. 'Start at the bottom, work your way up to the top and, unless you hear from me, don't stop.

'On second thoughts, just fetch me a new body.'

Thanks to Fraser and the debutant Dominic Cork, England had just levelled the series by winning the second Test at Lord's. Now, two days before the vital third Test, the man who was due to spearhead England's bowling attack was, to all intents and purposes, a physical wreck.

How he had got into that state tells you all you need to know to understand the phenomenon of burn out, and why the condition which is affecting Test players from all over the world has been particularly acute in our international cricketers.

In happier circumstances, the England team that achieved the 72-run win over West Indies at headquarters might have expected to celebrate in style. A few beers (or more) and fierce rejoicing should have been the order of the day, as much to enable the players to unwind and release the stress and excitement of the occasion as anything else, and an opportunity for team spirit to be fostered in a positive psychological environment.

In Australia, South Africa, West Indies, New Zealand and Zimbabwe, not to mention India and Sri Lanka, it would have been a case of 'Thick heads and lie-ins all round' and plenty of time to rest, recover and prepare for the next Test match.

But this was English cricket in 1995 and this is how Fraser's itinerary unfolded.

Almost immediately after the Lord's post-match formalities had been completed Fraser travelled the four-and-a-half hours south-west to St Austell to meet up with his Middlesex team-mates for their NatWest Trophy first round match against Cornwall the very next morning.

You might have thought that mighty Middlesex possessed more than enough talent to polish off minor county opposition without Fraser for once. Roberts certainly did and urged the player to try and persuade his county to allow him to take the match off. Of course, Fraser being Fraser, the thought never entered his head and county clubs being county clubs, it never occurred to Middlesex either.

When Fraser arrived at the team's hotel at around midnight he made straight for his room to sleep. Fat chance. The air-conditioning did not work, the windows were minute. The room was like a sauna. After having failed to get to sleep on the bed, which was uncomfortably soft and barely long enough to house his 6ft 4in frame, Fraser tried the floor. At around 3 am he gave up completely.

Less than eight sleepless hours later, Middlesex won the toss and decided to bat. Fraser hit the last ball of the innings for six in a total of 304 and when Cornwall replied, he took two wickets for three runs in five overs, before retiring to the boundary for the remainder of an inevitably one-sided contest won by Middlesex by 104 runs. Fraser travelled back to his North London home that night, arriving around 1 am.

Middlesex had employed Fraser to bowl 30 deliveries. In order to do so he had travelled more than 400 miles.

Wednesday was a day off. But on Thursday he reported to Lord's at 9 am for Middlesex's four-day championship match with Surrey. After helping bowl out Surrey twice in his side's three-day victory by an innings and 76 runs, he went out the following day to take part in their Sunday League match and finished with two for 23 from his full complement of eight overs.

The next day Fraser drove to Birmingham to check in with Mike Atherton's Test squad and to order his new body from the England physio.

Roberts told me: 'When Angus came into my room he was absolutely physically and mentally exhausted. He was stiff, sore and shattered. Then when he played in the match and bowled slightly below par on a helpful pitch, critics inside and outside the camp moaned that he looked jaded. "Gus doesn't look the bowler he was," they said.

'The fact is that when he arrived at Edgbaston he could hardly walk.'

Just for fun, minutes after England lost the Test match just before lunch on the third day, Fraser received a phone call from Middlesex asking him to drive to Bristol to play in their Sunday League slog against Gloucestershire the next day, which he duly did.

The most alarming aspect of the tale is that this kind of schedule has been the norm rather than the exception for as long as anyone can remember and still is to this day.

And from the point of view of giving England international cricketers the best chance to succeed at the highest level, it is, quite simply, madness. People ask: 'Why do our bowlers keep breaking down?' The answer is that they have been treated little better than slaves, to be used, abused and discarded.

Roberts found the same level of non-cooperation from a county club over Darren Gough during the Yorkshireman's first season in international cricket.

Gough had created a dynamic impression on his senior England debut, in the Texaco Trophy match against New Zealand at Edgbaston, removing both Kiwi openers, including Martin Crowe, then one of the best batsmen in world cricket, caught behind by Alec Stewart for a duck. Striving too hard for pace and fuelled by the adrenalin of the occasion, Gough strained a rib muscle during the game and, although the selectors were keen to include him in the team for the Test series, it was clear that he was struggling.

Gough missed the first Test at Trent Bridge, but prior to the second at Lord's Ray Illingworth and Keith Fletcher, the chairman of selectors and coach respectively, asked Roberts to travel to Bradford, where Yorkshire were playing Somerset, to check on his fitness.

Roberts duly made the journey and had just started discussing the matter in hand with Gough and Wayne Morton, the Yorkshire physio who was later to succeed Roberts in the England job, when he was summoned to see Steve Oldham, Yorkshire's director of cricket, and given a huge dressing-down for what Oldham called 'interfering with their player's welfare.'

'All I wanted to do was see Gough face-to-face rather than talk to him on the phone and ask him how he felt he was progressing,' Roberts explains. 'There was no question of interference or me trying to supervise his recovery programme. I was going along to show that, as he'd injured himself playing for England, England were interested in his well-being.

'I couldn't believe what happened. Oldham sat me down and bawled me out. He told me that Illingworth was a tosser, Fletcher didn't know his arse from his elbow and that I shouldn't even have set foot in the ground.

'On my way out, Martyn Moxon, the club captain took me to one side and apologised for what had happened. He told me that Morton, Gough and he were really embarrassed by the club's over-protective attitude. But when Fletcher asked me how Darren was I had to tell him I didn't know because the club hadn't allowed me to see him.'

The selectors had no option but to leave Gough out of the squad and the headline in the *Yorkshire Post* the day after it was announced was: 'GOUGH IGNORED BY ENGLAND.'

A year later the trouble between England and Yorkshire over Gough escalated even further. Gough had broken down on the England tour to Australia in the winter of 1994-95 with a foot injury and had been forced to return home. He played in the first three Tests of the summer series against West Indies but it was obvious to Roberts that his seriously inflamed left foot was still causing him problems.

He was picked for the squad for the fourth Test at Old Trafford, but left out of the final XI. The selectors publicly insisted that this was a tactical move to allow them to play two spinners, Mike Watkinson and John Emburey, on a pitch they fully expected to turn, while supplementing their seam attack of Fraser and Cork with all-rounder Craig White. In actual fact however, they had decided that Gough's foot could not be risked.

Their plan was that he should return to his county to rest, receive treatment and get himself fit and ready for selection for the winter tour to South Africa. They were surprised and not a little miffed, however, when Gough turned out for Yorkshire in their very next match, a NatWest quarter-final against Lancashire at Headingley. Ironically, Gough's single victim was the England captain Mike Atherton. The club had insisted that, no matter what the England management thought, Gough was fit for one-day cricket and went against the express wishes and interests of the national selectors in picking him.

Roberts was appointed England's physiotherapist to succeed Laurie Brown for the 1993 senior tour to India. Prior to that he had worked with the Zimbabwean national side and then Worcestershire, where his charges included Graham Dilley and perhaps his worst patient, me. From Worcestershire he graduated to the top position via England A.

He has no doubts over the causes for our inability to produce top quality pace bowlers at the highest level and keep them there for more than half an hour.

As he says: 'No one is expecting our players to be mollycoddled and it is quite clear that to reach the top you have to be extremely physically fit. But the fact is that, as a pace bowler, if you play the amount of cricket our international players do, both domestically and with England, and you undergo the amount of travelling, both home and abroad that is required in Test and county cricket here and on tour, I don't care how fit you are, you are going to be physically and mentally knackered most of the time.

'Patch up and mend was the norm when I worked with Worcestershire and England and although I never knowingly passed fit a player who was unfit to play, I've lost count of the number of times I've told a captain that so-and-so was "fit, but only just."

'To my mind, the success of the national side should override all other concerns. Yet the demands made on our top international bowlers by their county clubs mean that, from time to time, almost all of them have been operating in Test matches with their bootlaces tied together – and that's when they've had the energy left to drag themselves onto the field.

'The county clubs obviously want their best players to give them their best. They do, after all, pay their wages. But what they have failed to grasp is that, through national sponsorship, Test match receipts and television revenue, the England team pays their bills.

'I used to find it bloody farcical that the selectors would pick their squad on the Saturday night before a Test match starting on a Thursday, announce it, then spend all day Sunday panicking in case one of the players broke down in the 40-over slog.

'I would sit next to the phone all day Sunday with my heart in my mouth, waiting for the call to come from Micky Stewart, Keith Fletcher or later Ray Illingworth and then, on Monday morning, the players would all take the field again to finish off their championship matches. Absolutely crazy.

'Compare that to the procedure followed by the England football team prior to international matches, when the entire Premiership programme on the Saturday before a midweek match is cancelled. In the week before a Test match our cricketers play the equivalent of a five-day match – a four-day championship game with a 40-over throw-yourself-all-over-the-place Sunday match in the middle.'

I have witnessed at first hand the effects of burn out on a player around whom England would have hoped to build their side for years to come, Dominic Cork.

When he first came onto the international scene it was clear that he possessed a special talent. Seven wickets to win a Test match against West Indies on his debut, a hat-trick against them in his third appearance and 50 Test wickets within his first year of bowling for England.

Yet a year later not only was he not fit enough for the Texaco Trophy series against Australia but real doubts had been expressed over his future at the highest level. Clearly Dominic has had personal problems to deal with including the break-up of his marriage, as well as loss of form and fitness, and he has suffered from carrying around a huge burden of expectation.

All theses factors have contributed to his problems, yet to me the biggest single factor in his demise (temporary, I hope) has been burn out, pure and simple.

If ever a player was ripe for special treatment through being contracted to the national board rather than his county club Derbyshire, Cork is the one. I understand that Derbyshire have been as helpful as they feel they could have been, but the fact is that when you find a talent like Cork, the first and overriding priority should be to do everything possible to ensure you've got him for a long time.

Look at the example of Glenn McGrath of Australia, who has played more Test matches than he has state games. He regards himself, and is regarded by his country and his state, as a Test player first and foremost. And, as a result of doing the things necessary to maintain and improve fitness and technique over a period of time, without the unnecessary strains and workload of a crowded domestic programme, when he arrived in England at the start of the 1997 summer Ashes series he was rightly judged second only to Curtly Ambrose in the Coopers & Lybrand world rankings.

You had to look as far down the list as 16th position to find England's highest ranked bowler, Darren Gough, and down to 17th to see where Dominic Cork had landed, and their relative standings are no coincidence.

Right from the outset of his career in county cricket and more especially later when he won selection for the England A squad it was clear that

Cork's frame was never going to be able to withstand the workload he was bound to be confronted with. He had the priceless ability of bowling outswing at a reasonable pace, but his body did not seem equipped for a pace bowler's career.

Dave Roberts, then the A team physio, and many others who saw how much strain his knees were being put under were convinced that Cork required leg-muscle strengthening. But it was not until well into the time that he was making waves for England that anything was actually done about it. Instead he was subjected to the same old county grind that meant that by the time he began to do some serious training, his mind and body were knackered.

I'm not talking about wrapping players up in cotton wool, but if England had had the kind of access to Cork throughout his development that Australia have enjoyed with McGrath there is no doubt that many of his problems would have been avoided. Instead of No.22 he might even have been challenging McGrath and Ambrose at the top of the world rankings.

Yet what has happened again is that a promising young fast bowler has seemingly had the talent and the fire squeezed out of him by the county system.

Towards the end of the 1996-97 winter trip to New Zealand, Cork, having missed the first leg of the trip to Zimbabwe was struggling at all levels. His form had slipped to the point where he was just trying too hard to take a wicket with every ball. Far from letting the publicity over his talent go to his head and becoming complacent, as some would have had you believe, he was genuinely distressed at his failure to rediscover the form that he had shown during his spectacular entry to the world stage.

All you read in the newspapers, however, was criticism not only for his poor performances but for the fact that, in their opinion, he had just became arrogant and too big for his boots. When will we ever learn?

During his period as England physio, Roberts was particularly concerned with the workload inflicted on England players on tour. Time and again his tour reports to the Test and County Cricket Board urged the powers-that-be to take action over the physical and mental demands being placed on England's players overseas.

And, of course, it is not only the bowlers who suffer. I saw at first hand the kind of physical and mental toll taken on England players by the incredible workload they have to put up with when I travelled with them throughout the 1995-96 winter tour to South Africa before their ill-fated World Cup expedition in Pakistan and India.

For Michael Atherton, the captain, the story had begun in January 1994. For, following the long Autumn break at the end of the 1993 home Ashes series, Atherton's departure to the Caribbean was the start of a 26-month period in which he spent the best part of a year on tour in West Indies, Australia, South Africa, India and Pakistan (for the 1996 World Cup). During that time he played in 27 Test matches and 32 one-day internationals, not to mention two full six-month summer domestic seasons with Lancashire.

The full 26-month sequence reads:

Jan 1994-April 1994: West Indies v England (five Tests and five one-day internationals, plus several warm-up matches)

April 1994-September 1994: England v New Zealand (three Tests and two ODIs); England v South Africa (three Tests and two ODIs) plus full season for Lancashire

October 1994-February 1995: Australia v England (five Tests and six World Series Cricket ODIs, plus several warm-up matches)

April 1995-September 1995: England v West Indies (six Tests and three ODIs) plus full season for Lancashire

October 1995-January 1996: S Africa v England (five Tests and seven ODIs)

February 1996-March 1996: World Cup (six ODIs).

Such a gruelling workload and the almost non-stop travelling that went with it is simply absurd. And because England are the only Northern Hemisphere country playing Test cricket in our summer year after year, we are the country whose players face the 12-month season, season after season.

You only had to look at the faces of the players as the 1995-96 Test series with South Africa reached its climax to see the effects.

Atherton's innings of 185 not out to save the second Test in Johannesburg was a monumental effort of will, determination and concentration, but as time passed you could tell that it had drained him of almost all of his remaining reserves.

He made two in his only innings in the next Test in Durban and although he produced one final great effort to make 72 and 34 in Port Elizabeth, by the time the team reached Capetown for the final and what turned out to be deciding Test, his tank was empty. He made 0 and 10 at Newlands as England collapsed twice to defeat.

No wonder he went ballistic when, while he was out on the field for the post-match presentations, he heard over the tannoy that Ray Illingworth had arranged a day-night knockabout against a Western Province XI for two days hence.

Displaying just how tough he really is, Atherton helped win the second of seven one-day internationals with a well-paced 85. But that apart his batting fell to bits. In the World Cup his only score of any note was 66 in the final qualifying match with Pakistan.

On that final leg of the South African programme I looked into the eyes of some of our players and saw emptiness. When they performed so inadequately in the World Cup they were hammered but on reflection it amazes me that they even had the strength and stamina left to beat Holland and the United Arab Emirates.

Five months on the road during an English county season is just as arduous. During one season with Worcestershire I remember once being away from home playing and travelling for 27 out of 29 days.

Throughout the last ten years of my career I was extremely fortunate to have someone to do the driving for me. I took the decision that I was never going to last if I didn't employ someone to get me from place to place and I honestly believe I prolonged my professional career for a couple of years at least by doing so.

But how many others were in the same position? I heard some quite scary stories in various dressing rooms about players who had nodded off at the wheel, travelling late at night from one county ground to another. And when you eventually arrived at your destination, more often than not it was too late to get any decent food inside you. You would check in to your hotel late and it would be a case of grabbing a sandwich or nipping down to a fast-foot joint to get what you could. You don't often see soccer star Ravanelli at the bloody service station taking the wrapping off a pork pie or nipping into the nearest KFC, but that is the life of many of our top cricketers. As for the driving most of the guys know the road systems of Britain better than the RAC.

The constant travelling, packing and checking in and out of hotels becomes a routine, but unfortunately so does the cricket. It's physically and psychologically impossible to keep the freshness you require and that is when burn out takes its toll.

Quite apart from the physical and mental demands on the players themselves, the strain on domestic life can become intolerable. In fact, for county cricketers and their wives and children there simply is no such thing as normal family life. Divorce rates among first-class cricketers are constantly high, for the wife of a county cricketer must have the patience of a saint and the stamina of a Grand National winner. For a large part of their married life, the wives of cricketers are, to all intents and purposes operating as single parents.

Of course, people who feel cricketers moan too much about their lot will say that no-one forced them to take up the profession in the first place and will point to the improvement in players' wages in the recent past. That is all very well, but your body and mind suffer the same stresses and strains no matter how much you earn.

No player likes to be thought of as a moaner, someone who will pull up the ladder at the slightest hint of injury or even feign an ailment in order to take time off. But I have seen players so exhausted by the constant grind that they privately admit that an injury like a broken finger is a blessing in disguise. Spectators only see what state some of these guys are in when play starts at 11 am, after they have had the benefit of a couple of hours of treatment and warming-up exercises. They should see the carnage inside the dressing room when the players present themselves at 9 am. It is quite a different picture. For some, a few weeks off with a fracture was like being sent home from the front.

On the other hand some players are so desperate to play in case their place in the side comes under threat that they will go to disturbing lengths in order to mask injury, the most commonly-used device being anti-inflammatory drugs.

By the time I finished playing, in 1993, I estimate that 90 per cent of pace bowlers in county cricket were regular users of what the medics call non-steroidal anti-inflammatory drugs which, although effective in the short-term in disguising and lessening the symptoms of injury, were potentially extremely harmful in the long run. From my experience, the numbers have remained constant.

I speak from experience. For most of the last ten years of my career I dropped pain-killing anti-inflammatory drugs like they were Polo mints.

In simple terms inflammation, redness and swelling are nature's way of dealing with and healing muscle and joint injuries. Anti-steroidal inflammatory drugs, in the form of Brufen or Voltarol are used to dampen down the symptoms, reduce swelling and crucially, acting as painkillers, enable a player to play through an injury that would otherwise preclude him from doing so.

The amount of these being taken, often in the full knowledge of the county club's doctors is a joke – *in some cases three a day every day for the entire season.*

The most obvious problem is that by taking these pills players are going against the express demands of nature. If you feel pain or suffer swelling from an injury caused by playing sport, those symptoms are messages from the body telling you to stop in order to allow it to heal itself.

If you don't do so but choose instead to play on in spite of the body's advice, you are only going to make your condition worse. In the end you take more drugs to kill the pain and ease the swelling with the result that the injury never gets a proper chance to heal itself. But there are more sinister long-term side-effects as well; namely, damage to the stomach lining and potentially worst of all, the liver.

I recall the example of Graham Dilley, my fast bowling colleague for England and Worcestershire.

Dilley was a genuine pace merchant who had the priceless ability to swing the ball away, and on his day was among the most feared fast bowlers in world cricket. But his draggy action caused him many physical problems. At various times he suffered from back, neck, knee and Achilles tendon injuries, each one of which individually would have kept him off the field but the combination of all three meant it was a minor miracle that he could walk let alone bowl.

In fact, as his career progressed, in order to do so he relied more and more heavily on anti-inflammatory drugs. How much became evident when he underwent one of his many operations.

Prior to surgery Dilley was given a routine blood Test. When the doctors analysed the results they were shocked by what they saw. He was suffering from an abnormal liver function, the cause of which, the doctors established beyond doubt, was the high levels of anti-inflammatory drugs he had used over a number of years.

Yet players have become accustomed to treating these drugs as though they were sweets and I wonder how many of them actually paid attention to the long-term risks, or were even aware of them.

I've seen players in county and England dressing rooms so reliant on these drugs that the physical demands they are put through would be unbearable without them. So they drop the pills, sometimes as regularly as one in the morning when they arrive at the ground, one at lunchtime and one after play – over and over again, with scarcely a thought as to what long-term harm they might be doing.

Not only is that clearly dangerous for the players involved but that kind of common usage creates a dangerous environment for younger players, who, having seen one of their senior colleagues taking the drugs, automatically think this should be the accepted practice. It shouldn't be, of course. Sadly, it is.

The amount of anti-inflammatory drugs I took during my career would be inconceivable to the man in the street. They were rattling around inside me like coins in a spin-dryer. But for me and countless other bowlers they were just a fact of life.

There were various reasons why we took them, ranging from a player first coming into the side terrified that any impact he might have made would be overshadowed in his absence, through to established players seeking to maintain their position and, most obviously, to players up for selection for the Test side wanting to prove to the selectors that they were fit enough to play in the matches immediately preceding Test calls.

In the end I took them just to get on the field. During the early and mid-80s when I was struggling with back and shoulder injuries I would take them without thinking. I was lucky in that I had the ability to recover from injury fairly quickly. But there were times when only Brufen or Voltarol would do the trick. I was vaguely aware that taking large quantities of these drugs was potentially harmful but I just didn't think about the risks at the time. I simply reckoned I had no choice. Like so many other bowlers I was in the culture of taking these pills without a second thought and because there were no immediate side-effects I saw no reason not to. It was my career on the line as it was for everyone else who took the pills.

By the time I had become a regular user of these drugs I was fully aware of the side-effects. To deal with the acidity in my stomach I turned to Gaviscon in larger and larger doses. In the end I was drinking it like milk just to enable me to take the anti-inflammatory pills in the first place. And I didn't break out of that vicious circle until the day I packed it all in.

The highest-profile victim of this vicious circle is Mike Atherton, the England captain. Mike has struggled with a long-term back complaint for most of his career. During the 1991 Test series against West Indies, the condition became so serious that the doctors recommended surgery. Mike duly missed the 1991-92 winter tour to New Zealand and the World Cup and, after having the operation, spent weeks flat out in recovery. But the operation failed to cure the condition and since then only a strict regime of exercises and a constant diet of painkillers and anti-inflammatory drugs has kept him going. He himself reckons that if he is still playing Test cricket by the year 2000 he will have exceeded his own expectations but the main side effect of the medication is that Mike suffers unpleasant and uncomfortable stomach problems. No wonder he has sometimes earned the nickname 'Captain Grumpy'.

What amuses me now is that the use of these drugs is perfectly legal and accepted as part of the game, yet if you are suffering from a cold or flu on the eve of a match and decide to take some Night Nurse or its equivalent in order to help you get a good night's sleep, you will test positive for prohibited substances if called upon to give a sample the next day.

Even more potentially harmful as anti-inflammatory drugs, of course, has been the use of cortisone.

During the 1950s and 60s the game of professional football was full of players with dodgy knees who would regularly come off the field at half-time for a cortisone injection just to get them out again for the second half. At the time no one quite knew what the long-term effects of such treatment might be, but the number of ex-footballers hobbling around with serious knee problems in later life told its own story.

Only ten years ago cortisone injections in various parts of the body were reasonably commonplace in county cricket and nobody batted an eye-lid. While cortisone can supply the quick fix required to mask serious injury it has been proven that playing through cortisone-masked conditions causes severe long-term problems.

The example of Kerry O'Keefe, the Australian leg-spinner who played 24 Tests for his country in the 1970s, was one of the reasons why people started to turn away from cortisone to anti-inflammatory drugs. Kerry's career was finished by cortisone. He suffered from a long-term finger injury and, in order to get on the field to play would have regular cortisone injections into the finger joint. In the end he had so many that the joint calcified and seized up and he was simply unable to bowl.

But this is not just ancient history. Roberts recalls the example of Craig White having a make-or-break cortisone injection as recently as on England's 1994-95 tour to Australia.

'Craig was having a desperate time with his injured side,' Roberts remembers. 'No matter what we tried, nothing seemed to be working. In the end, and against my better judgement, it was decided that he should have a cortisone injection.

'I made my position clear. As far as I was concerned the rib injury he was suffering from was not going to be cured by the injection and even if successful in the immediate short-term the long-term risks were too great to make this a sensible option. In the event it didn't work, Craig broke down again and I've no doubt that the short-term measure delayed his long-term recovery.'

As players and physiotherapists seek to head off the effects of overuse and overwork, there is obviously scope for abuse. To my mind the use of anti-inflammatory drugs and cortisone are evidence of this.

But perhaps the most alarming proof I have come across concerned the England tour to South Africa in the winter of 1994-95 when the players were asked to take a substance the use of which the medical committee of the British Olympic Association refused to sanction in its athletes.

Creatine is a naturally occurring food protein substance that is created in the body. One gram a day, the amount that is found naturally in 250 grams of uncooked steak, is considered a safe natural limit.

Yet for some time many athletes have been taking larger amounts of Creatine supplements to provide high energy protein.

The benefits of Creatine mean that in spite of the fact that it is not officially sanctioned, it has been widely publicised in athletics magazines as a wonder drug. Although it is not illegal, its consumption in athletics has let loose a wave of debate over the moral justification for its use.

Among those who have been reported as using it to enhance performance are Linford Christie, Sally Gunnell, Colin Jackson, the British Lions rugby squad and the Cambridge Rowing Crew. In Jackson's case, he even advertised its use. At the Helsinki Games Jackson added the 1994 European sprint hurdles title to his world crown and world record yet his face could be seen beaming out from the glossy pages of sports magazines promoting Creatine's powerful effects.

The England cricketers were told that Creatine, used in conjunction with the concentrated carbohydrate drinks they consumed all tour would help them retain peak performance levels longer. As well as the storage of energy made possible by Creatine its proponents believe it can have long-term benefits in replenishing protein levels.

At least one of the England players I spoke with became worried, however, that he appeared to be putting on weight as a result of the Creatine supplements.

He was right to be concerned. For although no one has yet proved that regular use of Creatine supplements is dangerous, nobody has yet categorically proved it is not. Indeed, although as yet there is no definitive scientific evidence to prove whether Creatine is harmful or not, preliminary evidence suggests it could cause kidney problems if used in large doses.

According to Dr Mark Harries, the head of the British Olympic Association medical centre: 'The medical committee of the BOA does not recommend the use of Creatine substances.

'It is not a question of whether or not it enhances performance, but we do not want to endorse substances that can result in long-term harm.

'The danger of taking large or abnormal amounts of food substances or medicines is implicit in the fact that excessive intake of many natural substances can result in damage. For example, the correct intake of Vitamin A is clearly beneficial. Yet, in large quantities it is highly toxic. As far as Creatine is concerned, until studies prove that it does not cause harm we cannot endorse its use.'

England's cricket chiefs, however, thought otherwise.

There is no doubt that, in general terms, the approach to fitness and preparation has improved beyond all recognition in the past decade. Not so long ago the average county player's attitude to match-day preparation was to make sure he brought his knife and fork with him. The routine was straightforward: coffee and biscuits in the morning, what's for lunch, what's for tea, which curry house are we hitting and how many pints can we get down tonight? And when the first of the new breed of county physiotherapists came on the scene the trick among most of the old heads in county cricket was to see how much they could get away with.

Wayne Morton, the current England physio, for instance was amazed and delighted at the fitness levels of his charges when he took on the job at Yorkshire.

He recalls: 'I worked with the Leeds Rugby League club prior to taking on responsibility for the Yorkshire cricketers and one of the regular training exercises we would do was a 1.1 mile sprint around the ground at Headingley.

'The rugby boys used to take it very seriously and all would clock reasonable times. When I first asked the cricketers to do the same run I couldn't believe the results. As a general rule reasonably fit athletes would be looking to complete the run in around five and a half minutes. I would be happy doing that time regularly, but what amazed me was that this bunch of cricketers who I had assumed would be hopelessly unfit and out of condition would almost always finish only 20 seconds or so behind me.

'For them to run 1.1 miles in under six minutes I considered really quite impressive. When they reached the finishing point they were puffing and blowing and sweating and groaning, but they always finished in good time and when they tucked into their tea and biscuits and lit up the woodbines I was happy to let them have their reward for a job well done.

'What I didn't know at the time, and didn't actually find out for three years, was that they had been taking a short-cut that reduced the 1.1 mile circuit to less than one quarter of a mile.'

In fact even ten years ago the whole area of physiotherapy in cricket was just not taken seriously. Most clubs would rely on a doctor and a bloke with a sponge. Around the county circuit there were only a handful of qualified physiotherapists and as for the rest, the moment they came on the field was the time to make a miraculous recovery – there was no guarantee that their idea of treatment, or lack of it, wouldn't leave you on sticks for the rest of your life.

No one had anything but the greatest admiration for Johnny Miller, the partially sighted Middlesex physio, who had built a life for himself in the profession after suffering horrific injuries as a Test driver for Vauxhall in the 1960s but the players there were full of tales about him walking onto the field and treating the wrong man, let alone the wrong part of the body.

A lot has changed since then, of course, and how things have needed to, but there remain some areas of genuine concern.

I was more than a little surprised to discover that my first club Somerset actually started the 1997 season without a qualified physiotherapist. With no offence to the non-qualified physio they employed I wouldn't expect a county team would have been too happy about sending their players down to Taunton in those circumstances.

What is more, as most of the county physios will confirm, second-team cricket is still an accident waiting to happen. Although there is no requirement imposed by the ECB, and there certainly wasn't by the TCCB before them that all county clubs should make sure a qualified physio is present for all second team games, it amazes me that there is not.

I cannot for the life of me see why the ECB could not issue a directive to all clubs insisting that, during the hours of second team play medical cover in the form of a doctor, a qualified physio or at the very minimum a qualified first-aider must be on the ground.

Where vast strides have been made recently is in the area of prevention of injuries. Players are much more aware than they ever were when I was playing of the correct kinds of diet and proper pre-match training and stretching routines. As a result you simply do not get the volume of soft tissue injuries that used to be the case.

But as Morton confirms burn out and all its associated dangers is still prevalent.

'Cricket is unlike any other sport in terms of intensity. Whereas as football or rugby you play a game lasting only 80 or 90 minutes then at worst you normally have at least a couple of days off before you begin training and playing again, cricket never seems to stop.

'At the start of this season, the rain that affected the Benson & Hedges qualifying rounds meant that in a period which also included a championship game and two Sunday League matches, Yorkshire basically turned up to play from Monday to Monday two weeks running.

'Because of that, proper periods for rest and recuperation are virtually non-existent once the season starts. And this leads to real problems with the England international players. As physio of England Yorkshire I have a real dilemma. I may feel that Gough, for instance needs a break between Tests. What do I say to Yorkshire? 'Would you mind if Goughy took the next championship match off?' I can imagine them loving that.

'And when it comes to young bowlers coming into the game the problems are even more acute. Everyone is crying out for promising young fast bowling talent, so much so that the tendency is to try and rush them through.

'If you are a young guy with a bit of pace you can guarantee you will receive special attention from a county. Not in the way you should, perhaps, but you will be bowled all summer then put in the indoor nets in winter. Often the indoor surfaces on which these guys are running in to bowl are just not suitable and this is the reason why stress fractures and shin problems are so common. The seeds of these kinds of injuries are sewn very very young . Yet it is only very recently that people have been studying the problem scientifically ... Basically most of the problems of burn out and injury in young bowlers stem from the fact that we have been approaching a professional game in a far too amateur fashion for far too long.'

He can say that again. I hope that when the ECB start to confront the issues, they do so properly and with no half-measures. There must be a cogent, coherent plan for the fitness and physical and psychological well-being of all of our cricketers.

Above all the time has come for all our international cricketers to be contracted to the central Board rather than their county clubs. Quite apart from the necessary wholesale changes to the structure of first-class cricket we must ensure that when we find exceptional talent it is allowed to flower and flourish at the right pace rather than be burned out before its time.

BOTHAM'S
BLUEPRINT

TWENTY TWO
THE QUESTIONS

'The players are the ones who know how soul-destroying it is to play professional cricket in front of three men and a thermos. Cricket is nothing if no one wants to watch it.'

THE appointment of Sir Ian MacLaurin, later to become Lord MacLaurin of Knebworth, as the first chairman of the new England and Wales Cricket Board appeared to have brought a breath of fresh air to the national summer game.

Like the rest of us, the retiring chairman of Tesco, or 'Supermac', as he soon came to be called by some of the England players, had suffered too long watching England's Test cricketers lurch from one shambles to the next during the ten years of hurt since we last beat one of the leading Test playing nations in a full series on the 1986-87 tour to Australia.

Those progressive counties who pushed for his appointment did so for a purpose. For they knew that unlike many within the game content to stick their heads in the sand and hope for the best, MacLaurin was not impressed by the argument that fortunes in cricket are cyclical.

As he said in an interview in the *Mail On Sunday* immediately prior to taking on the job in October 1996: 'There are those who persist in claiming that success in cricket is cyclical, that if you wait long enough it'll all come right of its own accord. I simply don't believe that is true.

'You wouldn't last very long in my business if you just said "everything is cyclical." Imagine if you went to the shareholders and told them, "I'm terribly sorry that we've lost all this money this year, but I'm sure if you hang on and keep investing your cash, perhaps in a few years time we might make a profit." We have to be realistic. If nothing is done to turn things round, the most pessimistic scenario is that the game will wither on the vine.'

MacLaurin knew that he would not have the total support of the counties in his quest for change, as, predictably, a number of the more reactionary clubs saw absolutely no need for it in the first place.

Early in 1997 MacLaurin appeared to indicate his support for drastic restructuring of the county championship in order to make it more competitive and therefore produce tougher cricketers for the national side. In the end, MacLaurin drew back from the brink in his first version of his blueprint *Raising the Standard*. His consultations with county chairmen made it clear that the majority simply would not entertain the idea of splitting the competition into two divisions with promotion and relegation.

Rather than present a blueprint that had no chance of support, at first MacLaurin settled for compromise. Hence the proposal of a baseball-style conference for the county championship rather than straight promotion and relegation in two divisions. Ironically, but encouragingly, so baffling was that idea to many of the more reactionary counties that, as the date of ratification of MacLaurin's plans approached, there was a strong move to replace it with the real thing. A shaft of light in the darkness at last?

As he said prior to the publication of his strategy: 'I have been involved in many difficult and protracted business ventures. But I can honestly say this is the most complex thing I have ever undertaken, because, despite all the work and the conclusions, it is ultimately not my decision. At Tesco, I would put things in place, knowing that, if they didn't work, I would be sacked. Things work differently here.'

There is no doubt in my mind that fundamental change is vital for the future well-being of the game and in order to gauge the mood of those involved in the professional game as a whole, at the start of the 1997 season I canvassed opinion from all county chairmen, chief executives, captains and coaches, through a questionnaire of my own.

The results demonstrated the conflicts of interests between county and country that have undermined English cricket for more than a decade.

THE QUESTIONNAIRE

1. Are you satisfied with the overall performance of the England team in Test and international cricket?

Chairmen and Chief Executives: YES 0%; NO 100%
Captains and Coaches: YES 0%; NO 100%
TOTAL: YES 0%; NO 100%

Sample responses:
PAUL PRICHARD, captain of ESSEX: 'At times it seems we take the field with the vast majority of England players concerned only for their own performance. The sooner we get a squad of players who want to sweat blood for England the better.'
TIM MUNTON, captain of WARWICKSHIRE: 'The lack of continuity in selection leads to the team being made up of players thinking that if they don't perform they could be playing their last Test match – difficult to perform if you are under that sort of pressure. I sometimes wonder how many of the guys are really committed to playing for their country versus playing to enhance their ego/bank balance.'
MIKE HORTON, chairman of DERBYSHIRE: 'Lack of professionalism and low coaching standards. Amateurish organisational structure and understanding of sportsmen's psychology.'

Not surprisingly, given England's record in Test and one-day international cricket, this was the one question on which there was total agreement across the board from chairmen and chief executives to coaches and players. Clearly the performances of the team at the beginning of the summer did show a vast improvement on what had happened in Zimbabwe, but that was not difficult. What the response did show was a universal dissatisfaction with the status quo. But just how far were the interested parties prepared to go to change it?

2. Do you think the needs of the national side should outweigh the needs of the county clubs?

Chairmen and Chief Executives: YES 73%; NO: 27%
Captains and Coaches: YES 78%; NO 22%

TOTAL: YES 75%; NO 25%.

Sample responses:
JOHN HIGSON, chairman of GLOUCESTERSHIRE: 'No. If the counties' needs are subjugated this would detrimentally affect the national side.'
MARK ALLEYNE, captain of GLOUCESTERSHIRE: 'Yes. The whole point of county cricket is to provide us with a competitive national side. We shouldn't lose our edge at international level because of county commitments.'
JACK BIRKENSHAW, coach of LEICESTERSHIRE: 'We need to be the best international side in the world for financial reasons, e.g. Sky television, and also if we are to create national interest for our youngsters.'
TIM TREMLETT, coach of HAMPSHIRE: 'A successful national team will benefit county clubs in the way that their marketing departments and finance committees are really interested in – making money. England needs success. All the spin-offs will come with that.'

Good to see a large majority in favour of putting England first. The views of those administrators who fear that by doing so, county cricket could be seriously devalued are summed up by one chief executive who did not wish to be named. He said: 'I believe that the needs of the national side are very important, and that they are best served by a healthy partnership and shared vision by all concerned rather than a one-sided dominance which could devalue county cricket.' That's his opinion and the opinion of the more reactionary clubs. My response is this: how can county cricket with its premier competition, the championship, being watched by handfuls of die-hards and contested by players who to a large extent are going through the motions for half of every season, be any further devalued than it has already become?

3. Do you think the England selectors should have the power to instruct county clubs to rest Test players in the best interests of the national side?

Chairmen and Chief Executives: YES 68%; NO 32%
Captains and Coaches: YES 68%; NO 32%
TOTAL: YES 68%; NO 32%

Sample responses:
PETER BOWLER, captain of SOMERSET: 'Yes. Clearly it would be better

if clubs agreed to rest players when necessary, however views amongst counties differ and an overall power seems necessary.'

TIM TREMLETT, coach of HAMPSHIRE: 'Yes. To avoid mental pressure/tiredness apart from physical fatigue. England players play a hell of a lot. Ordinary county players can just about cope.'

PHILIP AUGUST, chief executive of GLOUCESTERSHIRE: 'No. County cricket must be competitive and the best players need to be involved as much as possible.'

My argument for investing selectors with total power in this matter is best explained by the case of Darren Gough. Goughie has been dogged by injury problems throughout his career. At the start of this summer he was fit and firing and the results were plain for all to see. His brilliant bowling in the first innings of the first Test helped reduce Australia to 118 all out and England went on to clinch the match. As the season wore on he started to complain of sore shins and an ankle injury. Neither were sufficient to cause him to miss games but the combination of both meant that he required careful 'nursing'. Instead he played on and on for Yorkshire so that by the time of the third Test at Old Trafford he was obviously struggling to bowl with the fire and menace with which he had previously caused so many problems for the Aussie batsmen. By the time England went to Trent Bridge for the fifth Test, he was done in and Mike Atherton was deprived of the services of his main strike bowler for a match that decided the series. Here we had a situation where a lad really did need to rest between Tests in order to have a chance of getting through the series. Which brings us to...

4. Should there be an elite group of players contracted to England rather than their counties?

Chairmen and Chief Executives: YES 36%; NO 64%
Captains and Coaches: YES 50%; NO 50%
TOTAL: YES 42%; NO 58%

Sample responses:
PETER MOORES, captain of SUSSEX: 'Yes. The ECB should contract the top 30 players, pay their wages then control the amount of cricket they play.'

TIM MUNTON, captain of WARWICKSHIRE: 'Yes. If the selectors wish to reserve the right to rest players then the 'England squad' should be employed by the ECB. There has to be an advantage in avoiding burn out to bowlers, as seen in recent years with Angus Fraser, Dominic Cork and Darren Gough.'

DON ROBSON, chairman of DURHAM: 'No. It is not sensible to prejudge selection in this way.'

DAVID ACFIELD, chairman of ESSEX: 'No. It would affect the standard of the county game and would be difficult to manage if Test players floated in an out. There would be little point in counties developing players only to lose them.'

To me, contracting the players to the ECB is a must. Those counties who feel that if they are merely developing talent for the national side there would be little point in having county cricket misunderstand the point. Once you establish that the needs of the national side should be paramount, you are saying that county cricket should then become the means to that end. The county clubs have to understand that they are only kept afloat financially by the revenue produced by the national side. Don't take my word for it. A report produced by a researcher from the University of Sheffield and a professor of the Leicester Business School entitled *The Financial Health of English Cricket* concluded 'County cricket has no significant support from the general public,' that 'the proportion of revenue provided by members' subscriptions is falling' and 'commercial income is insufficient to support the present structure'. If county clubs wish to survive in anything like their present form, the bottom line is that England must win and their best chance of winning will come through looking after the players, not forcing them to play second rate cricket. Tim Munton cites burn-out in Fraser, Cork and Gough. He's right, but he could add dozens more to the list. I can understand the reservations of some county clubs but surely we have got to look beyond the ends of our noses. We must put the England team first and we must do all we can to make it the best there is. I'm not saying that the contracted players should play no county cricket whatsoever, but the amount must be controlled and determined by the national selectors in order to make sure that every single time a player sets foot on the field to represent England he is ready for the challenge of facing the best players in the world and capable of excelling.

5. Do you think the present domestic structure is conducive to the development of young talent at international level?

Chairmen and Chief Executives: YES 42%; NO 58%
Captains and Coaches: YES 28%; NO 64%. Undecided 8%
TOTAL: YES 36%; NO 60%. Undecided 4%

Sample responses:
LYNN WILSON, chairman of NORTHAMPTONSHIRE: 'Yes. It has stood the test of time and is respected around the globe. It can perhaps be altered at the margin. What we need is a more professional approach to practice and skills etc.'
ROB BAILEY, captain of NORTHAMPTONSHIRE: 'No. The Under-19 set-up is disappointing. Counties should be able to use these lads but the England Under-19 side takes preference, e.g. David Sales of Northants.'
TIM TREMLETT, coach of HAMPSHIRE: 'The structure is killing off our best young bowlers too soon. There is a great shortage of bowling talent. Young bowlers are introduced and asked to do a man's job before their bodies are ready. The workload is too great.'
DAVID MORGAN, chairman of GLAMORGAN: 'No. Contracted staff numbers are too large.'
TOM MOODY, captain of WORCESTERSHIRE: 'Too much crap cricket on crap wickets.'

England's record in bringing youngsters through to thrive at the highest is a joke compared with that of other countries. When Ben Hollioake made his debut in the one-day international against Australia at Lord's, aged 19, he became the youngest England player for 48 years. Sure, Ben is talented and he has a great future in the game but can it be true that he has been the only 19-year-old or younger worth a try for nearly 50 years? My mind goes back to the example of Mark Ramprakash, of Middlesex and England. Ramprakash had earned rave reviews as a teenager playing club cricket alongside Angus Fraser for Stanmore in the Middlesex League. Middlesex were so impressed that they picked him for his first-class debut while he was still only seventeen and studying at college and, in the second innings of his first first-class match, against Yorkshire in April 1987, he made a sparkling 63 not out. On 3 September 1988, two days before his nineteenth birthday, and with only a dozen championship matches under his belt he set Lord's alight with a classy 56 against my county Worcestershire in the NatWest Final. Although I was absent recovering from surgery, Worcestershire boasted one of the most powerful attacks in county cricket, including a pace trio of Graham Dilley, Neal Radford and Phil Newport backed up by the spin of Richard Illingworth. When Ramps came to the wicket, Middlesex were heading for defeat. They had restricted Worcestershire to 161 for nine in their sixty overs, but had slumped to 25 for four in reply, with Wilf Slack, John Carr, Andy Needham out of the picture and, most importantly Mike Gatting, run out for nought without facing a ball. To an 18-year-old playing in his first big event match in front of a capacity crowd, the challenge must have been daunting. But he kept his head, showed maturity and coolness under pressure and with help from Roland Butcher and John Emburey, led Middlesex home. Such a display of skill and assurance should have encouraged the England selectors to pick him almost without delay. What happened instead was that he spent the next two years stuck in county cricket going nowhere fast. He was told that he needed to learn the game. The only game he was learning was the mediocrity produced by the daily grind of the domestic game. Frustration built up inside him to such an extent that, from time to time he allowed his impatience to get the better of him and gained a reputation for being difficult. By the time he was finally given his chance at Test level, against the West Indies in 1991, he appeared obsessed by occupation of the crease rather than playing his natural game, and since then his tentative play for England indicates what a waste those two years might have been. The upshot is that one of the most promising talents English cricket has been blessed with for years has been lost to the national side, possibly for good. Ramps is only the most obvious example of the failings of our domestic game in developing young players. But you only have to look around the county dressing rooms at the mediocre older players hanging on for their benefits to see that the way through has been blocked for too long by dead wood.

6. Are you in favour of a national cricket academy?

Chairmen and Chief Executives: YES 55%; NO 45%
Captains and Coaches: YES 50%; NO 28%. Undecided 22%
TOTAL: YES 54%; NO 36%. Undecided 10%

Sample responses:

DEAN JONES, (ex-) captain of DERBYSHIRE (former Australian Test star): 'Yes. But players should only be enrolled for terms of three months. The Australian system is too long. The Cricket Academy XI should play matches against counties in April and tour once. It would speed up the selection process.'

DAVE GILBERT, coach of SURREY (former Aussie Test player): 'Yes. It can only enhance a young player's cricketing education.'

PETER BOWLER, captain of SOMERSET (educated in Australia): 'Yes. Very important to make up for the lack of intensity in the game and provide a tough 'finishing school' for our talent much like the Australian system.'

DON ROBSON, chairman of DURHAM: 'No. We need eighteen centres of excellence provided by the first-class counties to keep the broad base of the pyramid throughout the country.'

ROGER GOADBY, chairman of LEICESTERSHIRE: 'No. It would not work successfully in this country. With our structure and playing professionally at both 1st and 2nd XI level it is better to put the resources into the counties for them to provide their own resources.'

JOHN BOWER, chief executive of LANCASHIRE: 'Yes. So that we have *one* centre of excellence supported by several regional centres. The notion of 18 centres of excellence is ludicrous.'

For me, the foundation of a national academy is essential. While each county should continue to operate as a regional focus for local talent, we need a national academy to set standards that can be followed throughout the game. Had a national academy been set up in time to catch hold of Ramprakash, for instance, there is no doubt in my mind that the guy would have gone all the way to the very top of the world game. At least he would have been given every opportunity to do so. Where the Australian system works so well is that they tailor their intake to suit the needs of the national side. If the national selectors are concerned that they need to find pace bowlers quickly, the next intake of Australian Academy 'students' will be made up almost entirely of pacemen. For example, the Aussies saw in advance that Craig McDermott would need replacing, so they instructed their coaches to concentrate on finding one. Glenn McGrath was one of a posse they rounded up and, thanks to intensive coaching from Dennis Lillee and others, he was fast-tracked into the Test side, having played no more than a handful of state games. According to the Coopers & Lybrand ratings, he is currently ranked the best bowler of all types in world cricket.

His performance in the Lord's Test, when he took eight for 38 to bowl England out for 77 was one of the greatest of all time. Although I am not in favour of parroting everything the Aussies do, there is no disgrace in copying something that works.

Questions 7, 8 and 9 were concerned with the selection process. Answers were sought to the following questions:

7. How should the chairman and other selectors be selected?
8. Should the captain and manager sit on the selection committee?
9. What would be your ideal system for the selection and management of the national side?

There were a wide range of responses. Interestingly, in view of the overall power vested in Ray Illingworth as supremo, only one response was in favour of such a system and it didn't come from Yorkshire. It is difficult to tell whether they, like the others, were put off the idea by the position or by the person who occupied it!

Sample responses:
PAUL SHELDON, chief executive of SURREY thought the captain and manager should both sit on the selection committee but insisted there should be 'One overall supremo with full power vested in him.'
PAUL PRICHARD, the ESSEX captain asked: 'Do we need a chairman of selectors?' His ideal selection system was: 'The captain, coach and three other selectors who are current or recently retired first-class cricketers.'

On the specific question of whether the captain and manager/coach should sit on the committee, the vast majority of players were in favour (YES 71%; NO 29 %), while, among the chairmen and chief executives, the voting was closer (YES 52%; NO 48%) According to TIM TREMLETT of HAMPSHIRE: 'The captain must have confidence in the players he is taking on the field with him. The manager has to have input if he is to take responsibility for the team's performance.' STEVE MARSH, the KENT captain wants more involvement from current players. He proposes that the players from every county should have some input in how the chairman and other selectors are selected. As for whether the captain should have a vote. Marsh goes further still. He said: 'A cricket captain lives or dies by the performance of the players under him, so he must have the players he wants.' CHRIS HASSELL, the chief executive of YORKSHIRE, makes this general comment not on the selectors but on the attitude of some of those they select: 'The best players are not necessarily dedicated enough. Pick those who will "die" for England. There are a lot of talented players in England, but do they really want it?'

I used to be totally in favour of the concept of a supremo. In the case of Ray Illingworth I just thought he was entirely the wrong man for the job. I still believe such a system could work, along the lines of the England soccer team, the selection of which is in the hands of one man, the manager, currently Glenn Hoddle. He is totally responsible for the selection, tactics and preparation of the team and is paid handsomely for the privilege of taking the plaudits when things go well and the stick when things go badly. Given the right support and the right man I believe a one-man band could work effectively. Whoever that man was would have to have the full support of the Board, the full confidence of the players, all possible resources available and a skin like a rhino.

10. Are you satisfied with the current format of the county championship?

Chairmen and Chief Executives: YES 63%; NO 37%
Captains and Coaches: YES 28.5%; NO 71.5%
TOTAL: YES 48%; NO 52%

Sample responses:
ROGER GOADBY, chairman of 1996 champions LEICESTERSHIRE: 'Yes. It provides four-day cricket which should be better for the national side and, at the same time, gives "unfashionable" clubs like our own the opportunity to develop young cricketers and introduce them gradually into the team at a comparatively early age.'
JACK BIRKENSHAW, coach of 1996 champions LEICESTERSHIRE: 'No. I would go for two divisions.'
DAVE GILBERT, coach of SURREY: 'Seventeen four-day matches is too much. There are about eight decent championship sides and the rest make up the numbers.'
PETER MOORES, captain of SUSSEX: 'The volume of cricket played means that not enough games are played while players are fresh. Also not

enough games have enough pressure on them to get players used to playing in tough situations.'

The split in voting between the chairmen and administrators and the players and coaches speaks volumes. Too many chairmen for too long have been too satisfied with the status quo. They fear change and its consequences, even though their memberships are dwindling and their crowds for championship cricket pitiful. Those who play and those who coach, on the other hand, are painfully aware of the lack of public interest in what they do and the lack of quality in what they play, not to mention the exhausting grind of a domestic programme that leaves them no room or time for proper rest, preparation and practice. Interestingly, according to a survey subsequently carried out by the Professional Cricketers' Association among their members, 73% of current players expressed dissatisfaction with the current four-day championship format. They should know. They want competitive cricket. They must be given it

11. Would you be in favour of a two-division championship?

Chairmen and Chief Executives: YES 31%; NO 69%
Captains and Coaches: YES 64%; NO 36%
TOTAL: YES 45%; NO 55%

Sample responses:
DAVID ACFIELD, chairman of ESSEX: 'At a time when we are asking all 38 counties to concentrate on youth development, this would simply produce a few top counties and little else.'
JOHN HIGSON, chairman of GLOUCESTERSHIRE: 'No. It would condemn certain counties to oblivion.'
JOHN BOWER, chief executive of LANCASHIRE: 'Yes. I would support anything to make the championship genuinely competitive.'
CHRIS HASSELL, chief executive of YORKSHIRE: 'Yes. Two divisions required.'
JACK BIRKENSHAW, coach of LEICESTERSHIRE: 'Yes. This would increase the interest in the competition. There is nothing wrong with change!'
STEVE MARSH, captain of KENT: 'Two divisions *must* come in, sooner rather than later. You might have to start with two equal Leagues with the

top two in each division playing a semi-final then a final. After that had been going for a couple of seasons it would be much easier and less severe to then start two divisions with promotion and relegation.'

I have argued for some time that a two-division championship with promotion and relegation for the bottom and top three teams is essential if the game is to progress. In the same survey by the PCA of their players discussed earlier, as many as 68% were in favour of such a scheme. The majority of county chairmen, on the other hand, are so fearful of change that they cannot see the obvious benefits. Sure, a transfer system would come in, but doesn't such a system exist already? When Chris Lewis became available at Nottinghamshire, didn't he go to the highest bidder, Surrey? In any case, as long as the premier players were contracted to the Board, the threat of the richer clubs merely buying all the best players would recede dramatically, as England players would then play so little domestic cricket as to be poor value in a transfer market. What are the reactionary clubs afraid of? I'll tell you. They are scared of being found out for what they are, second rate organisations happy to hide behind mediocrity. With promotion and relegation affecting six teams every year, not to mention the fight for the championship itself, almost every team would be playing for something every match. That would increase the level of interest dramatically whether your club was in the first or second division. Not only would revenue be increased through the turnstiles and the heightened media interest mean local sponsors would be far more likely to see value for money, the competitive level of cricket would be raised as well. While the best players would be the responsibility of England, those coming through and into the game would have a much tougher grounding and therefore be much better prepared to make the step up in class.

12. Is there too much domestic one-day cricket?

Chairmen and Chief Executives: YES 52%; NO 48%
Captains and Coaches: YES 64.2%; NO 35.8%
TOTAL: YES 57%; NO 43%

Sample responses:
TIM TREMLETT, coach of HAMPSHIRE: 'Yes. We have three one-day

competitions all with a different set of rules – mind boggling! Forty overs, fifty overs, sixty overs, circles, inner circles, Duckworth-Lewis!! Professionals should be able to adapt, but honestly.'

PAUL PRICHARD, captain of ESSEX: 'Yes. I think we play one competition too many. Bowlers need some rest before four-day cricket. Batsmen need fewer reasons to improvise.'

JOHN BOWER, chief executive of LANCASHIRE: 'Yes. With travel it is all but continuous for six months. Players need time to train, rest and relax.'

TIM MUNTON, captain of WARWICKSHIRE: 'No. It does need re-organising so that most of it is played at weekends. Most of it should also mirror the international one-day game, i.e. 50 overs per side as standard.'

DON ROBSON, chairman of DURHAM: 'No. Source of revenue and customers like the product.'

It makes no sense whatsoever for our players to be contesting three different varieties of one-day cricket at domestic level when at international level 50 overs per side is the norm. In the interests of the national side, whatever one-day cricket played should be standardised at 50 overs per side. In order to reduce the workload I would scrap one of the one-day knockout competitions, while the huge success of Warwickshire's experiment with floodlit cricket has opened up the possibility for real change in the AXA Equity and Law Sunday League. I was sceptical of night cricket in this country until I witnessed the AXA match between Warwickshire and Somerset at Edgbaston in the middle of the 1997 season. Warwickshire being one of the more progressive counties, they marketed the match aggressively and their hard work paid off when a crowd of 15,000-plus turned up on the evening of Wednesday, 23 July. For the uncommitted the game itself was disappointingly one-sided, with the home side winning easily, but it was a great occasion and a massive commercial success. The Warwickshire chief executive, Dennis Amiss, revealed that even with the hire of the lights (and the electricity bill that went with them), the club cleared £70,000 profit from the night. Bearing in mind the club's profits from the entire championship takings in 1996 was around £40,000, you can see what potential benefits this form of entertainment can bring. According to Amiss: 'We're keen to attract youngsters and families and this type of event works. It may not please the purists, but we have to face the fact that no-one comes to watch county cricket anymore. Clearly we need the four-day game in order to produce Test players, but anything that gets the public through the gates to watch any form of county cricket has to be good. I also believe that this kind of event helps produce better players. There's nothing that tests a player's mettle more than playing in front of a crowd, with the added pressure and intensity created by a full-house atmosphere. Sometimes some of the players who make the jump from county to Test cricket make their England debut having never played in front of a crowd before. Big-match temperament is something you don't know a player possesses until he is put in a big-match situation. Floodlit cricket would not be practical throughout the season, but there is window of opportunity in mid-summer. For those worried about the costs of lights, we were quoted at £250,000 for a permanent set. That kind of money could be made in one season. Alternatively, why not fund floodlights at all county grounds from the central Board hand-out?'

Having been at Edgbaston that night and witnessed the enjoyment and interest the event created, I agree. In fact I would go so far as to transfer all Sunday league matches to mid-week, where practical, with later start times in July and August for after-work audiences. I would also surround the game with razzmatazz. In this respect we could follow the lead of the New Zealand Cricket Board in their approach to the one-day international series against England on the 1997 winter tour there. Coloured clothing and numbers and names on the players' shirts for ease of identification have been common practice for some time, but the Kiwi board went even further, with the introduction of music to accompany each batsman out to the wicket. One of the great moments of the New Zealand tour for me came during the one-day match at Christchurch. England had been cruising to victory but a flurry of wickets put them under pressure. They still needed eight runs from four balls when Robert Croft, the Welsh off-spinner, strode to the crease to the strains of Tom Jones singing 'Delilah'. Croft promptly hit his first two balls to the boundary to win the match. It may not have been line and length, but it was fun, and that is what the short form of the game should be all about. One thing above all else struck me about Warwickshire's day-night game, namely the number of youngsters present and the great fun they had. Quite apart from the side-shows, including a demonstration from the local basketball team, the Birmingham Bullets with a chance for participating kids to win prizes for putting the ball through the hoop, the inter-innings entertainment gave them all an opportunity to feel they had been directly involved in the event. The club invited all youngsters present onto the field to take part in a party game involving mascots representing the five local soccer clubs; Birmingham, Wolves, Aston Villa, West Bromwich Albion and Walsall. Every single one of them went away with a prize and memories of a great night that will encourage them to come to the cricket again. My strategy for one-day cricket would be to focus on one 50-over knockout as the premier 'serious' one-day competition and treat a 50-over league as entertainment first, cricket second. Use this form of the game to develop innovations and attractions and experiment. Find out exactly what the public want to see and to experience and give it to them.

13. Should there be a total ban on overseas players?

Chairmen and Chief Executives: YES 31.5%; NO 68.5%
Captains and Coaches: YES 42.8%; NO 57.2%
TOTAL: YES 36%; NO 64%

Sample responses:
MATTHEW MAYNARD, captain of GLAMORGAN: 'Top overseas players certainly benefit county clubs and their supporters, but there are too many average overseas players currently playing, due to the increasing amount of international cricket being played around the globe. In 1999 we host the World Cup in England so let's use that as a starting point and see how we get on without them for two years.'
DAVID ACFIELD, chairman ESSEX: 'The TCCB cricket committee proposed an experimental ban for 1999 and 2000 (to include the World Cup year). Failed. I believe the pros and cons are finely balanced but overseas players take the responsibility from home players, hence failure under pressure.'
CHRIS HASSELL, chief executive of YORKSHIRE: 'No. They add something. We are devoid of stars.'
DAVID BYAS, captain of YORKSHIRE: 'Yes. I feel they take away far more than we obtain from them, i.e. lucrative deals and the place of one of our own English players.'
DAVID KEMP, chief executive of KENT: 'No. But I would only want one per county – and they should not be allowed to bat in the top six!'
ROB BAILEY, captain of Northamptonshire: 'Yes. I wouldn't be against

this as it would give the overseas Test players less insight into our game and players.'

JOHN HIGSON, chairman of GLOUCESTERSHIRE: 'Yes. Because they are keeping potential England players out of the game. They are taking too much money out of the game. Due to 'home' commitments their availability to play for counties is becoming more and more restricted.'

JACK BIRKENSHAW, coach of LEICESTERSHIRE: 'Yes. The difficulty in finding top overseas players is now severe. They cost a fortune and do not necessarily increase membership to offset the cost. We should start concentrating on our own.'

DAVE GILBERT, coach of SURREY: 'Overseas players in English soccer seem to have enhanced the quality of the national team. Why not cricket? But ensure the best are hired, not second stringers.'

Opinion here reflect the mixed views in county cricket. Certainly, with greater frequency of commitments to overseas players from their national board some of the highest quality players are no longer viable options for county clubs. Employed correctly, to help with coaching at all levels as well as marketing the club, top overseas players have a huge value. It was my privilege to play alongside two of the greatest servants to Somerset in recent history, Viv Richards and Joel Garner and no-one can tell me that in the performances they gave and the interest they created they were not beneficial to the game. The success we enjoyed together in the great Somerset side of the early 1980s created enough revenue for major ground developments. If a young county player is good enough he will be inspired to learn and improve by simply watching a world-class player in action as well as playing alongside him. Recently some counties have gone for an overseas player simply for the sake of it without bothering too much with the quality. I would keep overseas players in county cricket, but ensure that only the very best were hired and that means that those who have played international cricket.

14. Are county playing staffs too large?

Chairmen and Chief Executives: YES 73%; NO 27%
Captains and Coaches: YES 71%; NO 29%
TOTAL: YES 72%; NO 28%

Sample responses:

DEAN JONES, ex-captain of DERBYSHIRE: 'Yes. There should be a maximum of 18 players plus triallists to keep players on edge.'

LYNN WILSON, chairman of NORTHAMPTONSHIRE: 'Yes. Too many no-hopers.'

PETER MOORES, captain of SUSSEX: 'No. I don't agree with carrying dead wood but with the present structure we need cover for injuries, especially to bowlers.'

M J K SMITH, chairman of WARWICKSHIRE: 'Yes. The number of full-time players employed is to cover a full second XI fixture list which is not essential.'

PAUL PRICHARD, captain of ESSEX : 'Yes. Too much cricket leads to bigger squads mainly made up of bits and pieces players.'

TIM MUNTON, captain of WARWICKSHIRE: 'There are too many young pros there for the ride. Smaller staffs would mean higher wages for players who could be employed for twelve months of the year rather than six.'

STEVE MARSH, captain of KENT: 'Yes. Large numbers stifle the progress of young players.'

There is far too much dead wood in county cricket. Clubs have built up large squads in order to give themselves cover for second XI cricket which is largely meaningless if played by second rate county players. Second XI cricket should be full of young players bursting and busting a gut to win recognition for the first team. Eighteen players would be an ideal number to give a county cover for Test calls and injuries. Counties should be prepared to make tough decisions over whether or not a player is going to make the grade at the highest level. In my experience if a player hasn't produced evidence that he is worth persevering with by the age of 25, at an absolute highest ceiling, then he should be looking for another job. We must get out of the comfort zone mentality. Comparisons with Australia are not exactly relevant because they have so few state sides and so few professional cricketers, but their system ensures that there is not place to hide. I wouldn't want to do anyone out of a living, but we must face facts. We must become more ruthless in developing young talent or we will continue to flounder in the second division of world cricket.

15. Should those players who retire from international cricket be permitted to carry on in the county game?

Chairmen and Chief Executives: YES 89%; NO 5.5%. Undecided 5.5%
Captains and Coaches: YES 93%; NO 7%
TOTAL: YES 91%; NO 7%. Undecided 3%

Sample responses:
STEVE MARSH, captain of KENT: 'No. Not if international cricket is the most important area of our game.'
DAVID ACFIELD, chairman of ESSEX: 'Yes. A pity to deprive spectators for whom we play all cricket, of the likes of Gooch, Gatting etc.'
DAVE GILBERT, coach of SURREY: 'Yes. Their experience is vital. This is passed onto young players and is all part of the education process. However, a good young player should always get the nod over a good old player.'
TIM MUNTON, captain of WARWICKSHIRE: 'Yes. They have a lot to offer to younger players developing in the game. The county clubs need to manage the flow, though, so as to make sure too many aren't on a staff at the same time.'

An overwhelming majority were in favour of allowing former Test players to carry on in the county game once they have made the decision to quit international cricket – a majority which I believe are in the wrong. With the benefit system the only kind of financial safety-net currently available to county cricketers coming towards the end of their careers, a kind of slow death afflicts the senior citizens of the county game. And I believe the same condition settles on those who have quit Test cricket and then see out their days in the county game. Of course these guys could go on and on and on. But what is the point? Far better in my opinion for the clubs to employ guys like Graham Gooch and Mike Gatting as members of their coaching staffs, whether at first-team level, 2nd XI or youth development. That way they could pass on their experience and know-how without clogging up the development process for younger players. People will point the finger at me and ask why I played on until 1993? The reason was that I never retired from Test cricket. I always felt I could have done a job right until the moment I decided to pack in county cricket. I've no objection to players who have retired from international cricket being given a final year with their clubs as a thank you, but after that they should make way for younger blood.

16. Should the players' benefit system be replaced by pension funds?

Chairmen and Chief Executives: YES 58%; NO: 42%
Captains and Coaches: YES 86%; NO 7%. Undecided 7%
TOTAL: YES 70%; NO 27%. Undecided 3%

Sample responses:

DAVE GILBERT, coach of SURREY: 'Yes. The benefit system encourages players to hang around too long. If you've had your day, you should move on. Pensions would solve this.'

ADAM HOLLIOAKE, captain of SURREY: 'Yes. Because I don't want to beg, or sell my representative memorabilia for money.'

JACK BIRKENSHAW, coach of LEICESTERSHIRE: 'Yes. For many players the amount they earn from their benefit depends on which county they play for. A player like Gordon Parsons might have done ten times more and worked ten times as hard for Leicestershire than others who will earn ten times as much as him.'

CHRIS HASSELL, chief executive of YORKSHIRE: 'No, too costly. Leave system alone.'

MATTHEW MAYNARD, captain of GLAMORGAN: 'Yes. Some players who have given good service don't even qualify for a benefit, so receive nothing at the end of their first-class career.'

JOHN HIGSON, chairman of GLOUCESTERSHIRE: 'Yes. Because a benefit year can be a distraction for the beneficiary, accompanied very often by a loss of form and it detracts from county fund raising.'

PAUL PRICHARD, captain of ESSEX: 'Yes. Because it is almost impossible to do your job properly (which is the most important thing) when it is your benefit year, especially if, like me, you happen to be the captain as well!'

MIKE HORTON, chairman of DERBYSHIRE: 'Yes, starting in the year 2000 to allow transition. Players generally lack financial understanding. Clubs should take more responsibility.'

TIM TREMLETT, coach of HAMPSHIRE: 'In an ideal world a pension fund would benefit everybody. Players would be rewarded properly and not play with the thought of "Will I or won't I get one eventually?" Clubs would also be less morally bound to retain a player if they knew he was reasonable secure.'

The benefit system may have been introduced with the best of intentions, namely to reward outstanding service to individual clubs but it has developed into one of the great evils of the game. Quite apart from being manifestly unfair that players at fashionable clubs get far more than equally deserving cases at clubs like Derbyshire and Leicestershire, some players who are well past their prime will stay in the game merely to hang on in the hope that they will be granted a benefit. The obvious result is that, once again, the opportunities for young players to enter the county game at an early age are vastly reduced. I've seen and heard some of the old pros doing younger players down in front of the committee men just to safeguard their own positions. A sensible pension system with contributions from the club would help alleviate the problem. There might also be the chance, alongside such a scheme for one-off testimonial events to take place for particularly deserving causes. But the whole emphasis must be on bringing on young players more quickly, something the benefit system worked directly against. As far as the relationship between players and clubs is concerned, taking away the promise of a benefit (or the threat of not getting one) removes the noose from around the player's neck. If he feels he is being treated badly by a club or his career is going nowhere, he will not have to take the benefit into account when making a decision to leave. A proper pension fund would also take care of those players who give good and loyal service to a club over six years or so, then have to quite through injury. Clearly that period would not be considered long enough to warrant a benefit, but at least the pension would provide some semblance of reward and security.

17. Should players have more influence in the running of the game, as in other sports, like tennis?

Chairmen and Chief Executives: YES 58%; NO 37%. Undecided 5%
Captains and Coaches: YES 92%; NO 8%
TOTAL: YES 73%; NO 24%. Undecided 3%

Sample responses:
CHRIS HASSELL, chief executive of YORKSHIRE: 'No, this is the problem with cricket. Too many former players who couldn't run a fish and chip shop.'
ROB BAILEY, captain of NORTHAMPTONSHIRE: 'Yes. From a captain's point of view, it's very frustrating that most proposals we put

forward are ignored.'

PETER MOORES, captain of SUSSEX: 'Cricket, like all sports is changing all the time. It would be foolish not to take advice from those involved in the modern game.'

MIKE FATKIN, chief executive of GLAMORGAN: 'No. Haven't they got enough?'

ROGER GOADBY, chairman of LEICESTERSHIRE: 'No. The players already have a reasonable influence – directors should direct, managers should manage and players should play.'

TIM TREMLETT, coach of HAMPSHIRE: 'Yes. Administrators tend to act on new ideas too late. Administrators fear 'Player Power' for the wrong reasons. A sensible balance should prevail. Players need administrators and vice versa.'

JOHN BOWER, chief executive of LANCASHIRE: 'No. The Professional Cricketers' Association is the right channel. It is up to the players to make it effective.'

PAUL SHELDON, chief executive of SURREY: 'Yes. They know what happens in it. Administrators and ex-players usually don't.'

Hardly surprising that there is such a difference in voting between the two groups, but it is encouraging that the majority of both are in favour of giving players more responsibility for the running of the game. Of course there will always be the 'alternative view' and in this case Chris Hassell, the chief executive of Yorkshire and a man who in many other respects has progressive thoughts, champions it. I'm tempted to reply on behalf of the players in the same tone as that employed by a famous footballer of the 1950s and 60s whose autobiography included a chapter entitled 'What the average football club director knows about the game'. Under the chapter heading was a blank page. Seriously, I believe most players would find Hassell's assessment laughable, bearing in mind the mess created by those administrators charged with running the game. Surely it can only be good for the game if players do become more involved. For instance, the majority of players are in favour of promotion and relegation in the county championship, even though they realise half of them would end up in the second division. Their reasons are clear: they understand that the game is drifting nowhere at championship level and that in order to raise standards competition must be increased. Had the players carried more weight, a two-division structure would by now be in place for next season. Yet Lord

MacLaurin who himself was persuaded that some kind of restructuring was vital, found such intransigence on this issue among county chairmen that real and fundamental change was blocked. And so England's fortunes at Test level will continue to be subjugated to the needs of the county sides. And England will continue to do badly in the foreseeable future against the top Test playing nations.

18. Should players be allowed freedom of speech?

Chairmen and Chief Executives: YES 89%; NO 11%
Captains and Coaches: YES 86%; NO 14%
TOTAL: YES 87%; NO 13%

Sample responses:
PAUL PRICHARD, captain of ESSEX: 'Yes. We shouldn't be treated as lapdogs and puppets especially as our views are often more constructive that some offered by those who are allowed to talk on our behalf.'
MIKE HORTON, chairman of DERBYSHIRE: 'Yes. But players need support and training from the counties.'
LYNN WILSON, chairman of NORTHAMPTONSHIRE: 'Yes. But don't bite off the hand that feeds you. A delicate area.'

An interesting response from Paul Prichard here, reminding me of an incident that occurred at the end of the 1996 NatWest Trophy Final at Lord's between Essex and Lancashire. The match was made into a farce by the appalling pitch which started helpful to the bowlers and got worse as the day wore on. After winning the toss Prichard put Lancashire in and only John Crawley had any answers. He could have been out leg before first ball and had he been Lancashire might not have made 100. But his 66 helped them reach 186 in their full 60 overs. When Essex batted the pitch simply disintegrated. Glen Chapple and Peter Martin bowled well, but even they would not have dared take the credit for some of the deliveries. One stands out as a prime example of the impossibility that batting had become. Robert Rollins, the Essex wicket-keeper coming in at no.7, went back to his first ball from Chapple and was bowled by a shooter which pitched on leg stump and hit off. Even Graham Gooch, with all his vast experience and nearing the end of a season in which he made almost 2,000 runs in the championship including eight hundreds at an average of

67.03, was powerless. When Essex lost their sixth wicket, with the total on 33, there was a strong possibility that Gooch might carry his bat for about fifteen. Instead he soon became the third of three Essex batsman dismissed on the same score. Neil Williams and Ashley Cowan shared the batting 'honours' for Essex. They made eleven apiece as Essex were bowled out for 57 in 27.2 overs. Their dismissal at 5.26 pm ended the shortest NatWest Final on record. On his way to the post-match press conference in the pavilion, I bumped into Prichard. He was fuming and not just, I found out, because of Essex's disastrous showing. He told me that he had been instructed by a TCCB official not to mention the pitch. He said to me: 'It's bad enough being bowled out for 57 on a shit-heap but now I have to sit there and say nothing, as though it was all down to bad batting. My players are gutted. We've come here hoping for a great day. Our supporters were right behind us and excited at the prospect of watching us win a trophy. But the pitch was a shocker and the match was a joke. And I'm supposed to behave as though we've forgotten how to bat.'

Until the start of this season all players were bound by registration rules that effectively took away their civil liberties regarding freedom of speech. According to Appendix D of the Directives Of The Board published in 1995, applying in conjunction with the standard county contract, players were more or less bound and gagged. The document is full of legal jargon and split into sections and sub-sections, but the crux of it all was contained in paragraph 3(c), which read:

'Before any public statement of any kind in relation to cricket or any cricketer or body of cricketers is made by or on behalf of a registered Cricketer or an umpire of the Board, the registered Cricketer must obtain the consent of his County Cricket Club and the Board's umpire must obtain the consent of the Board, in each case on giving to the County Cricket Club or the Board, as the case may be, such reasonable notice and information as would enable the County Cricket Club or Board to determine properly whether such consent is appropriate...'

The Board's clarification of what constituted a 'public statement' was so wide-ranging as to make one question whether a player could leave a note for the milkman without their permission. It read:

'In the Board's Regulations 'public statement' means any statement which becomes or is made, or the gist of which becomes or is made public whether in its original or in an edited or serialized form and whether in a newspaper, magazine , periodical or book, or in any form of radio or television broadcast, OR IN ANY OTHER MANNER WHATSOEVER, REGARDLESS OF THE CIRCUMSTANCES IN WHICH THE STATEMENT WAS FIRST MADE and includes any repetition of any such statement.'

As far as books were concerned, paragraph 3(d) stipulated:

'Any registered Cricketer or any of the Board's umpires must notify the County Cricket Club or the Board, as the case may be, as soon as any such contract is entered into and shall keep the County Cricket Club or the Board regularly informed on the progress of publications including providing the County Cricket Club or Board with all drafts or proofs (whether final or preliminary) of the book as and when they are prepared and before they are submitted to a publisher, newspaper or any other body or concern.'

Restraint of trade? No court in the land would have upheld the legality of these regulations had they ever been put to the test. Allan Lamb was told he had a good case for doing so when the Board attempted to apply the 1995 directive retrospectively, insisting that he showed them proofs of his autobiography before they were submitted to his publishers. Lamby's contract with the publishers was drawn up before the directive came into force and the publishers insisted that if he did show the proofs to the Board he would be in breach of his arrangement with them. Lamby wanted to play on in 1996 and he had a case, according to counsel, who further advised him that he had a strong case for restraint of trade. But counsel also told him that costs might amount to something in the region of £500,000. Clearly, if Lamby wanted to be faithful to his contract with the publishers and tell his side of the ball-tampering story among others, he had to quit cricket, which, with regret, he did.

Finally, at the start of the 1997 season, at around the time when Jack Russell was due to publish his autobiography, the new ECB saw sense. From then on, they decreed players were to be allowed to say and write what they liked as long as they didn't infringe the laws by which we all have to abide, namely the libel laws of the land. But the fact that a player like Lamb could have had his career cut short shows just how much power the old Board wielded over individual cricketers. In essence it boiled down to this: if you wanted a job as a professional cricketer you had to sign away your right to basic freedom. There's a word for this: slavery.

19. Should leading players be permitted to negotiate individual sponsorship deals separate from their county sponsorships?

Chairmen and Chief Executives: YES 79%; NO 16%. Undecided 5%
Captains and Coaches: YES 64%; NO 36%
TOTAL: YES 72%; NO 25%. Undecided 3%

Sample responses:
M J K SMITH, chairman of WARWICKSHIRE: 'Yes. But must not impinge on county and England sponsorships.'
CHRIS HASSELL, chief executive of YORKSHIRE: 'No. They already have sufficient scope for additional earnings.'
STEVE MARSH, captain of KENT: 'Yes. If you are good enough, or able to do it, milk it. You will not have the opportunity for too long.'
DAVID ACFIELD, chairman of ESSEX: 'Yes, in principle, provided this does not affect the county sponsorship by advertising rival products. I'm against players going out looking like a racing car.'
JOHN BOWER, chief executive of LANCASHIRE: 'No. It would lead to conflict between club and player.'
MATTHEW MAYNARD, captain of GLAMORGAN: 'Yes, otherwise you would restrict a player's earning potential.'

To me, one major reason why English cricket is at such a low ebb is that the financial incentives on offer from playing at professional level bear no comparison with other sports. As I said when discussing the choice made by my son Liam, over whether to stay in cricket or opt for professional rugby as a career, were I now to be faced with the choice between cricket and soccer I made back in the 1970s, I would have no hesitation in choosing soccer. In order to attract the top ball-players and athletes among the younger generation cricket must do all it can to make such a career financially attractive. For some years I have believed that one way to do this would be to allow top players the right to negotiate individual sponsorship contracts. Clearly the leading stars are currently able to advertise what they like off the field, but why not allow some form of shirt or bat advertising on it. I could envisage a situation where players might carry discreet advertising logos on their shirts, trousers, pads, and even, most lucratively, on the back of their bats. Imagine how much a company like British Airways for example might pay to have their logo positioned on the back of Nasser Hussain's bat, obviously in conjunction with the player's own bat sponsor. The difference in potential earnings between cricket and football, rugby, golf or tennis is vast. If we are to attract and hold onto the very best sporting talent available we must be prepared to give a little where the traditions of the game are concerned. As far as the fear that such individual deals might cut across team sponsorships, I don't see any reason why they should. If a player is good enough to warrant such a deal he should have it. And that would encourage others to reach the same heights of performance.

20. Is the game properly marketed?

Chairmen and Chief Executives: YES 79%; NO: 21%
Captains and Coaches: YES 36%; NO 57%. Undecided 7%
TOTAL: YES 60%; NO 36%. Undecided 4%

Sample responses:
DAVE GILBERT, coach of SURREY: 'No. English cricket is poorly marketed. Sunday cricket provides the perfect vehicle for trying new strategies, yet little is done.'
TIM MUNTON, captain of WARWICKSHIRE: 'No. We need to make the game more appealing to the masses. We need to get cricket back in the schools – everywhere.'
DAVID ACFIELD, chairman of ESSEX: 'Counties vary, but nationally it's good.'
STEVE MARSH, captain of KENT: 'No. To me it seems that a professional sport is run in the main by amateurs.'
MIKE FATKIN, chief executive of GLAMORGAN: 'No. We need to retain a profile. We have no divine right to maintain our present status as the leading summer sport and cannot afford to take anything for granted.'
ROGER GOADBY, chairman of LEICESTERSHIRE: 'Yes. The marketing committee of the ECB do a good job to attract the funding which they do.'

ROB BAILEY, captain of NORTHAMPTONSHIRE: 'Yes I feel we market the game well. The Test matches and one-day internationals are always well supported. Other countries are turning to circus-type things because they cannot attract consistent attendances for international cricket.'

TOM MOODY, captain of WORCESTERSHIRE: 'No. We need to look forward, not back and learn from other countries.'

PAUL SHELDON, chief executive of SURREY: 'Yes, because the television and sponsorship deals are high for an underperforming England team, but we could be more aggressive and forward-looking.'

MIKE HORTON, chairman of DERBYSHIRE: 'It is improving but, for kids, the sport is not seen as exciting. There is so much competition from ice hockey, basketball and other emerging sports, not to mention football that I believe the sport faces a very difficult future, relying only on tradition.'

PAUL PRICHARD, captain of ESSEX: 'No. Cricket does not get the kudos the game deserves because marketing people generally haven't got a clue about the game itself, so don't know how to 'Talk it up.'

MATTHEW MAYNARD, captain of GLAMORGAN: 'No. We seem reluctant to change. What facilities are there to encourage kids to come to cricket matches?'

JOHN BOWER, chief executive of LANCASHIRE: 'No. But it is improving rapidly. There is still too much emphasis on tradition, and too little genuine willingness to accept and welcome change.'

MARK ALLEYNE, captain of GLOUCESTERSHIRE: 'No. We need to offer more encouragement to the younger children to come and watch. They are often ignored because they don't bring money through the gates, but these are the players and supporters of the future.'

The difference of opinion between chairmen and administrators and captains and coaches is stark. Most of the people that run county clubs believe they are doing more than enough to market the game properly. The majority of those who play feel exactly the opposite. This is not coincidental. The players are the ones who know how soul-destroying it is to play professional cricket in front of three men and a thermos. Cricket is nothing if no-one wants to watch it. At all levels interest could be increased by positive marketing, yet at the faintest suggestion of change to the product the chairmen reach for their smelling salts. They must wake up and face the facts before it is too late.

TWENTY THREE
THE ANSWERS

'Adapt or die. That is the stark and only choice
facing English cricket today.'

To sum up the points raised by the Questionnaire, here is my ten-point plan for the future of English cricket.

1. A TWO-DIVISION CHAMPIONSHIP WITH PROMOTION AND RELEGATION

For me this is the absolute priority if we are to get England back to the top of world cricket on a consistent basis. Three-quarters of the players polled by the Professional Cricketer's Association voted against retaining the current single division championship. Sixty-eight per cent voted in favour of a two-division structure with promotion and relegation for the bottom and top three clubs. To them and to me the benefits are clear: raising the level of competition and toughness required among county players for too long stuck in the mire of mediocrity and increasing interest by making every game mean something. For those who believe that this would not happen try the following thought for size. Imagine if you now announced that as of the season after next the championship would be split into two divisions of nine clubs each and that your position in Division One or Two would depend on where you finished in next season's championship. Now imagine how competitive that contest would be. We do produce some talented young cricketers, but by the time they have been put through the process of playing uncompetitive county cricket for two or three seasons, their mental edge is dulled. Then, when they come into Test cricket, the toughest examination of all, most of them simply do not know what it is like to confront and deal with the intense pressure involved because they have never experienced it at county level. Leave baseball-style conferences for baseball, give the game the breath of competition it needs. Only the weak and mediocre will not survive, the weak and mediocre that have dragged down our game for so long, the weak and mediocre we can no longer afford to carry. I would envisage nine teams playing each other twice to make the same number of championship fixtures as they currently play. It is not the amount of cricket players play that does them in, rather the amount of *meaningless* cricket.

2. CONTRACT AN ELITE SQUAD OF INTERNATIONAL PLAYERS TO THE CENTRAL BOARD

Those who fear a two-divisional championship on the basis that the rich clubs would buy up all the best players would have those fears eased if those top players were contracted to the Board. If they were, the number of games they were available to play in the championship would make them poor value for money. Under the same system in Australia, their Test players play hardly any state cricket. During the period when he dominated Australia's batting David Boon played two state games for Tasmania in two years while Glenn McGrath has already played many more Tests than domestic matches for New South Wales. The same applies in South Africa where recently Brian McMillan was pulled out of a packed-house domestic one-day match because he was being saved for a Test against Australia the following week. In England, the first item on the agenda for Test players after a gruelling five-day Test should be rest and recuperation. Yet every season the next thing they have to do after the second Test at Lord's is to make straight for a NatWest first round match. The benefits for England players of being contracted to England rather than their county clubs are manifold. By allowing them to concentrate on improving their fitness and technique under the supervision of expert coaches, then playing the amount of domestic cricket they and the Board would consider necessary to stay sharp, their best efforts would be reserved for England. Furthermore the curse of burn out and excessive use of anti-inflammatory drugs among the bowlers just to keep them standing would be eradicated at a stroke. Take the cases of Dominic Cork and Darren Gough among the current crop of front-line England bowlers. Neither want to be put in cotton wool, all they ask for is proper rest between key matches to let niggling injuries recover. We must give our players the best chance of performing at their best at all times. With more international and Test cricket on the horizon, England players will have more than enough on their plate just playing for England.

3. SCRAP ONE ONE-DAY DOMESTIC COMPETITION; STANDARDIZE AT 50 OVERS ONE LEAGUE AND ONE CUP CONTEST; JAZZ UP THE 50-OVER LEAGUE TO ATTRACT CASUAL AND YOUNG SPECTATORS

It is commonly held to be absurd that clubs currently play three different types of one-day domestic cricket – the 40-over Sunday League, the 50-over Benson & Hedges and the 60-over NatWest, when all international one-day cricket is now played over 50 overs. Leaving aside who sponsors what I would scrap the 60-over competition and replace the existing 'Sunday' League with a 50-over League competition played in two divisions, either on Sunday or during the appropriate months and with the proper facilities on mid-week evenings. (See Marketing Plan, Point 9.)

4. TRIM PLAYING STAFFS TO MAXIMUM 20 FULL-TIME PROFESSIONALS; REORGANISE 2ND XI CRICKET TO BE YOUTH-ORIENTED

Too many players mean too much dead wood. A playing staff of 20 to cover injuries, Test calls and loss of form would keep all players on their toes. Second XI cricket is currently populated by failed first-teamers who will never make the top grade in their own right. Fill these sides with young players, stipulating that at least three of the team must be under 20 years of age at the start of the season and at least six under 22. Make 2nd XI cricket equally competitive as 1st XI by mirroring the two-division championship with promotion and relegation to make young players better equipped for more intense cricket when they make the jump. From a practical point of view the decrease in the number of professionals would enable clubs to increase wages. Players would have more to lose by not working hard at their game at all times.

5. REPLACE THE BENEFIT SYSTEM WITH PENSION FUNDS; GIVE THE PCA FUNDS TO DEVELOP AFTER-CRICKET TRAINING PROGRAMMES

Too many players hanging on for their benefits clog up the system. Rewards for long service should come in the form of improved pension funding, with sizeable contributions from clubs via the central hand-out. Remove the shabby business of forcing players to sell their memorabilia, Test caps, bats, balls, bails, boxes etc to make a crust. At the same time I would divert resources to fund schemes devised by the Professional Cricketers' Association to train cricketers for life after the game.

6. INTRODUCE QUALITY CONTROL IN THE HIRING OF OVERSEAS PLAYERS

With England hosting the World Cup in 1999 some observers considered this a perfect opportunity to discover what affect the absence of overseas stars would have on the game. I have a degree of sympathy with that view but I do believe that, correctly used, the best overseas players can have a positive impact on the development of England-qualified youngsters. Such has been the desire of some county clubs to recruit from abroad that on some occasions they have done so for the sake of it, without any real degree of quality control. That is wrong. To my mind only the very best should be considered and, to that end, I would stipulate that, after the age of 25, only those players who have represented their country at Test or international level should be permitted to play county cricket. If a county cannot recruit one of those, far better to find other ways to spend the money sensibly, like development of local talent, than to waste it on second-raters. As part of their employment package, those high-quality overseas stars that do come should be paid to coach at county and schools level whenever appropriate.

7. ESTABLISH A NATIONAL CRICKET ACADEMY; APPOINT A NATIONAL DIRECTOR OF COACHING

There are those who consider that nineteen centres of excellence would be better than one. If they could all boast the same kind of high-tech facilities and top-quality coaches, fair enough. But that would be unrealistic. Far better to concentrate our resources in one national academy where the standards of excellence could then be set for the whole country and put the running of the facility in the hands of one man whose job it would be to organise and maintain the coaching of cricket in England at all levels. He would be charged with employing the experts in their fields from around the world to devise and supervise fitness and training programmes specifically geared for each department of the game. He would also be given carte blanche to hire the best cricket minds in the world to help coach the major skills of the game – for instance, Dennis Lillee for fast bowling, Abdul Qadir for leg-spin bowling, Sunil Gavaskar for opening, Allan Border for left-handed batting, Viv Richards for destructive batting, Geoff Boycott for defensive batting, Jonty Rhodes for ground fielding, Alan Knott for wicket-keeping and so on. The director of coaching would also employ leaders in sports psychology, diet and all areas of training and preparation. No, none of that did happen 'in my day', and look where we are now as a result. Is it coincidence that those countries who have invested in the future in this way are currently at the top of world cricket? No.

The national director of coaching would use all resources at the disposal of the academy to do devise a national plan for all coaches, so that when players are finished with playing the game they are given the opportunity to make a career helping others to play, whether at national, county club, representative, minor county, club or school level.

In conjunction with local education authorities I would invite schoolteachers from all areas to attend coaching classes at the national academy so that they could then pass on the best knowledge and experience and the latest technical innovations to their pupils (see creating a level school playing field). We mustn't be content to catch up because by the time we do, Australia and South Africa will be way ahead of us again. Let's set down a blueprint for training and coaching flexible enough to adapt to all facets of the changing game. Let's raise the standards as high as they can be, then work like mad to keep them rising.

8. CREATE A LEVEL SCHOOL PLAYING FIELD

Many schools have been left to do what they can with minimal and in some cases non-existent resources, putting too much responsibility on the shoulders of local clubs to keep youth cricket alive. I would establish a national development plan for schools cricket under the aegis of the national coaching academy and the director of coaching, and with the help of the government, seek to offer cricket as part of a national sporting curriculum. How can we expect to develop top quality cricketers among the young when they have no idea what the game is let alone how to play it? I would seek to attract national sponsorship for such a plan, and make the facilities of the national academy open to participating schools as and when appropriate. I would also establish a scheme whereby schools could send players to the county clubs for expert tuition from players and coaches all under the umbrella of the national academy's coaching guidelines.

9. REVAMP THE MARKETING OF THE GAME

Warwickshire showed what could be achieved by a club prepared to take risks when they staged the first competitive floodlit one-day match with Somerset at Edgbaston. Club chief executive Dennis Amiss recorded a profit of £70,000 from a crowd of more than 15,000. This was an unmissable signal to the powers-that-be, as that figure outstripped the total profit raised from the attendance of county championship games at Edgbaston during the 1996 season, by some £30,000. One-day cricket is the only money-spinner currently available to county clubs. But how much more appealing could it be made for the spectators? I would keep a 50-over knockout competition as 'proper' one-day cricket but let the marketing men loose on the League version, whether on Sunday or in mid-week, whether in natural light or under floodlights. Many would complain that this version of the game with its razzmatazz, music and the works just wouldn't be cricket. Maybe not, but it would be exciting, dramatic and popular. As for individual players, let them offer individual 3 x 3 inch sponsorship logos on their shirts or advertising strips on the back of the bats. Why are golf and tennis so appealing to young sportsmen as alternatives to cricket ? Because every club they use, every bag, every cap, every umbrella and every item makes them money. Decrease the differential in earning potential and watch the popularity of the sport as a career option increase.

As far as international cricket in England is concerned, five Tests and seven one-day internationals should be the norm, increasing the revenue for the central fund.

10. APPOINT A CHIEF EXECUTIVE WITH FULL AND UNFETTERED POWER TO MAKE ALL THE ABOVE HAPPEN

For too long the tail has wagged the dog in English cricket. Until and unless that principle is discarded, no real change will be possible.

Those counties who objected initially to promotion and relegation and forced MacLaurin to compromise in *Raising the Standard* with his baseball-style conference system, simply refuse to understand the depth of the crisis facing the game.

The future well-being of English cricket depends absolutely on the national team winning. Another prolonged period of failure and national interest will decline to such a level that the game will become a minority sport. Be serious, put the running in the hands of an appointment with vision and drive. Then leave his hands untied and let him get on with the job.

MacLaurin's 1997 version of a blueprint for cricket was not the first example of his involvement with moves to direct the way cricket is run in this country. Perhaps he should have known from experience how difficult it was going to be to get the counties to agree on truly revolutionary measures. As recently as 1992, he had been a member of the 1992 Structure Working Party that, under the chairmanship of Mike Murray produced *A Blueprint for the First-Class Game*. This working party did bring in four-day championship cricket across the board, in response to the amount of 'joke' cricket, manufactured games and agreed declarations in the three-day games that had become the norm in county cricket, but also decided: 'There is no justification and little support for the introduction of a divisional structure or a system of promotion and relegation.' Further, they decreed that, for the good of the game, the Sunday League should be played over 50 overs a side. and that the Benson & Hedges Cup should be converted to a straight knock-out competition in order to reduce the amount of early season cricket. Guess what? After just one year the counties insisted on reverting back to 40-over slogs on Sunday and Group rounds in the B& H. So much for progress in the best interests of the game.

Adapt or die. That is the stark and only choice facing English cricket today. For too long the county clubs have existed on a diet of complacency and romanticism. The complacency was founded on the mistaken belief that, in terms of its flagship, the England national team, fortunes in cricket were cyclical and that everything would turn out nice in the end. The romanticism existed in the sincere but misguided conviction that the traditions of the game and its history by themselves would enable the game to survive and prosper undamaged and unaffected by changes in modern culture and society. To put it bluntly, too many people have been living in the past for too long. Perhaps the most flabbergasting comment I heard on the state of the game came from one county club chief executive whose reaction to the possibility of change was to suggest that county cricket should be left as it is because it performed the vital function of giving pensioners something to do. For short-sightedness, this takes the cake. Let's forget those measures that might appeal to the young now. In 60 years time they'll be grateful we did. Well, as those counties who attempted to push through a two-division championship with promotion and relegation at the eleventh hour understood, the fact is that if we don't start changing the domestic game now, in sixty years time the nation might just be past caring.

INDEX